# JOURNAL FOR THE STUDY OF THE OLD TESTAMENT
## SUPPLEMENT SERIES
# 50

Editors
David J A Clines
Philip R Davies

JSOT Press
Sheffield

# THE CHRONICLER'S HISTORY

**Martin Noth**

Translated by
H.G.M. Williamson
with an introduction

Journal for the Study of the Old Testament
Supplement Series 50

Copyright © 1987 Sheffield Academic Press

Published by JSOT Press
JSOT Press is an imprint of
Sheffield Academic Press
The University of Sheffield
343 Fulwood Road
Sheffield S10 3BP
England

Typeset by Sheffield Academic Press
and
printed in Great Britain
by Billing & Sons Ltd
Worcester


British Library Cataloguing in Publication Data

Noth, Martin
    The chronicler's history.—(Journal for the
    study of the Old Testament supplement series,
    ISSN 0309-0787; 50).
    1. Bible, O.T. —Criticism, interpretation, etc.
    I. Title                    II. Ueberlieferungsgeschichtliche
    Studien. Teil 2. *English*   III. Series
    221.6                        BS1171.2

    ISBN 1-85075-043-2
    ISBN 1-85075-044-0 Pbk

# CONTENTS

## TRANSLATOR'S PREFACE

An English translation of the first part of Martin Noth's *Überlieferungs-geschichtliche Studien* was published in 1981 under the title *The Deuteronomistic History*. Steady demand soon led the publishers to commission a translation of the second part of the work, together with the important appendix, which properly belongs with the first. Although the present translation has thus been a quite separate enterprise, I have nevertheless made every effort to make plain its close connection with *The Deuteronomistic History*. Thus, for instance, the chapter enumeration has been continued unbroken, and the same system of bibliographical references has been adopted.

It is no secret that Noth's German is not always easily rendered into English. In a scholarly work of this importance, I have considered it right to make accuracy and clarity my first priorities. That this has resulted in a less felicitous English style than might otherwise be thought desirable I readily concede. I hope, however, that readers will regard this as a small price to pay for the advantage of being able to get to grips with Noth's tight argumentation at as close quarters as possible.

I happily express my thanks to the editors of the JSOT Supplement Series for their invitation to undertake this work and to Mrs Judith Hackett for her help in the preparation of the typescript.

H.G.M. Williamson<br>
Cambridge<br>
June 1985

# ABBREVIATIONS

| | |
|---|---|
| AB | Anchor Bible |
| ATD | Das Alte Testament Deutsch |
| BK | Biblischer Kommentar |
| BWANT | Beiträge zur Wissenschaft vom Alten und Neuen Testament |
| BZAW | Beihefte zur *ZAW* |
| *CBQ* | *Catholic Biblical Quarterly* |
| Chr. | Chronicles, the Chronicler |
| Dtr. | The Deuteronomist, the Deuteronomistic History |
| ET | English translation |
| FRLANT | Forschungen zur Religion und Literatur des Alten und Neuen Testaments |
| HAT | Handbuch zum Alten Testament |
| HSM | Harvard Semitic Monographs |
| *HTR* | *Harvard Theological Review* |
| *JBL* | *Journal of Biblical Literature* |
| *JJS* | *Journal of Jewish Studies* |
| *JSOT* | *Journal for the Study of the Old Testament* |
| *JTS* | *Journal of Theological Studies* |
| KAT | Kommentar zum Alten Testament |
| NCB | New Century Bible |
| *PJB* | *Palästina-Jahrbuch* |
| *RB* | *Revue biblique* |
| SBLMS | Society of Biblical Literature Monograph Series |
| SVT | Supplements to *VT* |
| *TLZ* | *Theologische Literaturzeitung* |
| *TRE* | *Theologische Realenzyklopädie* |
| *TynB* | *Tyndale Bulletin* |
| *VT* | *Vetus Testamentum* |
| WMANT | Wissenschaftliche Monographien zum Alten und Neuen Testament |
| *WTJ* | *Westminster Theological Journal* |
| *ZAW* | *Zeitschrift für die alttestamentliche Wissenschaft* |
| *ZDPV* | *Zeitschrift des deutschen Palästina-Vereins* |

# INTRODUCTION

Noth's work on the books of Chronicles, Ezra and Nehemiah might appear at first sight to have been less influential or significant than his celebrated theory of a Deuteronomistic History. This initial impression is not altogether justified, however. Of course, in the generation after the appearance of Noth's book in 1943, the post-exilic historical works suffered a period of quite exceptional and wholly unjustified neglect which the last fifteen years have only begun to restore. It is thus no surprise that in scholarly literature as a whole Noth's work on the Chronicler received less mention and in consequence his views did not become so readily identified as was the case in regard to the earlier historical work.

There is, however, a far more significant factor than this to consider. For whatever reason, there was a long gap after Noth's work before commentaries in any language appeared which treated his theory of a Deuteronomic History with sustained consideration. This is especially true of the books of Kings, on which Noth himself left an unfinished major commentary at his untimely death in 1968.[1] For this reason, scholarly monographs and articles were obliged to work directly from Noth's own statement of his theory, and since for a considerable period his principal conclusions largely went unchallenged his achievements in research on this literature stood out as unrivalled.

The situation with regard to Chronicles, Ezra and Nehemiah is quite different. Here, in the wake of Noth's treatment, W. Rudolph produced two superb commentaries, one on *Esra und Nehemia* in 1949 in the Tübingen 'Handbuch zum Alten Testament' series, and the other in 1955 on *Chronikbücher* in the same series. So outstanding were these commentaries and so clear their lines of argument and modes of expression that in a period when little first-hand research was being undertaken on the books in question a whole generation of scholars appears not to have felt the need to

consult further than them. In a situation quite unlike that of the
Deuteronomic History, therefore, the name of Rudolph became
closely associated with the work of the Chronicler.

Now, there is no intention whatever to detract from Rudolph's
achievement if we observe at this point how indebted he frequently
was to Noth's earlier publication. Of course they did not agree in all
details, and indeed as we shall see later they diverged quite markedly
on some important matters. Furthermore, precisely because Rudolph
was writing commentaries there is much in his work which is fresh
and independent. My point here, rather, is to observe the extent to
which a comparable method pervades their approach to literary and
historical criticism so that their works stand out as the products not
just of the same period but of the same school of scholarship. It thus
came about that Noth's profound influence was not so readily
perceived as such in this area, since it was refracted through the
prism of Rudolph's commentaries.

This influence can best be seen by contrasting the approach of
Noth and Rudolph with the state of research on Chronicles prior to
Noth's work. During the nineteenth century from de Wette to
Wellhausen[2] the books of Chronicles featured prominently in
research on the Old Testament. Broadly speaking, however, interest
was less in the books themselves than in two other areas for which
the books of Chronicles were adduced merely as evidence. The first
such area was the history of Israelite religion, which itself was
integrally bound up with the development of theories of Pentateuchal
origins. The second area, which developed by way of conservative
reaction to the first, was the testimony of Chronicles to earlier
historical 'sources'[3] which might then be used in the enterprise of
constructing a critical history of Israel from the national and political
points of view.

With the general acceptance of a critical approach to the Old
Testament this second area of interest fell away as a serious focus for
research during the early decades of the present century. Naturally,
historians continued to pay lip-service to Chronicles,[4] but little fresh
or creative work resulted.[5] The first area of interest, however,
continued to attract a certain amount of attention, but in a manner
which tended to suggest that the method was beginning to go to seed.
Instead of Chronicles serving as part of the backdrop against which
to unravel the composition-history of the Pentateuch, the documentary
hypothesis came itself to influence the framing of theories about how

Chronicles was written. It would seem that it was impossible to move forward in research on Chronicles without relating one's results to the results of Pentateuchal criticism. Furthermore, it is a notorious fact that during these decades the literary analysis of the Pentateuch became excessively elaborate, some scholars apparently feeling no qualms about confidently postulating multiple layers of both sources and redaction,[6] and this too had an impact on the study of Chronicles.

The most obvious example of these trends was the massive commentary *Das erste Buch der Chronik* (KAT; 1927) by J.W. Rothstein and J. Hänel.[7] Here it was suggested that 1 Chronicles had as its basis a narrative which continued the Pentateuchal source P—still known as a separate document—and that this then went through an elaborate series of subsequent redactions which gradually accommodated it more closely to the Pentateuch as a whole, including, as of particular importance, Deuteronomy. Very different in tone, but apparently still sensing the need to justify its proposals in terms of the documentary hypothesis, was the monograph of A.C. Welch, *The Work of the Chronicler* (1939). Welch believed that the 'original' Chronicler's work was to be dated before the post-exilic restoration and that it was written by a member of the community who had never been in exile. It 'must be set alongside the proposals in Ezekiel as one of the programmes which were put forward, before the final settlement was reached' (p. 156). Thus not only did Welch inevitably regard 1 Chron. 1–9 as secondary, but also all passages which betray the influence of P. He therefore devoted much of his monograph to the task of isolating the work of a later reviser who shared the outlook of P. The original Chronicler, he argued, compiled his book within a community which still accepted D as its authoritative law-code.

The one work of this period to make a sustained effort to break this impasse was G. von Rad's *Das Geschichtsbild des chronistischen Werkes* (BWANT 54; 1930), a contribution whose value Noth himself acknowledged (see below, pp. 97ff.). In seeking to penetrate the historical, religious and theological framework of the Chronicler's mental horizons, von Rad naturally paid considerable attention to the law which the Chronicler presupposed. In direct response to the theory of Rothstein and Hänel, he succeeded in demonstrating that the Chronicler drew on both P and D, and indeed that in certain important respects the latter was especially important for him. In this regard, von Rad's work has been widely accepted (though Welch is an obvious exception) and Noth clearly believed that there was no need to add anything further on that score.

Despite the welcome fact that von Rad's monograph evidenced interest in the Chronicler himself and not just a desire to consult him for evidence on some other matter, it nevertheless left a number of important issues unresolved. First, it made no pretence of dealing with the questions raised by historical criticism. Second, perhaps by way of reaction to the excesses of Rothstein and Hänel's commentary, it paid little attention to literary-critical issues either. Only in his treatment of the Levitical singers was von Rad obliged by the results which his traditio-historical method produced to isolate a small number of short passages as having been added secondarily to the work of the Chronicler. On the whole, however, von Rad seems to have assumed that his conclusions would stand regardless of the results of literary analysis.[8] Third, von Rad paid little attention to such standard introductory questions as date and setting, despite the fact that he regarded a good deal of the Chronicler's work as arising directly out of the concerns of the writer's own day. In short, therefore, whilst von Rad marked the path for a return to an interest in the Chronicler for his own sake, he pursued this in only one area of study, and one which is generally taken to be the conclusion, not the starting point, of Old Testament research. There thus remained an all-too-obvious need for a thoroughgoing and comprehensive analysis of these books on their own terms, that is to say, with methods of study that were appropriate to them as opposed to being imposed upon them from the very different situation presented in the Pentateuch. It was this requirement that Noth was the first to fulfil.

It is not necessary to give a full summary and appreciation of Noth's study at this point. It may, nevertheless, be helpful to point out a few of the areas where his work may be seen to have had a lasting effect. First of all, he injected a healthy dose of realism and common sense into the literary-critical study of Chronicles. Whether or not one agrees with Noth's conclusions, it is difficult to read his first chapter on this subject (see below) without appreciating the clarity and logic of his argument. Freed from the constraints of external sources, Noth looked simply for internal narrative coherence as the key that should reveal secondary insertions. Thus, for instance, the narrative connection between 1 Chron. 23.1-2 and 28.1

suggested to him, as it already had to others, that the intervening chapters (23-27) were all added later, and should not, therefore, be included in a consideration of the Chronicler's own thought and purposes.

This straightforward approach to the literary-critical enterprise was taken up by Rudolph in his commentary, and though he did not agree with Noth in every detail, much of his analysis is broadly comparable. The outline of their conclusions then came to be adopted in most of the textbooks of the following decades. Furthermore, of the monographs which attest to the recent revival of interest in Chronicles, several accept these conclusions at points which are of fundamental importance for their own hypotheses. It would have been difficult, for instance, for Willi to pursue his theory that the books of Chronicles are intended to be an 'exegesis' of their authoritative counterparts in the former prophets had he not been able to follow Noth in regarding as secondary a good deal of that material which has no parallel in earlier Biblical books, material which had often been thought to serve the very different purpose of pro-Levitical propaganda.[9]

A comparable influence may be traced with regard to Noth's treatment of extra-Biblical sources available to the Chronicler[10] and hence of the historical value of those parts of his work for which no other source has survived for us. For a long time discussions of this topic had revolved around the Chronicler's apparent citation of sources at the end of the reign of each king. Indeed, this approach is still often repeated today. Even if it were valid, however, it would still only allow us to speak in the most general terms about the historical value of the Chronicler's special material because there would be no means of knowing which parts of it were drawn from these hypothetical sources.

Noth responded negatively to this 'method' by arguing that these source citation formulae were a purely literary device based on the practice of the books of Kings and so devoid of all value as testimony to the existence or otherwise of sources behind Chronicles. His own approach, whilst unable, in the present state of our knowledge, to be so comprehensive, is far more satisfactory and convincing from the point of view of method. He endeavoured first to isolate those two or three items which the Chronicler alone recorded for which there was sufficient reasonable evidence from other sources to uphold their authenticity. Since the Chronicler could not have fabricated them, he must in these few cases have been dependent on other sources. The principal examples which Noth adduced in this regard were the construction of Hezekiah's tunnel (2 Chron. 32.30) and the account of the death of Josiah (2 Chron. 35.20-24). From these two certain cases, Noth believed that it was reasonable to proceed to other examples of royal building projects and of military matters similarly recorded only in Chronicles. In many of these cases, though authenticity could not be proved, there were nevertheless reasons which made it seem likely. This likelihood would be strengthened if these passages were drawn into relationship with the undoubtedly authentic passages already noted by postulating on the basis of similarity of subject matter that they all came from the same source.

In this field of research, too, it has been Noth's approach that has largely dominated more recent work. The search for 'certain' or 'probable' items of reliable information in Chronicles is to be found in all the commentaries as well as in a number of specialized articles. Generally speaking this has been in the direction of expanding Noth's list in the light of archaeological and other historical research.[11] However, in 1973 the whole issue was drawn together in a fresh examination by P. Welten,[12] who adopted a method which may be regarded as a direct development of the procedure outlined by Noth. Welten groups the relevant material into categories that he labels *topoi*, such as building or details about the army. He then studies each text belonging to that *topos* in turn, looking for both literary and historical evidence by which to evaluate it. He also, however, considers each *topos* as a whole in relation to the Chronicler's literary methods and purposes. On the whole, Welten's conclusions are closer to Noth's than most others who have written on this subject. He regards as most certainly historical the information included in 2 Chron. 11.5b, 6a-10aβ; 26.6a and 10; 32.30a; next in order of probability come 2 Chron. 11.22f.; 21.1-4; and 35.20-25 (cf. pp. 192-93). The important point here, however, is not so much to compare the detailed results with those of Noth as to observe the compatibility of the methods which each scholar has pursued.

It is to be hoped that these examples will be sufficient to illustrate the extent to which Noth's study of the books of Chronicles set the agenda for subsequent research right down to the present day. It would be a mistake to imply, however, that new approaches have not also intervened during the past forty years; they have, and it would be idle to pretend that anyone can simply put the clock back to Noth's day. In order further to appreciate his position within the history of scholarship in this field we may conclude this part of our introduction with an indication of those areas which have been developed since Noth's time, those which are still being actively exploited, and those in which some of the positions he maintained are, inevitably, being modified.

First, the discovery of the Dead Sea Scrolls has had a significant impact on the study of Chronicles. When Noth was working, he was able to assume that the Masoretic text of Samuel and Kings represented quite closely the *Vorlage* which the Chronicler followed. In consequence, any differences between the texts in parallel passages could be taken without further ado as evidence of the Chronicler's *Tendenz*. Such an assumption cannot be so simply made today. With regard to the books of Samuel in particular, the discovery of 4QSam[a] has shown[13] that there once existed a Hebrew text which differed to a sometimes significant extent from the MT and that it was from this that the LXX was translated.[14] Whilst it is theoretically possible that this text has in places been influenced by parallel passages in Chronicles, it is usually believed with good reason that in fact it existed before Chronicles was written and that it was this text, or something very like it, which the Chronicler followed rather than the MT. If so, not every difference between the MT of Samuel–Kings and Chronicles need inevitably reflect the Chronicler's *Tendenz* or bias.

There can be little doubt that some exaggerated conclusions were drawn from this state of affairs when first it became widely known.[15] Comparison of synoptic passages is still important for the study of Chronicles, even though now it must be conducted with greater attention to witnesses to the text of Samuel other than the MT and in full recognition of the dangers of placing too much weight on a single deviation. Nonetheless, scholars can never move in this area with quite the same confidence that Noth did, and for future research the possibility is opened up that in some cases there may have been even more substantial differences between Samuel–Kings and the *Vorlage* of the Chronicler than has hitherto been suspected.[16]

Second, and to some extent as a consequence of this first point, a number of recent studies of Chronicles have tended to draw their conclusions about the Chronicler's views and aims from a much broader appreciation of his overall narrative structure. If detailed differences in synoptic passages are a less reliable guide, it seems reasonable to concentrate instead on the general shape of the work, for this at least must have been due to the Chronicler himself. Thus the exegete needs to give due attention to the type of material which the Chronicler chose to include and to omit, the major themes to which he gave emphasis by his own additions and the arrangement of all this material in one order rather than another, if he is to do justice to the Chronicler's composition. Thus, to give but a few examples, R. Mosis,[17] to some extent both anticipated and followed by P.R. Ackroyd,[18] has argued that the Chronicler presents the history of Israel in terms of a recurring cycle of 'exile' and 'restoration', with the age of Solomon depicted as a third potential situation, that of ultimate, even eschatological, blessing. Words such as 'paradigm' characterize this fruitful approach as they seek to do justice both to the Chronicler's evident dependence on the earlier history and his ability to work creatively with it. Again, I have myself suggested that appreciation of narrative patterns spanning more than a single passage can advance our understanding of such disputed questions as the Chronicler's attitude towards the northern kingdom of Israel and towards the future of the Davidic dynasty.[19] Finally, in addition to a number of useful articles in similar vein by R.L. Braun and others,[20] mention must be made of the magisterial volume of S. Japhet, *The Ideology of the Book of Chronicles and its Place in Biblical Thought* (in Hebrew; 1977), in which, not uncontroversially, the full range of material in these books is drawn together in a sustained attempt to present a synthesis of their outlook. The result of all these studies has been (so far as one may justifiably speak of a consensus) to modify some of Noth's cardinal points in his evaluation of the Chronicler's thought and purpose, especially his emphasis on the anti-Samaritan *Tendenz* which he believed he could detect in the Chronicler's work.

Third, whereas the significance of Noth's contribution to the development of literary-critical method with regard to the books of Chronicles has been emphasized above, there are signs of unease about the manner in which he pursued it in isolation from other considerations. To be sure, Noth's conclusions were broadly followed by Rudolph; Myers was unwilling to commit himself in detail, but on occasion, at least, indicated his general acceptance of Noth's position.[21] The same is true of the monographs of Willi (pp. 194-204), Mosis (who generally follows Noth's and Rudolph's literary-critical judgments, though without full discussion) and Welten, in so far as the latter's position on this issue can be determined.

In the modern climate of opinion, however, it is somewhat disquieting that Noth never stopped to ask who was responsible for the multifarious additions to Chronicles which he had detected and what was the rationale for their inclusion.[22] In addition, Noth showed no interest in literary structure and patterning. This has become a fashionable subject of study in modern scholarship and is undoubtedly open to the abuses of excess; nevertheless, there are cases where it has provided convincing examples of planned literary composition which cut across some of the results of earlier critical work. Along with these modern studies there have also been attempts to establish some of the literary devices which authors of antiquity used. Without access to the facilities of modern book production and the flexibility afforded by such devices as the footnote and appendix, Biblical authors were obliged to use other conventions. Admittedly the use of these cannot be proved any more than can the results of any other form of literary-critical analysis, but for some, such as the device known as 'repetitive resumption', there is impressive evidence, and their identification invites modifications of Noth's conclusions. Next, it is difficult to see how the literary-critical exercise can be pursued in total isolation from the consideration of sources. In the genealogies of 1 Chron. 1-9 in particular, modern research has adduced analogies for some of the types of material which suggest that they may have belonged together from the start and so should not be broken up in the manner Noth suggests. Finally, whilst it is to Noth's credit that his proposals were detailed and explicit and his reasons for them stated quite clearly, it also means that his proposals are open to modification or refutation as new evidence is brought to bear.[23] Thus, whilst it is clear that there can be no going back to 'pre-Nothian' approaches, it is also the case that he did not speak the last word on the issue of determining the precise shape of the work which left the Chronicler's hands.

There is one final matter which has affected the study of Chronicles since Noth's time but which has not been referred to in the foregoing. Readers will have noticed that so far nothing has been said about Ezra-Nehemiah. In setting about his work, Noth shared in the almost complete consensus of his time that the Chronicler's history originally included these two books. So confident was he about this that his opening paragraph concludes with the sentence:

'In this case, therefore, in contrast with our analysis of the Deuteronomic History, there is no need to start with a demonstration of the work's literary unity'.

Credit is due to Japhet for reopening this issue in so forceful a way as to draw others after her.[24] Previously, those such as Welch who had adopted the minority opinion of treating Ezra and Nehemiah separately from Chronicles had been almost completely ignored. Following Japhet's work, however, a number of scholars turned their attention to this issue, albeit embarking from quite varied critical starting-points. One group, for instance, finds a setting for the core of Chronicles in the earliest days of the post-exilic restoration and so postulates a series of redactions of the work which embrace Ezra and Nehemiah at only a secondary stage of the work.[25] Others, such as Willi and Welten, find it incompatible with their understanding of the purpose of Chronicles as a whole to accept Ezra and Nehemiah as part of the work, although they nevertheless allow the possibility that they may be two quite separate works of the same author. Yet a third group follow Japhet more closely in examining the two works and concluding that the differences between them preclude unity of authorship on the one hand whilst on the other hand the traditional arguments for unity are flawed.[26]

Of course, not all scholars by any means have been persuaded that Chronicles should be separated from Ezra–Nehemiah;[27] however, that the question is genuinely open may be judged from the fact that the newer view has found favour in several recent textbooks.[28] The important point to stress here, however, is that this obviously makes a difference to an appraisal of the Chronicler's 'Central Theological Ideas' (Chapter 20 below). As I have tried to show elsewhere (*Israel*, pp. 2-4), one of the major features which Noth expounded, the Chronicler's supposed anti-Samaritan polemic, was based entirely on a prior analysis of Ezra–Nehemiah. Once that plank is removed, a completely different picture comes into view, as several of the recent monographs have recognized from their different angles. Thus, just as Noth correctly perceived the need to modify von Rad's characterization of the Chronicler's theology in the light of his literary-critical conclusions, so Noth's own sketch is open to modification as further preliminary critical work develops.

These remarks serve as a useful bridge to a consideration of the significance of Noth's work on Ezra and Nehemiah, and here it will be possible to be brief. Because these books are our major witness for

Jewish history in the Persian period, they have inevitably been studied with greater intensity than Chronicles. Moreover, they have not been bedevilled by some of the problems which we noted in connection with Chronicles in the period before Noth; and some aspects, at least, of their literary history have received a general degree of assent amongst scholars. Finally, since Noth recognized the extensive use of sources in Ezra–Nehemiah whereas his own interest was primarily in the work of the Chronicler, he did not touch on several of the major issues in the study of the books. A particularly noteworthy example of this concerns the Nehemiah Memoir. Noth was happy to accept the usual view of its extent and authenticity and, in contrast with his thorough treatment of pre-exilic sources in Chronicles, he showed little interest in it thereafter, even though its genre and purpose are widely debated and far from agreed.[29] In addition, he quietly dismissed (cf. pp. 153f. n. 62 below) the relevance of the apocryphal Greek work 1 Esdras, even though a number of scholars both before and since have argued that its ending (roughly Ezra + Nehemiah 8) represents the 'original' ending of the Chronicler's work.[30] For these reasons amongst others Noth's work was bound to have less influence on subsequent scholarship than was the case with regard to Chronicles.

In fact, there is only one major subject on which he advanced a fresh suggestion which has had a significant impact on subsequent study, and that concerns the nature of the so-called 'Ezra Memoir'. The account of Ezra's activities is found in Ezra 7–10 and Nehemiah 8 (with which Neh. 9–10 are frequently associated). Many questions are raised by this material: why is it split into two parts? Why is some transmitted as third-person and some as first-person narrative? Why is its Hebrew style apparently so similar to that of the Chronicler? How reliable is the Aramaic edict of Artaxerxes in Ezra 7.12-26? To these questions, scholars have suggested several answers encompassing the whole range of possibilities between the fully conservative view which takes the narrative at face value as Ezra's own account of his mission (apart from the editorial recasting of some first-person material as third-person narrative) through to the radical view of C.C. Torrey[31] to the effect that Ezra never existed and that the whole account was a fabrication by the Chronicler.

Noth's proposed solution to this dilemma was characteristically straightforward in its essential details. He accepted that the Aramaic edict in Ezra 7.12-26 and the list of those who returned to Jerusalem with Ezra in 8.1-14 were sources antecedent to the Chronicler. (This in itself, Noth hastened to affirm, did not settle the question of their historical authenticity.) The Chronicler also knew the Nehemiah Memoir. On the basis of this material, the Chronicler himself wrote the whole of the Ezra account, for Noth could find nothing in this material which demanded other independent knowledge. He was thus able to explain why the style of writing so closely resembled that of the Chronicler, why Nehemiah 8 was not included with Ezra 7-10 (the Chronicler wrote it from the first for its present setting for theological reasons), and why part of the account was in the first person (imitation of the Nehemiah Memoir, but characteristically not pursued consistently by the Chronicler). The influence of Noth's views on this matter may be gauged by the fact that they have been adopted with only minor changes by both Kellermann[32] and In der Smitten.[33]

On this occasion in particular, Noth was not followed by Rudolph. In his commentary, Rudolph went to considerable lengths carefully to justify a more conservative position. The result has been that in recent decades scholars have found that their agenda for discussion of the Ezra material has again largely been set by these two scholars.[34] Whilst this is not the place to set out the reasons why Rudolph's approach may be preferred to that of Noth,[35] it is clear that such a preference cannot be expressed without the most careful attention to the pioneering work of Noth on this topic and the supporting arguments which those who have followed him have adduced.

In drawing this introduction to a close, it should perhaps be emphasized that there has been no intention of providing a comprehensive survey of work on Chronicles, Ezra and Nehemiah. My aim has been rather to set Noth's contribution into its context in the history of scholarship and to outline something of his influence and of how matters have since developed in those particular areas. We may conclude, in the light of this discussion, by venturing the opinion that despite all the advances and changes that have taken place since he wrote, it is nevertheless to Noth's contribution here presented in translation that the modern era of Chronicles studies may be traced.

H.G.M. Williamson

# NOTES

1. M. Noth, *Könige*, I. Teilband (BK; 1968).
2. Cf. T. Willi, *Die Chronik als Auslegung* (FRLANT 106; 1972), pp. 33-45. Willi says of de Wette that his 'Stellungnahme . . . zur Chronik ist zwar nur ein Nebenprodukt der Beschäftigung mit der pentateuchischen Frage—genau wie später das Chronik-Kapitel in J. *Wellhausens* Prolegomena' (p. 33); J.W. Rogerson, *Old Testament Criticism in the Nineteenth Century: England and Germany* (1984).
3. Cf. especially C.F. Keil, *Apologetischer Versuch über die Bücher der Chronik und über die Integrität des Buches Esra* (1833).
4. E.g. the brief commentary of R. Kittel, *Die Bücher der Chronik* (HAT; 1902). Typical of the period is T.H. Robinson's judgment when discussing the sources available for the history of the Israelite Monarchy in the standard textbook on the subject in English, W.O.E. Oesterley and T.H. Robinson, *A History of Israel*, I (1932), p. 177: 'Our Biblical evidence is contained in the books of *Samuel* and *Kings*, with some doubtful additions from *Chronicles*. But the extent to which this latter compilation can be used as an authority independent of *Samuel* and *Kings* is very uncertain.'
5. These remarks naturally apply only to the books of Chronicles. Ezra and Nehemiah, which constitute our main source for the history of the post-exilic period, will be discussed separately below.
6. See, for instance, the introductory survey in O. Eissfeldt, *The Old Testament: an Introduction* (1965; ET of the 3rd edn, 1964, of *Einleitung in das Alte Testament*), pp. 168-70.
7. See also J. Hänel, 'Das Recht des Opferschlachtens in der chronistischen Literatur', *ZAW* 55 (1937), pp. 46-67.
8. See von Rad, p. 133, where he appears to concede Rothstein's analysis of 'two Chroniclers' but goes on to assert that this is irrelevant to his investigation.
9. T. Willi, *Die Chronik als Auslegung*, pp. 194-204.
10. It is also worth observing that Noth cut through another area of earlier speculation by affirming in the case of passages which have a Biblical parallel that the Chronicler worked directly from the texts as we know them and not from the sources which may have lain behind them. This view, which has not been seriously challenged since (though cf. A.G. Auld, 'Prophets through the Looking Glass: Between Writings and Moses', *JSOT* 27 [1983], p. 3-23), is not materially affected by more recent textual discoveries (see below).
11. An extreme exception is R. North, 'Does Archeology Prove Chronicle Sources?', in H.N. Bream, R.D. Heim and C.A. Moore (eds.), *A Light unto my Path: Old Testament Studies in Honor of Jacob M. Myers* (1974), pp. 375-401.
12. P. Welten, *Geschichte und Geschichtsdarstellung in den Chronikbüchern* (WMANT 42; 1973).

13. This text has still not been published, and studies based upon it by the pupils of F.M. Cross, in whose care it is, do not always agree in every detail over readings. However, from the publications of those who have had access to photographs of the manuscript we can learn enough to substantiate the points made above; cf. W.E. Lemke, 'The Synoptic Problem in the Chronicler's History', *HTR* 58 (1965), pp. 349-63; E.C. Ulrich, *The Qumran Text of Samuel and Josephus* (HSM 19; 1978); P.K. McCarter, *I Samuel* (AB; 1980); *II Samuel* (AB; 1984). Of the numerous secondary discussions, it is necessary to mention here only E. Tov, 'The Textual Affiliations of 4QSam[a]', *JSOT* 14 (1979), pp. 37-53.

14. The peculiar importance of the LXX for the textual criticism of the books of Samuel has long been recognized; cf. in particular J. Wellhausen, *Der Text der Bücher Samuelis* (1872) and S.R. Driver, *Notes on the Hebrew Text and the Topography of Samuel* (2nd edn, 1913). For the significance of the Greek versions for synoptic studies, cf. M. Rehm, *Textkritische Untersuchungen zu den Parallelstellen der Samuel-Königsbücher und der Chronik* (1937), and G. Gerleman, *Synoptic Studies in the Old Testament* (1948). Note also L.C. Allen, *The Greek Chronicles* (2 vols., SVT 25 and 27; 1974).

15. For a single example of how such exaggeration is now being modified, cf. P.E. Dion, 'The Angel with the Drawn Sword (II [sic!] Chr. 21, 16): An Exercise in Restoring the Balance of Text Criticism *and* Attention to Context', *ZAW* 97 (1985), pp. 114-17.

16. Cf. my 'The Death of Josiah and the Continuing Development of the Deuteronomic History', *VT* 32 (1982), pp. 242-48.

17. *Untersuchungen zur Theologie des chronistischen Geschichtswerkes* (1973).

18. Cf. especially out of numerous publications on these books *The Age of the Chronicler* (1970); *I & II Chronicles, Ezra, Nehemiah* (1973); and 'The Chronicler as Exegete', *JSOT* 2 (1977), pp. 2-32.

19. Cf. *Israel in the Books of Chronicles* (1977), pp. 87-131; 'The Accession of Solomon in the Books of Chronicles', *VT* 26 (1976), pp. 351-61; and 'Eschatology in Chronicles', *TynB* 28 (1977), pp. 115-54.

20. R.L. Braun, 'Solomonic Apologetic in Chronicles', *JBL* 92 (1973), pp. 502-14; 'Solomon, the Chosen Temple Builder', *JBL* 95 (1976), pp. 581-90; 'A Reconsideration of the Chronicler's Attitude toward the North', *JBL* 96 (1977), pp. 59-62; R.B. Dillard, 'The Chronicler's Solomon', *WTJ* 43 (1980), pp. 289-300; 'The Literary Structure of the Chronicler's Solomon Narrative', *JSOT* 30 (1984), pp. 85-93.

21. See, for instance, J.M. Myers, *I Chronicles* (AB; 1965), pp. 12 and 110.

22. This is an appropriate point at which to refer to the attempt by K. Galling, *Die Bücher der Chronik, Esra, Nehemia* (ATD; 1954), to distinguish two 'Chroniclers' throughout the work, each with an identifiable

individuality. In regard to 1 Chronicles, Galling's second Chronicler coincides to a considerable extent with the material which Noth simply characterized as 'secondary'. In 2 Chronicles, however, matters change dramatically because here, unlike Galling, Noth detected only a few brief and isolated additions. Probably because of the publication of Rudolph's commentary the following year, Galling's proposals received very little attention, critical or otherwise, from other scholars. So far as I know, apart from reviews of the commentary, only Welten, himself a pupil of Galling, has given his theory considered attention (pp. 189-91), and then only to reject it.

23. For illustration and justification of all the points made in the foregoing paragraph, I would refer to my *1 and 2 Chronicles* (NCB; 1982) on the passages discussed by Noth in chapter 14 below and to the modern literature which is cited there.

24. S. Japhet, 'The Supposed Common Authorship of Chronicles and Ezra–Nehemiah Investigated Anew', *VT* 18 (1968), pp. 330-71.

25. Cf. F.M. Cross, 'A Reconstruction of the Judean Restoration', *JBL* 94 (1975), pp. 4-18; J.D. Newsome, 'Toward a New Understanding of the Chronicler and his Purposes', *JBL* 94 (1975), pp. 201-17; D.L. Petersen, *Late Israelite Prophecy: Studies in Deutero-Prophetic Literature and in Chronicles* (SBLMS 23; 1977); J.R. Porter, 'Old Testament Historiography', in G.W. Anderson (ed.), *Tradition and Interpretation* (1979), pp. 125-62; M.A. Throntveit, *The Significance of the Royal Speeches and Prayers for the Structure and Theology of the Chronicler* (Unpublished Dissertation, Union Theological Seminary, Richmond, Virginia, 1982); and note the brief, but in many ways programmatic, essay by D.N. Freedman, 'The Chronicler's Purpose', *CBQ* 23 (1961), pp. 436-42.

26. Cf. H.G.M. Williamson, *Israel in the Books of Chronicles* (1977), pp. 5-70; R.L. Braun, 'Chronicles, Ezra, and Nehemiah: Theology and Literary History', *SVT* 30 (1979), pp. 52-64.

27. Of those who have discussed the issue in any detail, note H. Cazelles, *VT* 29 (1979), pp. 375-80; S.J.L. Croft, *JSOT* 14 (1979), pp. 68-72; A.H.J. Gunneweg, 'Zur Interpretation der Bücher Esra–Nehemia —zugleich ein Beitrag zur Methode der Exegese', *SVT* 32 (1981), pp. 146-61 (and cf. the Bonn dissertation of Gunneweg's pupil T.-S. Im, *Das Davidbild in den Chronikbüchern* [1984]); D.J.A. Clines *Ezra, Nehemiah, Esther* (NCB; 1984), pp. 9-12 and 25-31; M. Haran, 'Book-Size and the Device of Catch-Lines in the Biblical Canon', *JJS* 36 (1985), pp. 1-11.

28. E.g. M. Saebø, 'Chronistische Theologie/Chronistisches Geschichtswerk', *TRE* 8 (1981), pp. 74-87; O. Kaiser, *Einleitung in das Alte Testament* (5th edn; 1984), pp. 192-94; and J.R. Porter (above, n. 25).

29. Cf. U. Kellermann, *Nehemia: Quellen, Überlieferung und Geschichte* (BZAW 102; 1967).

30. Cf. K.-F. Pohlmann, *Studien zum dritten Esra. Ein Beitrag zur Frage*

*nach dem ursprünglichen Schluss des chronistischen Geschichtswerkes* (FRLANT 104; 1970), with a full and helpful survey of earlier discussions. Of these, we would mention only two here as being of particular influence: G. Hölscher, 'Die Bücher Esra und Nehemia', in E. Kautzsch and A. Bertholet (eds.), *Die heilige Schrift des Alten Testaments* (4th edn, 1923), and S. Mowinckel, *Studien zu dem Buche Ezra-Nehemia* I (1964), pp. 1-28. Significant work which has been influenced by Pohlmann includes that of Mosis, Ackroyd and Cross (see above, notes 17, 18 and 25). In my opinion, however, Noth's opinion on this matter was sound; cf. *Israel*, pp. 12-36 and *JTS* n.s. 34 (1983), pp. 2-8.

31. C.C. Torrey, *The Composition and Historical Value of Ezra-Nehemiah* (BZAW 2; 1896); *Ezra Studies* (1910).

32. See above, n. 29.

33. W.Th. In der Smitten, *Esra: Quellen, Überlieferung und Geschichte* (1973).

34. The only major alternative proposal in the meantime has been that of S. Mowinckel, *Studien zu dem Buche Ezra-Nehemia III: Die Ezrageschichte und das Gesetz Moses* (1965), but on the whole he has not attracted much scholarly support.

35. See my *Ezra-Nehemiah* (Word Biblical Commentary, 1985).

# THE CHRONICLER'S HISTORY

*Chapter 14*

## THE ORIGINAL FORM OF THE WORK

To all intents and purposes, the work of the Chronicler has come down to us as a literary unity. The last book of the Old Testament canon forms the main part of it. Adopting Jerome's nomenclature, we generally call this 'Chronicles'; the division into two 'books' did not occur until the Greek translation of the Old Testament. However, the final part of the work, which we know as Ezra–Nehemiah (here again the division into two derives from the Greek translation), has been subsequently detached and placed before the main part. Despite this, it is generally accepted as certain that in 1 and 2 Chronicles + Ezra and Nehemiah we have but a single work. In this case, therefore, in contrast with our analysis of the Deuteronomic History, there is no need to start with a demonstration of the work's literary unity.

There is, nevertheless, good reason to ask in what shape the work left the hand of its author, the so-called 'Chronicler'. (The abbreviation Chr. will serve hereafter for both this author and his work.) As yet this question has by no means been properly or conclusively resolved. It must first be emphasized that the basic work goes back to a single, specific author. It is to him alone that the conventional designation 'the Chronicler' (and hence the abbreviation Chr.) belongs. Despite all its unevenness in matters of detail, the work is so clearly dominated by a particular outlook—which will be treated more precisely later on—that its existence must be attributed to the careful planning of a single author. On the basis of all kinds of literary sources which were available to him, he fashioned a historical narrative marked by quite distinct underlying concerns and with fairly definite characteristics as regards both form and content. In order to grasp the exact nature and aim of Chr. (without which, moreover, there can be no proper understanding of the details of its content), the attempt must be made to determine as accurately as possible the original contents as they left the hand of the work's main author. This is necessary because it can scarcely be doubted as a presupposition, nor is it in any case seriously disputed by anyone, that the work of Chr. has fared no differently from practically all other parts of the Old Testament tradition. As a result, its original shape will have been altered to a greater or lesser extent into what we have now by various subsequent additions and expansions both small and large. Only the extent and nature of this alteration are initially uncertain and have yet to be determined. Indeed, it may even be said that all previous descriptions of the character of Chr. have suffered either from failing altogether to attempt seriously to determine the work's original shape, which is the only proper starting point, or from understanding the task in an inadequate manner or in a way that is clearly at fault in its method.

It must certainly be acknowledged that this undertaking runs up against greater difficulties in the case of Chr. than is usual elsewhere. The main reason for this is the carelessness which the form of the Chr.'s historical narrative displays. It is well known that we are confronted here with an unusually careless style of Hebrew. Chr.'s linguistic usage is strikingly uneven; it is lacking in uniformity and is clearly dependent upon very varied sources. Consequently, a demonstration of the originality or additional nature of any given unit in the tradition can hardly be pursued on the basis of linguistic evidence; at best, it can only be a very rough guide. Alongside this must unfortunately be set the considerable unevenness in the separate elements which make up the whole. In cases where Chr. is giving a word-for-word transcription of sources which are known to us from elsewhere, he may without hesitation cut across the existing context and narrate incidents without having recorded the matters which they presuppose, or he may pass over their necessary consequences in complete silence. In cases where he was not so tied to the fixed verbal form of the sources at his disposal but was himself composing freely, it may certainly be supposed that he paid greater attention to the present context of what he was narrating. Even in these cases, however, one cannot without qualification build on the likelihood that he has traced the course of the narrative completely smoothly, without any gaps or contradiction. The foregoing all relates primarily to numerous matters of detail. The work as a whole, by contrast, is by no means constructed without design. There are certain leading themes which come so prominently to expression that they provide clear guidelines for tracking down the original form of the work.

This search for the original form of the work is a purely literary-critical task. In no way must it be combined with historical considerations about the reliability of the narrative. Nor should a discussion of Chr.'s use of sources be admitted as part of this initial task, for without any doubt the extensive extracts from sources which he demonstrably includes are pressed into the service of his primary aims. For this reason the question of sources can only be taken up when the original form of the work has been broadly ascertained. Of course, we have to allow for the possibility that sometimes he continues with the citation of some more extensive passage from his source even if it was not all of particular significance for him, so that here and there it was the source which determined the form which his work took.

In an attempt to analyse the work as it has come down to us, the best starting-point is *the section about David's preparations for building the temple, 1 Chron. 22–29.* It is generally recognized that 23.(2b), 3-27.34 is a massive insertion; it clearly interrupts the original connection between 23.1, 2a and 28.1ff.[1] 22.1-13[2] tells how, after he had determined the site for the future temple, David prepared the workforce and material for the building and commissioned his son Solomon to carry out the work. Then, according to 23.1, 2a, when David was 'old and full of days', he made Solomon king and summoned 'all the princes of Israel'.[3] At this assembly, as 28.1–29.25 goes on immediately to relate, David makes a public announcement about the work of temple building which Solomon is to complete, hands over to Solomon the model of the future temple,[4] and addresses Solomon with a few further words of encouragement. He announces in addition that further donations of costly materials will be made from the royal treasury for the building of the temple, and invites the 'princes' to do likewise, whereupon David's prayer of thanksgiving, together with sacrifices and the public enthronement of Solomon, brings the whole celebration to a close. The coherence of this self-contained narrative is interrupted just after the notice about the summoning of the assembly of the 'princes'[5] by a great conglomeration of lists of all sorts of temple personnel and the like. This is seen to be all the more out of place for the fact that neither before nor after[6] is there mention of priests, Levites or other temple officials.[7] The strange nature of this insertion has, of course, been noted before. Commentators on Chronicles have usually tried to explain it by saying that Chr. was following some otherwise unknown source for the account of the preparations for the temple building and that into this he in turn inserted off his own bat the lists of priests, Levites and so on.[8] Generally speaking, the basis for this explanation lies in the presupposed view that lists of all kinds of temple personnel were a matter of special interest to Chr. and that therefore such lists must in principle be attributed to him.

Now, following what has been said above, it may be felt that it is not sufficient to argue against this conclusion by referring to the extremely disorganized nature of this collection of lists (in which it is certainly possible to isolate a basic core from later additions), nor to the mere fact of the unattractive interruption of the narrative between 23.2a and 28.1. However, the account of David's care over the preparations for the future building of the temple is in fact bound up so closely with Chr.'s total presentation that it cannot but be traced back to Chr. himself. By the same token the collection of lists at once proves itself to be a subsequent expansion.

In this account of his Chr. ventures to enter a correction to the old and historically reliable tradition about the construction of the Jerusalem temple by Solomon. The ascription to David of the decisive resolve to build the temple and of all the necessary preparations is indeed such a correction; it stops short only at an outright contradiction of a historical fact which was so securely embedded in the tradition. In no way can this correction be separated from the role which Chr. attributes to David. Chr. already brings this role into play by the way in which, in the interests of Jerusalem and the Jerusalem sanctuary, he departs from the literary sources at his disposal and opens his whole historical narrative with the elevation of David to be king over 'Israel' and with David's capture of Jerusalem. Hypothetically to adduce some otherwise unknown source for the section about the preparations for building the temple means attributing one of the fundamental leading themes of Chr.'s work to an author whose very existence is merely postulated. One would therefore have to assume that Chr. had a double, but for his existence we have otherwise no kind of positive support. Such an assumption lacks even the barest probability. What is more, in 1 Chron. 22.1-13; 23.1, 2a; 28.1–29.25 we find some evident characteristics of Chr.'s literary style which can be observed elsewhere in his work. To this category belongs the dependence on the style of Dtr. (cf. 22.9aβ, 12, 13; 28.8, 20), which is due to the fact that Dtr. was one of Chr.'s chief sources, and also the way in which echoes of other Old Testament literature (principally passages from the Prophets and Psalms) are worked into the composition (cf. 28.2 with Ps. 132.7, 8, 14; 28.9 with Gen. 6.5; 8.21; Jer. 29.13f.).[9] If this is due elsewhere to the author of Chronicles, and hence to Chr., then the same will apply here also.

The lists of temple personnel in 1 Chron. 23–27 are thus certainly to be regarded as a later addition to Chr. The purpose of fitting them in at this point was to trace back to David the origins of the late post-exilic divisions of the various cultic servants. Why did this happen to the history of David preserved in Chr. and not to that in 2 Samuel? The answer is bound up with the fact that, by the time these lists originated, not only the Pentateuch, but also the books of Joshua-Kings, had become such fixed and venerated items in the literary tradition that no one dared any longer to make large insertions in them.

Once 1 Chron. 23–27 is recognized as a secondary addition to Chr., then the present literary state of these chapters, with their varied and closely intertwined lists, can also be explained in a simple and unforced manner: to this first core more lists, and additions to the individual lists, were subsequently added one on top of another. We are presented here with a typical picture of the gradual proliferation of literary growth. At the same time Chr., whose work admittedly exhibits elsewhere enough in the way of formal and factual unevenness, is exonerated by this recognition from a particularly disturbing aesthetic shortcoming. It is not necessary in the present context to follow through the gradual development of the insertion in more precise detail;[10] the important point, rather, is the general conclusion that in 1 Chron. 23–27 we have a definite example of the fact that Chr.'s narrative work was secondarily expanded by a presentation in the form of lists of various arrangements and orderings of the late post-exilic community.[11]

*The first part of the historical narrative about David in 1 Chron. 10–21* is dealt with ·in a relatively clear manner. Using the David narrative in 2 Samuel as a guiding source, Chr. directs the history of king David towards the goal of the preparations for the building of the temple. David's elevation to be king over 'Israel' after the death of Saul is forged into a chronologically and factually self-contained event with the conquest of Jerusalem by 'David and all Israel' and the decision to bring the holy ark into the new capital (1 Chron. 10–13).[12] In ch. 14 Chr. makes skilful use of the interruption in the bringing up of the ark to work in the material found in his source at 2 Sam. 5.11-25. He probably did this mainly for the sake of the introductory statement about David's building of a palace in Jerusalem. The note in 15.1 about the place which David prepared for the ark then joins on smoothly to this. This is followed by an important passage—the bringing of the ark into Jerusalem (chs. 15 and 16)—and further by the great promise of Nathan to David, which is of equal significance to Chr. (ch. 17). After Chr. has then followed both the outline and the wording of his source to relate the accounts of David's successes in war (chs. 18–20), he partly reshapes (ch. 21) the history of the census of the people (2 Sam. 24) in order to arrive at the choice of the site for the future temple. The way is then clear for the preparations for the building of the temple to begin. Jerusalem, ark and preparations for the building of the temple are the major themes of Chr.'s presentation of the history of David, and for these he makes use of his own free composition in addition to the source he is following. Alongside these themes he goes on to cite from his source the notices about Nathan's promise and the wars against the surrounding peoples.

In this whole section only ch. 12 and parts of chs. 15 and 16 arouse the suspicion that secondary expansions are included. First, the list in 12.24-41 is certainly a later addition. If Chr. had already known this detailing of the representatives of all the tribes of Israel who came flocking to Hebron at David's coronation,[13] he would have been able to spare himself the bother of running through the list of many individuals in 11.10-47 who, according to his version, supported David's elevation to the throne. So originally 12.24-41 was certainly added as an expansion of 11.10-47 in order to serve as a further contribution to the same theme. In that case, however, the stories which come in between in 12.1-23 are presumably even later additions. In any case they hardly fit into Chr.'s structure, because they list those who came to support David during the time of his stay at Ziklag and so refer to the period of David's gradual rise to power, a period which Chr. leaves quite outside his purview. Unfortunately we can no longer determine with any assurance the origin of the names and lists which make up all these additions.

When we turn to ch. 15,[14] verses 4-10 are first of all clearly a late expansion. By coming in secondarily they render the material in v. 11 quite superfluous. As he generally does in such cases Chr. has enumerated the names of some Levites in v. 11—probably names which were current in his own day. A reviser has subsequently expanded this by working these names into a Levitical genealogy in vv. 4-10, which was possibly only constructed *ad hoc*. Further, the interlude in 15.16-24, which deals once more with the disposition of the cultic personnel who were to officiate at the bringing up of the ark, is an addition. This can be seen by the fact that it should follow v. 13 at the latest but comes too late after v. 15, while v. 25 provides the smooth continuation of v. 15. 16.5 intrudes quite abruptly, while on the other hand 16.39 can originally only have been the continuation of 16.4;[15] the verb in 16.4 must at first have governed 16.39 as well.[16] According to Chr.'s version in 16.4, 39 and 40, after the transfer of the ark David briefly made arrangements for the division of the cultic personnel between the two cult centres of Jerusalem and Gibeon.[17] This information has given rise to a secondary insertion in vv. 5-38 (with which vv. 41 and 42 belong) concerning official Levitical duties. This insertion is again not a unity in itself, for the Psalm in vv. 7-36, at any rate, is a more recent element within it.[18]

Thus on the basis of purely literary-critical considerations it has so far been established that the work of Chr. has been subsequently expanded, primarily by all sorts of lists; and amongst these secondary lists arrangements concerning the organization and official functions of cultic personnel make up an especially large part. Within this the condition of the expansions, which is often very complicated from a literary point of view, together with the fact that the divisions of the cultic personnel are presented in very varied forms, shows that we are not dealing by any means with a unified redaction of Chr., but with a rank growth of all manner of literary accretions.

Concerning *the history of Solomon in 2 Chron. 1-9* there is not a great deal to be said in the present context, for there is no reason to doubt that we read this section, on the whole, in the form in which it left the hand of Chr. Although the digression in 5.11b-13a interrupts the original connection between 5.11a and 13b, it could nevertheless go back to Chr. himself, for he is citing his source verbatim both before and after and he is often quite careless about such formal matters. There are just a few individual elements in this digression which appear to be added in the wake of 1 Chron. 23–27—for instance v. 11bβ and the special mention of the singers in vv. 12a and 13a. The same may apply to 8.14 and 15, where again secondary reference is made to 1 Chron. 23–27.

The section dealing with *the history of the Judaean kings in 2 Chron. 10–36* also offered little motive for the insertion of later expansions into the work of Chr. Apart from the usual small textual distortions which crop up in the course of any manuscript tradition, it lies before us in the form which Chr. gave it. In the present context only 23.18 and 35.15 deserve mention. In the former, the passage from the word 'the Levites' (which is introduced without connection with what precedes) to the end of the verse looks like an addition; again, it probably refers to 1 Chron. 23–27. Similarly in the latter (35.15), the passage 'Asaph, and Heman, and Jeduthun the king's seer' obviously originated as an addition intended on the basis of 1 Chron. 25 to correct the reference to 'the sons of Asaph' in Chr.'s original text.

It stands out in even bolder relief, therefore, that secondary material has grown up round the work of Chr. in *the introductory genealogical section in 1 Chron. 1–9*. In the form in which it has come down to us the condition of this section is one of unusually great disorder and confusion, but for this, as will be shown immediately below, Chr. cannot be held responsible. Here again it is innumerable genealogies and lists which have been subsequently added in to Chr.'s work.

It is true that no serious objection can be raised against any part of the first chapter. Here, in concise genealogies which are often reduced merely to the bare outline, the line is followed from Adam to the ancestors of the twelve tribes of Israel. Coupled with this are various subsidiary lines which are, strictly speaking, unnecessary for the immediate context. The various slight overlaps, such as that between v. 17 and v. 24 and between v. 28 and v. 34a, can be explained simply enough by Chr.'s use of diverse sources and are not indicative of significant unevennesses. Moreover, the fact that two larger segments of this chapter are lacking in one branch of the Septuagint tradition[19] does not justify the conclusion that they did not belong to the original. The omission of the passage from v. 17aβ to the second word of v. 24 is merely the result of homoioteleuton,[20] and accordingly the omission of vv. 11-16 is no doubt also to be traced to the carelessness of the translator or of the manuscript tradition of the Septuagint.[21]

The genealogical trees of the Israelite tribes in chs. 2–9, on the other hand, are laden with obviously secondary material. This circumstance has led to the most varied attempts to work out the original basic form of these chapters. It is not necessary to discuss these attempts in detail because, it seems to me, they have not been successful in their aim. The solution of this literary-critical question is to be found in 7.12-13; these verses are apparently hopelessly corrupt and so have always remained unexplained. The original text here evidently read:

> .... and Shupham and Hupham.
> The sons of Dan: Shuham.
> The sons of Asher ...
> The sons of Naphtali: Jahziel etc.

One needs only to compare Num. 26.39ff. with this to see at once that we are dealing, in 1 Chron. 7.12f., with the fragment of an extract from the great tribal and clan list of Num. 26, a list which deals only with the generation immediately following the sons of Israel.[22] Furthermore, the order of the tribes can be explained only on the basis of Numbers 26 and Numbers 1: this order is not attested in any other place in the Old Testament. Conversely, the agreement with Numbers 26 confirms the correctness of the proposed textual reconstruction of 1 Chron. 7.12f. This recognition seems certain to me. Once accepted, however, it has far-reaching consequences. The fragment contained in 1 Chron. 7.12f. cannot be regarded as a later addition, for there could be no motive for introducing an addition of this sort at just this point. In particular a secondary reference to Asher would be out of place at this point in view of the section about Asher in 7.30ff. The only possibility which remains, then, is that we have here a fragment of the basic core of the material; and this basic core, which rests on a reworking of Numbers 26, we have traced back to Chr. In fact an extract from Numbers 26 forms the basic element of almost all the sections dealing with the individual tribes (cf. 2.3-5; 4.24; 5.3; 7.1; 7.12, 13; 7.*14-19; 7.20; 7.30; 8.1). To this are attached the other genealogies and lists. The situation in 1 Chron. 7.12f. thus immediately teaches us that for the tribes which are mentioned here

Chr. has merely provided a short extract from Numbers 26, a chapter in which the tribes follow one another in quick succession. Certain details, which remain to be discussed, show that in addition Chr. probably took the list in Gen. 46.8-27 into account. This was only to be expected. In any case, from a literary point of view Gen. 46.8-27 is itself dependent on Numbers 26. Of course it cannot be convincingly proved from the brief formulation in 1 Chron. 7.12f. that in the case of some of the tribes which were of especial concern to him (one thinks in the first place of the tribes of Judah and Levi) Chr. did not offer more than the extract from Numbers 26. In the main, however, the great bulk of that which we now read in 1 Chron. 2-9 is shown on the basis of 1 Chron. 7.12f. to be a secondary accretion to the work of Chr. This has now almost completely concealed the original basic material and has also caused serious disturbance of the original arrangement.

In 1 Chron. 2ff., accordingly, Chr. continues to follow his procedure in 1 Chron. 1 of extracting from the Pentateuch all kinds of lists for his genealogical introduction. And just as in 1 Chron. 23-27, so here, countless further lists have subsequently been added one on top of another. In most cases it is impossible to ascertain their origin in detail. These supplements have mostly been slotted in with little careful regard for the context which already exists. Thus in the course of time there developed the confused picture which chs. 2-9 now present. With all due reserve, the attempt can nonetheless be made to determine the original core which derives from Chr.

By a link with the name 'Israel' in 1.34b, Chr. first lists the twelve sons of Israel in 2.1f. roughly in accordance with Gen. 35.23-26.[23] He then proceeds in 2.3 to a treatment of the individual sons of Israel— or rather of the Israelite tribes—on the basis of Numbers 26. By contrast with Numbers 26, however, he has altered the order of the tribes at various points according to some important aspects of his viewpoint. Thus he has understandably started off with the tribe of *Judah* (2.3ff.) and devoted to it a quite exceptional treatment. To the extract from Num. 26.19ff. (Gen. 46.12) he has added in some associated statements from Gen. 38 (vv. 3 and 4)[24] and exceptionally he has here in addition carried the genealogy on to the second generation (v. 5),[25] obviously so that he could attach further items of information to it. In fact the genealogy of David and his brothers which comes in vv. 9-15,[26] and which links up with v. 5, should most probably be attributed to Chr. himself because Chr. manifests a particular interest in the figure of David. This interest adequately explains the deviation from the procedure which Chr. otherwise adheres to in his genealogical introduction of reworking material from the Pentateuch in the form of extracts. The only question which remains unanswered is, where did Chr. get this family tree of David from?[27] It is hardly to be expected that anything which follows in 2.18–4.23 is to be attributed to the basic core which can be traced back to Chr.[28]

In the case of *Simeon* (4.24–43), where obviously only the extract from Num. 26.12f.[29] in v. 24 belongs to the original material, it may be doubted whether it was Chr. himself who brought about the close association with Judah in dependence upon the proximity of Simeon's dwelling place with that of Judah, because geographical considerations were far from his mind in this context. Perhaps it was the one responsible for expanding this passage by adding in the list of Simeon's dwelling places (vv. 28-33) from Josh. 19.2-8a who on the basis of the geographical considerations just mentioned changed round the order of the section dealing with Reuben and Simeon. As far as Chr. himself is concerned, after having put Judah first he will then have reverted to following the order of Numbers 26 (Reuben, Simeon, etc.). At any rate, in the case of *Reuben* (5.1-10) the original basic element is again only the extract from Num. 26.5f. (Gen. 46.9) in v. 3. This can be seen from the lack of any connection between v. 3 and what follows it in either form or content.[30] As v. 11 explicitly notes, the present order of what then follows (5.11-26) is determined by attention to the geographical association by settlement of the three Transjordanian tribes. That, however, applies only to the stage of the later expansions, for they are all that we now find in the section 5.11-26, where there is no trace of the work of Chr. Consequently, it can no longer be definitely ascertained whether at first Chr. included an extract from the list concerning *Gad* in dependence on Numbers 26, this having afterwards, and as an exception to what happened elsewhere, been suppressed completely by the later material about Gad in vv. 11ff., or whether Chr. did not rather follow the order in Gen. 46 and his own enumeration in 2.1f. and move on immediately to Levi after Simeon–Reuben (or more probably Reuben–Simeon). In the latter case he would have introduced Gad at some later point and his notice about Gad would then have been lost secondarily.[31]

In the long section about *Levi* (5.27–6.66) the bulk of the material is undoubtedly of secondary origin. This is certainly so for the extensive passage in 6.39-66 dealing with the priestly and Levitical cities. Its geographical content marks it out as foreign to the genealogical introduction. So too, however, is the presentation in 6.16-33 of the Levitical singers whom David appointed to minister before the ark. If Chr. had wanted to give information about this arrangement, he would undoubtedly have introduced it in connection with 1 Chron. 16.4. Finally, a similar verdict applies to the high priests' genealogy in 5.27-41. Its addition has given rise to an anticipation of the original opening of the list concerning Levi in 6.1-4. Most commentators have rightly judged that it is an addition. Everything else may, perhaps, be attributed to Chr., on the assumption that Chr. devoted an exceptionally extensive treatment to the tribe of Levi, as in the case of the tribe of Judah. The core of the original material, at any rate, comes in 6.1-4, where Num. 3.17-20 is repeated. No serious objection can be raised against 6.34-38 either; it traces the Aaronic line down to the time of David, the point at which Chr. later begins his own historical narrative. The most that could be said against it is that Aaron himself is not firmly integrated into the general Levitical genealogy, even though Chr. could have found information about this in the Pentateuch which he was using. It is very doubtful whether 6.5-15 belongs to the original material;[32] the secondary character of similar lists of names in the case of other tribes tells in favour of 6.5-15 being a later addition.

According to Numbers 26 the tribes of *Issachar* and *Zebulun* should follow next. We do in fact find the extract from Num. 26.23f. (Gen. 46.13) concerning the tribe of Issachar in 7.1, to which the further details about Issachar in 7.2-5 have been subsequently added. Chr.'s information about Zebulun, however, which we expect to follow in succession to Issachar, has been completely lost. It fell victim to the severe disturbances which affected the original order at this point and which will be discussed immediately below. 7.12f. was the passage from which we ascertained the plan of the original material. It emerges from this that, following Issachar and Zebulun and in complete conformity with the arrangement in Numbers 26, the extracts relating to the tribes of *Manasseh*, *Ephraim* and *Benjamin* originally came next. However, in the present form of the text there is nothing about Manasseh and Ephraim at this point, while in the section about Benjamin in 7.6-11 there is no trace of an extract from Numbers 26. On the contrary this all follows only later, in 7.14ff., 7.20 and 8.1. Why this group of Rachel-tribes was subsequently displaced to the end can no longer be certainly stated;[33] at all events, this happened in connection with the expansion of the original basic material. The first two words of 7.12, which are the names of the last two sons of Benjamin in Num. 26.39, show that the Rachel-tribes were represented here merely by the extracts from Numbers 26. This, then, is the place where once there was found the extract from Num. 26.29ff. concerning Manasseh. It now clearly underlies 1 Chron. 7.14-19, albeit in a form which has secondarily become severely confused. The same applies to the extract from Num. 26.35 concerning Ephraim which is present in 1 Chron. 7.20 but which has subsequently been amalgamated with further lists of names and other incidents. Finally, the same can be said for the extract from Num. 26.38f. (Gen. 46.21)[34] concerning Benjamin in 1 Chron. 8.1ff. Again, it has been confused with further Benjamite lists of names and it has been expanded extensively. Presumably, as in the case of Asher further on, the headings, at least, were at first left standing in their original place ('the sons of Manasseh, the sons of Ephraim, the sons of Benjamin'), and this gave the later reviser his opportunity to slot in an obviously quite secondary section about Benjamin in 7.6-11.[35]

In the basic material according to 1 Chron. 7.12 there next followed the extract from Num. 26.42 (Gen. 46.23) about *Dan*, and then the extract for *Asher* from Num. 26.44f. (Gen. 46.17). Of the latter only the heading was preserved in its original place, and, what is more, for reasons unknown to us, it was later transferred to 7.30-40, where it now stands very awkwardly between Ephraim and Benjamin.[36] The extract for *Naphtali* from Num. 26.48f. (Gen. 46.24) in 7.13[37] formed the original conclusion to Chr.'s information about the tribes of Israel. Apart from the secondarily displaced sections concerning a few of the tribes, everything which now follows up until the end of ch. 9 is to be analysed as follows: first and foremost the list of the inhabitants of Jerusalem in 9.1-34, which certainly does not derive from Chr. since only later does he tell of the capture of Jerusalem by David, and then the short list of Gibeonites in 8.29-32 (= 9.35-38), which Chr. scarcely had reason to introduce. It may be conceded that Chr. might have had cause to include the genealogy of Saul in 8.33-40 (= 9.39-44) because of the account of the death of Saul which follows in ch. 10. This genealogy, however, is traced down much too far, and besides, 7.12 shows that, although Saul's genealogy must have originally been included with the tribe of

Benjamin, Chr. introduced no more of this latter than the list extracted from Numbers 26.

It may thus be concluded that in his introductory genealogical section about the Israelite tribes Chr. included only quite short notices derived from Numbers 26 (Gen. 46). These were enriched only by a Davidic genealogy in the case of Judah and probably by a genealogy of the high priests in the case of Levi.[38] The great bulk of that which is now found in 1 Chron. 2–9 is a confused and secondary mass of rank textual growth.

*The books of Ezra and Nehemiah* pose the most difficult questions with regard to the original shape of Chr. To start with, of course, following the results of our discussion so far, the numerous lists of names must fall under suspicion of having been added secondarily. Thereafter, it remains to be determined to what extent the arrangement of these books as we now have them (especially in regard to Neh. 8–10) goes back to Chr. and how far it is the result of secondary disruptions.

*The section about the return and temple building in Ezra 1–6* may in all essentials be ascribed to the hand of Chr. as it now stands. Small additions are naturally to be found here too. Noteworthy in this regard are the notices about the celebration of the feast of Tabernacles and the institution of the regular burnt offerings in 3.4–5, because they interrupt the direct connection between vv. 3 and 6.[39] In addition, the listing by name of the Levites who supervised the temple building in 3.9[40] is out of place after the generalizing statement of v. 8.

The main question in this connection, however, is whether the large list in 2.1ff. of those who returned, itself in any case an independent element in the tradition, was already included by Chr. within his narrative or whether it represents a later addition. Sound method demands that we should first try to answer this question in terms of the literary composition of Ezra 1–6—that is to say, without consideration of the repetition of this list in Neh. 7.

First of all, a not insignificant question concerns the correct determination of the extent of this list, or to be more precise, the question of its ending. To begin with, it seems certain to me that 2.70 is not part of the list but must belong to the narrative framework. This is because of the necessity that between the notice in 1.11 that the exiles returned to Jerusalem under Sheshbazzar and the statement in 3.1b that, at the beginning of the seventh month (as 3.1a observes) 'the people, who were in their towns, gathered together as one in Jerusalem', there must have been some statement to the effect that those who returned had settled in the Judaean countryside as well as in Jerusalem; and such a statement is clearly to be discerned in 2.70 despite the precise form in which the text has come down to us.[41] The only remaining question, then, is whether the preceding passage (2.68, 69) should be included in the list or ascribed rather to the narrative framework. Consideration of the present text of v. 68, with its talk of an arrival at 'the house of the Lord in Jerusalem', might lead one to think of the latter possibility, and 2.68 could follow on smoothly from 1.11. However, as v. 68 is unusually badly phrased even for Chr., it is preferable to regard this abbreviated relative clause in 2.68 as an addition.[42] Its purpose will have been to forge a special link with the historical situation described in the narrative framework. In that case, 2.68-69 can then best be regarded as the conclusion of the main list.

Concerning the main list, whose extent we have thus defined as 2.1-69, there is unfortunately no positive evidence that it already stood in the work of Chr. It could be removed without leaving a gap. Moreover, nothing in what follows makes explicit reference to it. The citation of 2.40 in 3.9 has been shown to be an addition. The fact that in 3.10 the Asaphites are named as Levitical singers cannot be viewed as a particular reference to 2.41 alone, because in the main list the 'singers' are not yet regarded as Levites, whereas elsewhere Chr. knows of Asaph (and Asaph alone) as a Levitical singer in David's time and of the Asaphites as Levitical singers (2 Chron. 20.14; 29.30; 35.15[43]). On the other hand, it has to be admitted that there is also no sound proof against the presence of 2.1-69 in the work of Chr. The fact that the original text of 2.70 speaks only of priests and Levites in contrast with the list's divisions of cultic personnel shows no more than that the list was not compiled by the same author as the narrative framework; it does not prove that this narrative could not have included the list from the very beginning as a separate item. All that will have happened in 2.70 is that, in accordance with later practice, all the non-priestly cultic personnel will have been summarized under the heading of 'Levites'.[44] On the principle of *in dubio pro re*, it is therefore best to accept that the main list was originally included in the work of Chr.

In Ezra 1-6, therefore, we have first the decree of Cyrus and the consequential return of the exiles under Sheshbazzar to which is joined the long, inserted list. Then, with a rather abrupt appearance of Zerubbabel and Joshua[45] as leaders, there follows the reinstitution of the sacrificial cult in Jerusalem together with the start made on the building of the temple. This, however, was immediately hindered by 'the enemies of Judah and Benjamin' and, as 4.5 remarks in conclusion, it had to be suspended until the time of the Persian king Darius. Following this, the temporary hindering of the temple building as well as the eventual completion of the work is described in detail in the long insertion in Aramaic, 4.6-6.18.[46] After this insertion, 6.19-22 merely remarks that this completion of the work was celebrated with the ceremonies of Passover and Unleavened Bread just as had been the case in their turn with the major temple reforms under Hezekiah and Josiah (2 Chron. 30.1ff.; 35.1ff.).

The history of Ezra is joined on quite loosely in 7.1. Its first section, *the account of Ezra's journey to Jerusalem in Ezra 7-8*, manifests several clearly later expansions of the work of Chr.[47] That 7.7 is an addition[48] with which v. 8 does not connect smoothly is obvious. It seems to me, however, that 7.8-9 is also an expansion, albeit one that is earlier than v. 7. It anticipates the following narrative and separates v. 10 from v. 6 even though the generally expressed substantiation in v. 10 fits by far the best as an explanation for the last words of v. 6. Admittedly this expansion has been fitted relatively well into the contxt,[49] so that its secondary character is not immediately apparent. Nevertheless, it seems clear enough to me that it is indeed an addition. An important consequence of this is that in the basic text of Ezra 7 Ezra was at first dated only generally within the reign of Artaxerxes; no specific year was mentioned.[50]

It is also uncertain whether the list in 8.1-14 belonged to Chr.[51] There are reasons for believing, however, that it was an independent piece which was worked into the original form of the narrative. The unusual way of referring to those who accompanied Ezra simply as 'heads' in 7.28 is best explained as a reference to the heading of the following list. Furthermore, 8.15 does not join smoothly on to 7.28; rather, the resumption of the verb of 7.28bβ at the start of 8.15 is most simply understood as due to regard for the list which has been inserted. Finally, the curious story in 8.15bff. about the initial lack of Levites may be traced back to the fact that no Levites were named in a list which the narrative inherited and used. The Levites who were then eventually fetched by a commission of 'heads'[52] were not explicitly named, for the way in which 8.18d-19[53] is joined on betrays it as an addition;[54] similarly, the repetition in 8.24 of the two Levitical names mentioned here is obviously an expansion. Finally, the date in 8.31 arouses suspicion because elsewhere in this narrative short periods of time are mentioned only occasionally and then without dates (8.15, 32) and because the note in 8.31 is clearly related to the secondary verses 7.8-9.

Though *the account of Ezra's handling of the mixed-marriages affair in Ezra 9-10* is attached loosely,[55] no objection need be raised against it. Basically, everything in this passage runs along smoothly; the only open question is whether the list in Ezra 10.18, 20-44 belonged to the original form of the text. The way in which it is joined on arouses misgivings: there is no motive for the position of 10.19 in the middle of the introduction to the list, there being no apparent reason why only the first group of priests should have pledged themselves on oath to dissolve their mixed marriages and why only they should have brought a guilt offering.[56] Verse 19 follows on immediately from v. 17, and the list, whose opening interrupts this connection, must therefore be regarded as a later addition to the work of Chr.

In Ezra 7-10, then, there is first, after an introduction, the edict of Artaxerxes about Ezra's mission in Aramaic (7.11-26) and then, after a brief expression of praise in hymnic form by Ezra (7.27-28a), the account of Ezra's journey and of those who went with him from Babylon to Jerusalem (7.28b—8.36), and of Ezra's handling of the mixed-marriages affair (9.1-10.17, 19). In all this the most striking feature is the abrupt appearance of the use of the first person by Ezra in the hymnic expression, a form of narration which is retained thereafter until, equally abruptly, it is replaced again by the third person after Ezra's great confession caused by the mixed marriages (9.6-15). This feature is all the more curious because of the fact that the section which is marked out by the use of the first person cannot be distinguished in any other way as regards its literary form from what follows and because, furthermore, no break can be discerned on the ground of content between 9.15 and 10.1. On the contrary, the whole is marked by an inevitable continuity. Unless we want to assume that someone has subsequently changed part of a first person account into the third person, or *vice versa*, we have no alternative but to conclude that, after the hymnic expression (where the first person was fully appropriate), the author of the narrative then carried on somewhat thoughtlessly with 'I' or 'we', and that he finally reverted again to the use of the third person for Ezra after the prayer, in which once more 'I' had been used for a particular reason.

After Ezra 10, Neh. 1.1 introduces *the history of Nehemiah* most abruptly. As is well known, Chr. starts out here by following the Nehemiah memoir, which he retains in the first person. On the basis of this memoir he narrates the sending of Nehemiah to Jerusalem as governor and the successful undertaking and completion of the task of building the walls of Jerusalem in the teeth of all opposition. He also includes some social measures which Nehemiah undertook (Neh. 5). Throughout this passage (1.1-7.3) there are only occasional supplements to the Nehemiah memoir. In particular, the list of participants in the wall-bulding (3.1-32) has been explained as secondary.[57] However, the reasons adduced in support of this opinion are hardly convincing. It cannot be maintained with any degree of certainty that the list must properly come after 2.18 and before 2.19-20, because 2.19-20 does not necessarily presuppose the start of the wall-building but only the preparations for it. If that were not the case, 3.33-38 would have to go as a doublet of 2.19-20 just as much as the list. In reality, however, 3.33-38[58] shows that the list stands in its appropriate place. Nor can it be said that the list ascribes the initiative for the wall-building to the High Priest Eliashib; it is simply that, for understandable reasons, he is listed first of those who participated in the wall-building under Nehemiah's direction. I can see no decisive reason why the list should not have belonged to the Nehemiah memoir; at any rate, it certainly belonged to it by the time Chr. came to use this memoir as the basis for his history of Nehemiah.[59] For his part, in 1.1-7.3 Chr. did not add anything of great significance to this source which he took over. To him must be ascribed the prayer of Nehemiah in 1.5-11a, which is formulated in the Deuteronomic style, together with the remark in 6.11aβ, which adds a point of view concerning the sanctity of the temple to the words of Nehemiah, and the verb 'to sin' in 6.13 which goes with it.[60]

In this light it stands out all the more strongly that the Nehemiah memoir has been expanded secondarily in 7.4ff. With 7.4-5a the

Nehemiah memoir begins to deal with the topic of increasing the population of the newly-walled town, and for this purpose Nehemiah summons an assembly of the people to Jerusalem. Leaving aside for the moment the repetition of the long list of Ezra 2.1-3.1a in Neh. 7.6-72, this last remark provided the opportunity to include *the account of the reading of the law by Ezra to the assembled population and its consequences in Neh. 8-10*. It is obvious that this account represents the fulfilment of Ezra's mission according to Ezra 7.14, 25f. (cf. earlier 7.10) and that it therefore belongs very closely with the Ezra history in Ezra 7-10. Consequently, the nowadays frequent suggestion that these three chapters should be transferred to the book of Ezra (i.e. the assumption that they originally stood there in the work of Chr.) seems entirely reasonable. It can be further shown that Neh. (7.6-72;) 8-10 is an insertion from the fact that Neh. 11.1 picks up again the threads of the Nehemiah memoir which were dropped at Neh. 7.5a. The weaving together of the activity of Ezra and Nehemiah which this insertion presupposes is obviously based on the idea that Ezra's main task, the enforcement of the law, could only be carried through once the condition and security of the post-exilic community had been guaranteed by Nehemiah's completion of the wall-building. The resultant order of the various events can only have developed before Ezra's journey to Jerusalem was fixed precisely in the seventh year of Artaxerxes by the addition of Ezra 7:(7)8-9,[61] an addition which meant that Ezra would have had to wait quietly for thirteen years before fulfilling his real task; but more than this, it must also have developed at a time when Ezra was dated in only a quite general way to the the reign of Artaxerxes so that a chronological overlap with Nehemiah could be assumed without difficulty.

We are still faced, however, with the question whether the order of the chapters as we now have them goes back to Chr. or to a subsequent redactor. The content of Neh. 8-10 belongs in such an obvious way with Ezra 7-10 that it would be utterly impossible to understand how a later redactor could have arrived at the decision secondarily to separate these two elements which *ex hypothesi* once stood together.[62] Consequently, only the author of the complete work, that is to say, Chr., can have been responsible for the order which has come down to us. As a result of so doing, Chr., after introducing Ezra with his task of enforcing the law of God (Ezra 7.10), first had him dispose of the most striking abuse—the mixed marriages (Ezra 9-10). Then, however, he had Nehemiah take care of the wall-building in order after its completion to use the opportunity provided by Nehemiah's summoning of a general assembly in Jerusalem to have Ezra appear once more to read the law.[63] This conclusion is of a literary-critical nature only, and should not be confused in any way with historical considerations; it is purely a matter of determining the arrangement in Chr.

Amongst the secondary material must be reckoned above all the repetition in Neh. 7.6-72 of the long list from Ezra 2 with 7.5b as a redactional link. Even if we disregard the argument that there is no decisive objection against the list in Ezra 2 having belonged to the work of Chr. and that Chr. would hardly have used the same list twice,[64] the secondary nature of Neh. 7.6-72 is nevertheless apparent. This can be seen from the fact that a part of the narrative continuation in Ezra 2 (namely Ezra 2.70-3.1a) has been taken over by Neh. 7 (Neh. 7.72);[65] however, this is only partially suitable in the context of Neh. 7,[66] whereas it is in its proper place in Ezra 2. A later editor who took a particular delight in lists used the remark of Neh. 7.5a that Nehemiah had a genealogy drawn up of those who had been summoned to Jerusalem for the resettlement[67] as an opportunity for the complete citation of the whole of the long list in Ezra 2. In Chr., 8.1 would have followed on immediately from 7.5a. If the connection is a bit harsh, that is only because at this same point Chr. stopped following the Nehemiah memoir and began a completely new account. The list of signatories in Neh. 10.2-28[68] is also secondary. It interrupts the flow of the narrative which is in the 'we' form; the sentence which begins in 10.1 is continued in the first two words of v. 29,[69] in the first word of v. 30,[70] and further in v. 30aβff. Finally, 10.38b-40a interrupts its context and so is a later addition.

Concerning the text in detail, we may note that it is hardly necessary to change anything in Neh. 8.7-8. The Levites who give instruction in the law are so much a part of Chr.'s world (cf. 2 Chron. 17.7-9; also 19.4-11) that he could easily have introduced them here even though the context is not very suitable. It is difficult to determine for certain what the original subject of Neh. 8.9 was. According to v. 10 it was in the singular, so that we can first eliminate the Levites as an addition; besides, they are introduced afresh in v. 11. After that, we have to make a choice between the two remaining possible subjects. It is such an obvious step for someone to have introduced Ezra here secondarily that his name has presumably been added. We may note that his name is here amplified by his double title—'the priest, the scribe'—which otherwise occurs only at Ezra 7.11 (on the basis of the heading to the following document) and at Neh. 12.26b, where it is an addition.[71] Working from the Hebrew text alone one might soon conclude that the original subject was 'the Tirshatha', in which case it would remain an open question whom Chr. had in mind. However, precisely this word is lacking from the Septuagint.[72] It must probably be concluded, therefore, that the phrase 'who was the Tirshatha' has been added to the name of Nehemiah, exactly as at Neh. 10.2, and that 'Nehemiah' alone would have stood as the original subject. That Chr. should have thought of Nehemiah at at least one point in Neh. 8–10 would not be surprising. At the same time it would demonstrate that the present position of Neh. 8–10 was original to Chr. We also find a secondary introduction of Ezra in the Septuagint of Neh. 9.6. Once again it was so obvious a step to introduce Ezra at this point that we cannot seriously entertain a preference for the Septuagint text. That the prayer which follows should properly be ascribed to the assembled people[73] can be seen from the fact that in the immediately following 10.1ff. the same people continue as those who are doing the talking.

In *Neh. 11–13* the lists which come between the note from the Nehemiah memoir about the resettlement (11.1-2) and the account of the dedication of the wall (Neh. 12.27ff.) are only very loosely attached to their context. The various lists of priests and Levites in 12.1-26 have nothing whatever to do with the theme of resettlement. They in particular so clearly manifest indications of a growth which has run riot that they must be regarded as additions to the work of Chr. The most appropriate part for the general theme is the list of the inhabitants of Jerusalem in 11.3-19. This in turn, however, is unmistakably related to 1 Chron. 9.1-17, so much so that the dependence of one list upon the other cannot be proved.[74] It is much more probably a case of two separate and independent reworkings of a common original. If 1 Chron. 9 has already been shown to be an addition to Chr., then the same will also hold true for Neh. 11.3-19. Added to this is the fact that Chr. generally classes the gatekeepers amongst the Levites, whereas here (v. 19) they appear as a separate class alongside the Levites.[75] And if that is correct, then the catalogue of towns in Judah and Benjamin, Neh. 11.20-36,[76] must also be regarded as additional to Chr. because from a literary point of view it serves merely as a supplement to Neh. 11.3-19.

*The remainder of the book of Nehemiah (Neh. 12.27–13.31)* supplies the concluding portion of the Nehemiah memoir as worked over by Chr. Here too the work has been expanded by various later hands. In the account of the dedication of the wall the introductory section, Neh. 12.27-29,[77] must be judged to be a post-chronistic addition: Chr. has the Levites living in Jerusalem (Ezra 2.70), whereas here they have to be fetched in to Jerusalem from outside, and this undoubtedly represents the actual circumstances prevailing at the time of the redactor.[78] Another post-chronistic addition is found at 12.46-47, for here the singers (and gatekeepers) have subsequently been put on a par with the priests and Levites, who are treated in vv. 44-45.[79] Finally, 13.1-3 may also be adjudged a very much later addition. It is joined only very loosely to what precedes with the colourless phrase 'on that day'. This passage, which makes no mention of Nehemiah, was certainly no part of the Nehemiah memoir; but it does not belong to Chr. either, because Chr. has already dealt at length with the issue of the exclusion of everything foreign and the punctilious enforcement of the law. He therefore had no need to return to the issue, especially not at such an obscure point. It must therefore be the result of later reflection on Deut. 23.4-6.

## Chapter 15

## THE SOURCES WHICH HAVE BEEN USED

So far, the attempt has been made to establish in general terms the original shape of Chr.'s work. We are now in a position to move on to inquire about the sources which Chr. drew upon and used. It is important to be able to answer this question as precisely as possible, first for the sake of an accurate assessment of Chr. as a literary work in its own right, and also in order to arrive as well at some kind of evaluation of Chr. as an historical source. Chr. was too far removed chronologically from the events which he relates for us to regard him as an historical witness in his own right. He can therefore be consulted by a historian only when he is demonstrably, or at least probably, working on the basis of older literary sources. Now the extent to which Chr. used sources, and the way he has handled them, can be easily and clearly established in those places where the sources themselves are known to us from elsewhere in the Old Testament tradition. The question only becomes difficult when it is a matter of evaluating sources which are otherwise unknown to us— those whose existence and content can be determined only indirectly from Chr. itself. There is at present a definite predominating tendency to be generous in assuming the existence of such sources.[1] Whether such a view is justified deserves to be carefully examined. In undertaking this we must first take the *whole* of the Chronicler's work into account and then move to the investigation of his sources.

It was the Pentateuch in the finished form in which it has come down to us which served Chr. as the main source for the basis of his *introductory genealogical section (1 Chron. 1-9)*. Rothstein-Hänel's attempt[2] to prove that Chr. used the priestly writing as an independent document must be judged unsuccessful. We have already shown above on pp. 36-37 that there is no cogent reason for regarding any significant part of 1 Chron. 1.1–2.5 as secondary;[3] in no way does a literary-critical analysis of this section naturally produce a basic text which could have been derived from P alone.[4] In particular, there can be no serious doubt that Chr. made use of Gen. 10 in a form in which J and P were already joined. It is easy enough to explain why Chr. was predominantly dependent on priestly material for his genealogical extracts from the Pentateuch: for the most part, the genealogical lists in the Pentateuch belong to P.[5] On the other hand, the Pentateuch was practically the only source at Chr.'s disposal for the genealogical introduction. The only passages not from the Pentateuch which it was conjectured above (pp. 38-39 and 40) were part of Chr.'s original work were the Davidic genealogy in 1 Chron. 2.\*9, 10-15 and the genealogy of the high priests in 1 Chron. 6.34-38. These two lists are probably not Chr.'s personal fabrication; it is, however, equally uncertain that they should be regarded as authentic documents. It would not be surprising if in the post-exilic period such genealogies were developed artificially on the basis of some older, inherited material,[6] and so became the subject of wider interest; it is equally understandable that Chr. should have considered them genuine and used them for his own purposes.

For *the history of the Judaean kings (1 Chron. 10–2 Chron. 36)* Chr.'s main source was the traditional books of Samuel and Kings in the form that we now know them; that much is obvious and uncontroversial. While Chr. was thus following the work of Dtr., he obviously did not know of it in its original form. It had already been split up into individual 'books' and had been expanded with all kinds of supplements into the form in which we find it today. This latter point can be established from the fact that Chr. not only had 2 Sam. 21.18-22 (cf. 1 Chron. 20.4-8) and 2 Sam. 23.8-39 (cf. 1 Chron. 11.10ff.) but also 2 Sam. 24 (cf. 1 Chron. 21) in his source.[7] On the whole Chr. stuck pretty closely to the narrative thread of Samuel–Kings. Most of the places where he deviates from this source of his, whether by omissions, changes or expansion, can be satisfactorily explained as being due to his own particular purposes.[8]

It is difficult to know the extent to which for this part of his work Chr. made use of other ancient sources which were still available to him but which have since disappeared. In such cases, Chr. would be indispensable as the only channel through which they have reached us. This question should not be settled at the level of general probability; precise evidence is necessary in each individual case. Consequently, we may only assume that Chr. has made use of ancient sources, otherwise unknown to us, in those cases where we have made full allowance for the overall character of Chr. and where cogent arguments can be advanced in favour of such a claim. In uncertain cases we shall do well to leave a decision open until, maybe, new arguments will enable us to advance a more convincing case. The possibility can never be excluded *a priori* that Chr. may have personally developed his narrative from Samuel–Kings and even embellished it with quite specific-looking material.

In dealing with the question of the use of otherwise unknown sources it is usual to start with the citations of sources which Chr. includes in the concluding formulae of each reign. In fact, however, these citations are completely unsuitable for this purpose. Chr. here simply adopts a literary convention, following the example of Dtr. The only difference is that Dtr. regularly quotes 'the annals of the kings of Israel (or Judah)' while with remarkable inconsistency Chr. names all kinds of prophetic writings, either alongside the royal annals or instead of them[9] as sources in which further details can be read.[10] Almost without exception he refers in this matter to prophets who are known from Samuel–Kings to have been contemporaries of those kings whose history they are supposed to have recorded.[11] It can be clearly demonstrated that this is simply a case of following a literary convention in the wake of Dtr. and not of actually citing sources that have been used. For his presentation of Solomon Chr. had no other *Vorlage* than Dtr.'s history of Solomon (1 Kgs 3–11).[12] All he did was to vary it by some omissions, by various minor changes in the order of material and by introducing a couple of additions for which he was himself responsible.[13] There is not the slightest indication that Chr. made use of any other source in this 2section. Nevertheless, in the concluding notice about Solomon (2 Chron. 9.29) Chr. writes, 'The rest of the acts of Solomon, first and last, are they not written in the history of Nathan the prophet, and in the prophecy of Ahijah the Shilonite and in the visions of Jedo the seer concerning Jeroboam the son of Nebat?' After all that has been said, this cannot be a genuine item of information about sources, intended to name the material that was available for use and to direct attention to it for further study. Moreover, in case anybody should appeal to the idea that the way Chr. has phrased his formula ('The *rest* of the acts of Solomon') points to sources which Chr. did not himself use for his history of Solomon but which he knew were available, we would merely refer to the corresponding situation in the case of the history of David's reign. Here, Chr. formulates his concluding notice in 1 Chron. 29.29 as follows: 'Now the acts of David the king, first and last, behold they are written in the history of Samuel the seer, and in the history of Nathan the prophet, and in the history of Gad the seer'.

Similarly, for the history of David[14] Chr. had no *Vorlage* other than the traditional books of Samuel. On the whole this is quite obvious and does not need to be proved in detail. In places where Chr. goes beyond his *Vorlage* (e.g. the full involvement of the Levites in the account of the transfer of the ark to Jerusalem in 1 Chron. 15.1ff.[15] and the completion of David's preparations for the building of the temple in 1 Chron. *22–23.2a + 28-29), it is obviously a case of Chr. making his own additions to themes which were of fundamental importance to him. There are only three places which require brief discussion because it has been thought that they can be used to show that at these points Chr. had access to a source separate from the books of Samuel.[16] In the main, the account of David's conquest of Jerusalem in 1 Chron. 11.4-9 follows 2 Sam. 5.6-10 word for word.[17] However, Chr. has omitted the rather obscure references to the lame and the blind from 2 Sam. 5.6bβ and 8aβb and introduced instead some references to Joab in vv. 6 and 8b without any basis in 2 Sam. 5. Did he have access to a separate source for this? Hardly: by far the simplest explanation of the differences is that he merely passed over those phrases in his source which he did not understand.[18] Then, finding that 2 Sam. 5 had no intelligible sequel to the words 'and David said on that day, "whoever smites the Jebusites ... "'", he himself composed the very simple piece of narrative about Joab so as to make what results in a pleasing unity.[19] It is evident, therefore, that Chr. had no alternative source here, but already knew 2 Sam. 5 in the obviously corrupt form in which it has reached us.

Next, it is striking that the list of David's heroes which is transcribed in 1 Chron. 11.10ff. from 2 Sam. 23.8-39 is continued further in vv. 41b-47 with material that is lacking from 2 Sam. 23. Was Chr. maybe not composing on the basis of 2 Sam. 23? Did he rather have in front of him the original list[20] which had been only partially included in 2 Sam. 23?[21] In that case he would still have been in a position to consult the sources which were used for compiling the appendixes to 2 Samuel. Now, 2 Sam. 23.8-39 belongs only to the second layer of these appendixes.[22] More than that, however, we must remember that these appendixes cannot have been added to the books of Samuel before Dtr. had been divided up into 'books',[23] and that this in turn was bound up with the redaction of the Pentateuch. That being so, it is not so remote a possibility that 2 Sam. 23.8ff. and 1 Chron. 11.10ff. should both have been dependent upon a common source which was still known in the post-exilic period. Nevertheless, the facts of the matter are probably quite other. It is not the case in 1 Chron. 11.10ff. that the continuation of the list in vv. 41b-47 beyond 2 Sam. 23 'joins on so smoothly in form and content to what precedes'[24] that there is no justification for thinking of a secondary addition. For one thing, in contrast to the personal names in the passage which runs parallel with 2 Sam. 23, those in this continuation belong for the most part to the stock of personal names which became common only in the post-exilic period;[25] for another, it is striking that in vv. 26-41a = 2 Sam. 23.24-39 (i.e. in the list of the 'Thirty'), *every* name has joined to it a note about the person's place of origin.[26] This pattern is broken at once by the name in 1 Chron. 11.41b and such information is omitted spasmodically thereafter. We should conclude, then, that 1 Chron. 11.41b-47 actually represents a secondary lengthening of the list. We could then go on to ask whether this lengthening was already included in Chr. or whether, like so many of the other lists of names, it did not rather get incorporated later into the Chr.'s work.[27] Either way, Chr.'s *Vorlage* here was again no more extensive than the books of Samuel as they have come down to us.

Finally, it has been suggested that the source for 1 Chron. 21 is not 2 Sam. 24 itself, but rather that perhaps both forms of the account of David's census should be traced back to a single common source.[28] However, there is really not a single cogent argument for this view. Detailed comparison of 1 Chron. 21 and 2 Sam. 24 reveals to what a large extent they agree verbally with each other. This shows that without doubt Chr. was following the traditional text of 2 Sam. 24 as his source. All the deviations can be satisfactorily explained on the basis of Chr.'s methods, intentions and theological outlook. Leaving various changes of wording aside, these factors account for the introduction of Satan in v. 1, the omission of the textually corrupt and therefore scarcely intelligible itinerary in 2 Sam. 24.5-7,[29] the changes to the various figures given,[30] and above all the portrayal of the closing scene. Though there has not been major interference here, nevertheless this scene was of central significance to Chr., because it resulted in the choice of the site for the future temple.[31] As regards the messenger of Yahweh who appeared between heaven and earth (v. 16) and the divine fire from heaven which ignited the burnt offering (v. 26),[32] there is no more need to worry about a special source for these than there is for the reference to the 'tabernacle of Yahweh' in Gibeon (vv. 29 and 30a).[33]

For his history of David, Chr. had nothing but the books of Samuel in their present form as his *Vorlage*; despite this, he makes a statement about sources in his concluding notice which was quoted above.[34] Just as in the case of Solomon, so here this cannot be understood as referring to sources which are otherwise unknown to us. And what is true for David and Solomon is naturally true for the other Judaean kings. We cannot set about dealing with the real question of Chr.'s sources from the statements made in his concluding notices. This should in any case be already apparent from the simple fact that these concluding notices belong to the material which Chr. took over from Dtr.[35] The only differences are that, on the one hand, with his characteristic carelessness in such matters Chr. varies the wording of Dtr's concluding remarks in a variety of ways,[36] and that, on the other hand, he makes frequent, though thoroughly inconsistent, reference to all kinds of prophetic writings instead of to the royal annals. This is obviously due to the general assumption that the ancient history of the people of Israel was at that time recorded by contemporary prophets.[37] Because all this merely concerns a narrative element adopted from Dtr., it is idle to speculate about what Chr. thought of these statements about 'sources'; it is certain that he had in view the work of Dtr. which served as his *Vorlage*. Consequently, if in this connection he also follows Dtr. blindly in making statements about where even *more* can be read, that does not justify the conclusion that he himself, let alone his readers, had Dtr.'s sources at his disposal. His work reveals no certain clue in favour of such a conclusion.

Now it is true that Rothstein and Hänel[38] have tried again to offer proof that Chr. must have had access to 'the *Vorlage* of the books of Samuel and Kings', that is to say, some hypothetical earlier form.[39] This demonstration has not succeeded, however. Of the many arguments advanced in favour of this theory, some are simply a matter of text: more than once Chr. has preserved the original because a textual error arose in Samuel–Kings only after Chr. had used them as his *Vorlage*;[40] others are cases where Chr. has followed his usual practice of changing the wording of his *Vorlage* somewhat. As concerns the remainder,[41] they are simply a string of comments which, though found only in Chr., nevertheless all serve his own special interests. They cannot, therefore, be traced back to a separate *Vorlage*, but must be attributed to Chr. himself. They are: the changes in 1 Chron. 11.6 and 8a which we have already discussed, the additions which develop the story of the transfer of the ark (13.1ff.; 15.1ff.; 16.1, 4 + 39f.), the slight alterations in the account of the census (ch. 21) and most especially the comments about the preparation for the temple building (chs. 22, 28, 29). Apart from occasional references to Pentateuchal material, there is nothing in the passages about David and Solomon which points to any ancient source other than the traditional books of Samuel and Kings.

Turning now to the presentation of the history of the Judaean kings after Solomon, we have to start with two individual pieces of information which do not come from Dtr. As can be shown on the basis of other evidence, they are so accurate historically that we are compelled to adopt the assumption that Chr. derived them from a pre-exilic source. The first is the note about Hezekiah's tunnel in 2 Chron. 32.30. What it says agrees so precisely with the so-called Siloam tunnel[42] that it must be based on an exact knowledge of the situation. It is therefore not possible that it was made up from the short and very ambiguous statement of Dtr. in the concluding notice about Hezekiah in 2 Kgs 20.20. One might, of course, consider the possibility that Chr. here had local knowledge of Jerusalem and used this in order to present the vague note in Dtr. in a more detailed and accurate manner.[43] In fact, however, this is quite out of the question. Not only has he erratically inserted his account into the middle of his abbreviating and divergent version of 2 Kgs 20.12-19, but in 2 Chron. 32.3f. he has in addition already made some mention of the topic using partly the same wording but in a way which shows all too clearly that he himself was far removed from any such local knowledge. It follows that 2 Chron. 32.30 must be a word-for-word citation from some source otherwise unknown to us.

The other case is the Chronicler's description of King Josiah's last battle and death in 2 Chron. 35.20-24. Things are a bit more complicated here, however, because clearly Chr. was himself responsible for the composition as a whole. To him we must attribute, first, the negotiations between Necho and Josiah, which are meant to show that Josiah was guilty before God and so responsible

for his own fate (vv. 21-22), and, second, the description of the
wounding and death of the king (vv. 23-24a), which is partly
dependent on 2 Chron. 18.33=1 Kgs 22.34. The remainder, however,
cannot have been derived from 2 Kgs 23.29-30a because here Chr.
deviates from 2 Kings in his account of Necho's purpose in going to
war. What is more, only since C.J. Gadd's publication in 1923 of part
of the Babylonian Chronicle[44] have we been in a position to know
that in place of a factually mistaken remark by Dtr.[45] Chr. provides a
statement which, though somewhat general, is nevertheless in
harmony as it stands with the historical facts (v. 20).[46] Here too there
can be no question of Chr. having had personal knowledge of an
historical incident which was so far removed from him in space and
time; we must therefore assume that Chr. made use of an ancient
written source other than Dtr. Even stranger, Josephus, *Ant.* 10.74
has a quite detailed and factually accurate comment about Pharaoh
Necho's objective in this campaign which goes back neither to 2 Kgs
23.29 nor to 2 Chron. 35.20; so Josephus too must have had a good
historical source at his disposal, and it could even be the same as the
one which Chr. used.

It is a reasonable assumption that if Chr. had some additional
ancient source or other at his disposal he may have constructed other
statements out of it even though we may not be in a position to
mount such a precise demonstration of their historical reliability.
Alongside the note about Hezekiah's tunnel we may reasonably
range various other statements about the Judaean kings' fortifications.
They do not come from Dtr., but they give the impression of being
reliable tradition. The primary example is the list of Rehoboam's
fortresses (2 Chron. 11.5b—10aα). We can see at once that this is an
element of inherited tradition from the fact that it does not fit
completely smoothly into the Chronicler's surrounding text. The
list's heading in v. 5b speaks of 'cities for defence in Judah'.[47] In his
added comment in vv. 10aβb, 11, and 12a, Chr., by contrast, uses
'fortified cities', an expression which he also uses commonly
elsewhere (cf. 11.23; 12.4; 21.3). Furthermore, in line with his usual
historical conception he speaks of 'Judah and Benjamin'. Thus Chr.
quoted vv. 5b-10aα from a source. What is more, an examination of
the content of this paragraph[48] demonstrates the overwhelming
probability that here we have a genuine document, one which was
available to Chr. within the framework of some older *Vorlage*.[49]
Further, in this connection, mention should be made of the note

about the building of some fortifications in Jerusalem in 2 Chron.
26.9. Its description is so straightforward and detailed that it is
clearly to be distinguished from all the generalized bits of information
of the same kind; consequently, it is much better ascribed to an
ancient source than to Chr. For similar reasons, we should also
probably include here the brief report of Uzziah's installation of
catapults on the Jerusalem fortifications in 2 Chron. 26.15a and the
information about Manasseh's construction of various fortifications
in 2 Chron. 33.14a. Elsewhere, whenever it seems appropriate to
him, Chr. repeatedly makes reference to fortification construction
projects, the disposition and arming of troops, the preparation of
supplies for military purposes and the like, sometimes even with
details of the numbers involved. This clearly shows that he had a
general idea of what was appropriate for a genuine national
mobilization but does not reveal any evidence for the use of an
ancient source. Under this category should be included the Chronicler's
addition to the list of Rehoboam's fortresses in 2 Chron. 11.10aβb,
11, 12a; the information about Asa in 2 Chron. 14.5-7; the relatively
detailed description of Jehoshaphat's armaments in 2 Chron. 17.2a,
12b-19; the statement about Amaziah in 2 Chron. 25.5[50] together
with its continuation in vv. 6-10 + 13, which deals with the
recruitment of Israelite mercenaries (a story whose origin is obscure
but whose style is pure Chr.); the description of Uzziah's armaments
in 2 Chron. 26.11-14,[51] which comes in between the sentence
reckoned above to have been cited from sources; the comments about
Jotham's building activities in 2 Chron. 27.3b-4, which are added to a
quotation from 2 Kgs 15.35b; and finally the account of the measures
which Hezekiah took in the face of Sennacherib's threatened attack
in 2 Chron. 32.3-6a[52] (an account which makes secondary use of the
archival note about Hezekiah's tunnel), together with the continuation
in 2 Chron. 33.14b of the material judged above to have come from a
source concerning Manasseh's building activity.[53] It seems, therefore,
that Chr. had available to him an ancient source in which he found
various items concerning the defensive building work undertaken by
the kings of Judah. On the basis of this, he seems to have developed
his own presentation of the royal armaments which he applied
primarily to his favourite characters in the history of the kings of
Judah.

We dealt above with the account of the military encounter of
Josiah with Pharaoh Necho. With this should be linked some further

accounts of the wars of the kings of Judah which do not come from Dtr. and yet which do not look like Chr.'s invention. Consequently, as Chr. can no longer have had a direct knowledge of these events, they must be traced back to an old written source. To this may be attributed the basis of the accounts of Uzziah's wars with the Philistines, Arabs and Meunites in 2 Chron. 26.6-8a,[54] the information about Jotham's Ammonite campaign in 2 Chron. 27.5,[55] and especially the notice in 2 Chron. 28.18 about the cities which the Philistines captured from King Ahaz. Chr. probably also had a basis in some source other than Dtr. for the account of Abijah's war against Jeroboam I in 2 Chron. 13.3-20, though he himself then developed it much further. It may have taken the form of a note about the Israelite towns which passed into Abijah's jurisdiction after he had conquered them (cf. v. 19). At any rate, Dtr.'s unfavourable portrayal of king Abijah could hardly have been a trigger for Chr. to fabricate a victorious war against Israel. It is more likely that Chr. had some alternative source material at his disposal which enabled him to correct Dtr.'s negative assessment of Abijah (1 Kgs 15.3-5) by omitting it. The situation is similar in the case of Asa's campaign against the Cushites in 2 Chron. 14.8-14. Here again, the exact details about the places involved make it a likely assumption that Chr. was making use of source material, even though he has again reworked it heavily.[56] It thus seems as though Chr. was able to draw some material on the theme of the wars of the Judaean kings from an alternative tradition to which he had access but which has since been lost to us.

Having said all that, however, this is the sum total of what can be assumed with any real basis about Chr.'s use of otherwise unknown sources for the history of the kings of Judah.[57] Since the themes of fortification and war belong together, it may be suspected that Chr. made use of just one, single source document besides Dtr. for the period of the monarchy. In view of the small amount included in Chr., it would, of course, be idle to speculate about the extent and nature of this unknown source. The wording of the notices[58] which are presumably included word-for-word from this source are reminiscent of the quotations from the royal annals in Dtr.; the possibility might thus at least be considered that this source was some sort of (unofficial) extract from the official annals dealing with those matters. The very existence of the work of Dtr. is sufficient to show that the annals themselves or at least some extracts of this sort were not all destroyed in 587 BC. This hypothetical source can hardly have presented Chr. with an elaborate history of the Judaean kings; otherwise, he would scarcely have used the traditional books of Samuel–Kings so exclusively as in fact he does as the real basis of his presentation.[59]

In the case of *the history of Ezra and Nehemiah*, it seems to me that it is not so difficult to deal with the question of the sources which Chr. used. There is not the slightest hint that the materials which make up the books of Ezra–Nehemiah had already been combined together before Chr. Consequently, to a far greater degree than in the period of the monarchy, for which Chr. had the work of Dtr. at his disposal, we shall have to take him more seriously as the one responsible for devising the framework and for arranging the material.

Throughout *the narrative of the return and temple-building in Ezra 1–6* we have a continuous text. Into this there have been inserted several particular items which the author of the continuous text came across and reckoned to be valuable 'sources'. To these belongs first of all the inventory (whether genuine or fictitious) of the temple treasure given back by Cyrus (Ezra 1.9-11a).[60] This now forms an important link in the narrative chain, because its heading has been woven into the wording of the continuous text in v. 8,[61] while the latter carries on directly from it in v. 11b. Another of these separate elements is the great list of those who returned in Ezra 2.1-67(69).[62] As 2.68 (70) follows on smoothly from 1.11, this list sits so loosely in its present context that there can be no certainty as to whether it was really an integral part of this narrative from the start. The final one of these separate elements is the Aramaic passage in 4.6[63]–6.18, which is an indispensable part of the narrative as a whole. Its different language is a strong argument in favour of regarding it as a unity. There is no compelling reason to attribute its narrative portions to the continuous Hebrew text and then to assume that they have been translated at a secondary stage into Aramaic.[64] If we take it just as it stands, it presents us with a report of various documents set in a narrative framework on the theme of the rebuilding of the temple. The narrative framework ends appropriately with the account of the dedication of the new temple and the installation of the cultic personnel which makes possible again the running of the cult to its full extent. Only the start of the narrative framework seems to have been omitted by the author of the continuous Hebrew text out of consideration for his own narrative.

There is no trace of the use of another, otherwise unknown source for the composition of the continuous text; it is constructed out of data supplied in the Aramaic passage and in the traditional writings of the prophets Haggai and Zechariah who are mentioned in the Aramaic passage (5.1; 6.14), and on the basis of some simple conjectures. There can be no reasonable doubt that its author was Chr. himself; his characteristics are everywhere apparent.[65] From the decree of Cyrus (1.2-4), which he formulated freely on the basis of 6.3-5, he concluded that the building of the temple must have been started immediately after the return. Consequently, though he drew his knowledge of the historical events from Haggai–Zechariah, he brought them forward chronologically to follow on directly after the edict of Cyrus. He allowed Sheshbazzar (1.8, 11), of whom he knew from 5.14, 16, immediately to fall from view and replaced him with Zerubbabel and Jeshua (3.2, 8; 4.2, 3),[66] in line with Haggai–Zechariah, and then had them start straightaway on the rebuilding of the temple by setting up the altar for burnt offerings.[67] New Year's Day furnished a suitable date (3.6; cf. 3.1a) for the recommencement of cultic activity, which had now become possible again. Similarly, the second month of the following year (3.8) was appropriate for the start of the temple building, because the Solomonic temple had itself been begun in the second month (2 Chron. 3.2=1 Kgs 6.1). Likewise, the gathering of the materials for the Solomonic temple (cf. 2 Chron. 2.14, 15) served as a prototype for the description of the corresponding activity in the case of the present temple building (3.7). The reference to Esarhaddon in 4.2 may have been inspired by no more than the obscure Osnappar in v. 10 in conjunction with a recollection of 2 Kgs 19.37. Finally, after Chr. had used his Aramaic source to recount the completion of the temple building and its dedication, he added off his own bat the account of a first celebration of Passover and Unleavened Bread (6.19-22). In this connection he let drop an accidental anachronism by referring to 'the King of Assyria', no doubt referring to the Seleucid king of his own day.[68]

The *first part of the history of Ezra, Ezra 7–10*, which is only loosely joined by 7.1 to what precedes, provides us once again with a basic text into which several separate elements have been inserted. Right at the start the genealogy of Ezra in 7.1b-5 interrupts the narrative connection between 7.1a and 6 + 10[69] in such a striking way that it must be regarded as a separate item. We are then faced with two possibilities: either Chr. knew of this undoubtedly apocryphal genealogy of the great teacher of the law from some tradition familiar in his own day and himself slotted it somewhat abruptly into the Ezra narrative, or else it is an altogether later addition to his work. The second alternative is favoured by the relationship of the genealogy to the secondary passage 1 Chron. 5.29-32, 37-40a, since the genealogy of Ezra seems to be a later compilation out of the two lists of names in that passage. On the other hand, the Aramaic royal decree in 7.12-26 giving authority to Ezra[70] is a separate item which is securely anchored in the basic text, as can be seen from the fact that its introduction in v. 11 is based on material drawn directly from its contents. It was shown above on p. 44 that the list in 8.1-14 was also incorporated from the first into the basic text; clearly, therefore, it was available to the author of the basic text as something which he inherited,[71] though of course this does not prove anything about whether it is 'genuine' or not. By contrast, we concluded above on p. 45 that the list in Ezra 10.18, 20-44 was an addition to the work of Chr.

The most important question, however, concerns the author of the basic text, for once the various inserted items discussed above have been removed it creates the impression of having been basically a unity. Now, are we dealing here with an account of Ezra's activity which Chr. was able to use as a source—even, as is so popularly assumed,[72] an 'Ezra Memoir' (that is to say, a record which goes back to Ezra himself)—or was this basic text simply Chr.'s own composition? The answer can only be in favour of the latter possibility. First, Ezra 7-10 is strikingly similar to Ezra 1-6 from a literary point of view. Coupled with that is the fact that the language and style throughout are typical of Chr., as the lists compiled by S.R. Driver[73] and C.C. Torrey[74] make clear. Furthermore, the historical outlook and interests of the author are particularly those of Chr.

In view of all this, strong arguments would have to be advanced to favour the hypothesis of an older written source, but there are none such. In no way can the use of the first person singular and plural in 7.27-9.15 be advanced as an argument for an 'Ezra Memoir'. The immediate and necessary continuation in 10.1ff.[75] speaks of Ezra in the third person; there are therefore two possibilities: either we should have to assume that there had been a secondary change of person for one or other part, in which case there would be no proof that the use of the first person was the original, or, as was shown on pp. 45f. above to be the correct view, it is simply a matter of inconsistency on the part of the author of the whole narrative. He simply has Ezra speak in the first person for one stretch of narrative, but then after the long prayer in 9.6-15 gives no further thought to the form in which he himself chose to start off with and speaks of Ezra in the third person;[76] in this case too there can be no question of an 'Ezra Memoir'. The partial use of the first person is clearly dependent on the Nehemiah Memoir; the latter, moreover, has clearly influenced the story of Ezra in Ezra 7-10 in other ways; this is shown above all by the use of the expression 'according to the (good) hand of God upon someone' in Ezra 7.6 (9), 28; 8.18, 22, 31, which is obviously drawn from Neh. 2.8, 18. Even without further arguments, this dependence tells against the assumption of an original source in Ezra 7-10 and favours rather the view that these chapters were composed by Chr., who both knew and worked over the Nehemiah Memoir.

Besides this, there is nothing in Ezra 7-10 which Chr. himself could not have deduced from the sources which he used (Ezra 7.12-26; 8.1-14 and the Nehemiah Memoir) or have added on his own account. The outline of the whole—Ezra's journey from Babylon to Jerusalem and his appearance there to carry through the law of God—derives from Ezra 7.12-26. It was deduced from Neh. 13.23-25 that the prevalence of mixed marriages was an abuse of much longer standing,[77] and must have been reckoned by Chr. to be so major an offence against God's law that he could not allow Ezra, who had responsibility for this law, to overlook it. It was therefore natural that Chr. should have made Ezra's first activity in Jerusalem his action against the mixed marriages.

Nor are there any details which can prove Chr.'s use of a source. The dates in Ezra 10.9, 16, 17 belong to the numerous chronological indications which Chr. calculated for himself:[78] the business of the mixed marriages must have been settled by the New Year's Day following Ezra's arrival (v. 17); the work of the commission which was set up to deal with them lasted exactly three months (hence the date in v. 16); and the negotiations and preparations leading to the setting up of the commission took up exactly ten days (hence the date in v. 9). Alongside that the conventional short period of three days crops up repeatedly (Ezra 8.15, 32; 10.9).[79] The use of common personal names to fill out the narrative (8.16, 33) is one of Chr.'s well-known literary characteristics, and the same may be true of the striking appearance of a few named individuals (10.2, 15).

The only items which remain as apparently very specific and so attributable to a source are the Babylonian place name Ahava, the place of departure for Ezra's journey to Jerusalem (8.15, [21,] 31) and the name of the Levitical settlement, Casiphia, which was thought to be nearby (8.17). On their own, however, they are hardly sufficient to establish the existence of an 'Ezra Memoir'; Chr. was certainly aware of the existence of a Babylonian diaspora in his own day, and he must have known something of its settlements. This knowledge could easily have served him for filling out the history of Ezra.[80] Thus when all is said and done there is no trace to be found in Ezra 7–10 of a continuous special source; and in view of what can be seen elsewhere of Chr. as an independent narrator,[81] there is no argument of any substance to be raised against the interpretation which we have expressed above.

For *the history of Nehemiah* Chr. had the Nehemiah Memoir available to him to serve as a basis. After Ezra's settlement of the business of the mixed marriages he slots this source in quite abruptly, heading and all (Neh. 1.1), without so much as a hint at the chronological relationship with what is related before and after.[82] He then simply follows this source word for word until 7.5a; only in 1.5–11a does he put the words of a prayer into Nehemiah's mouth.

There then follows in Chr.'s presentation *the account of Ezra's reading of the Law and its consequences, Neh. 8–10*;[83] this is where Ezra's real work reaches its climax. After what we concluded with regard to Ezra 7–10, we would not expect to find an extract from some 'Ezra Memoir' in Neh. 8–10, but rather a further passage of Chr.'s own narrative about Ezra. And in fact here again we come across the language and style,[84] the outlook and interests of Chr. Moreover, the content of what is related does no more than direct us to Chr.'s two sources with which we are already familiar (Ezra 7.12–26 and the Nehemiah Memoir), and not to some further special source about Ezra.

All the problems raised by this section are most easily resolved on the presupposition that it is Chr.'s own work. For instance, there is a genuinely harsh transition between chapters 8 and 9, because after two days the joy of the celebration of the Feast of Tabernacles switches without warning to a penitential mood consequent upon the awareness of having transgressed the Law. This can be easily explained, however, if Chr. was from the first aiming at the great communal confession[85] when he had Ezra start to read the Law on New Year's Day (8.2) with the associated explanation of the Law by the Levites.[86] However, he believed that first of all he had to complete the celebration of New Year's Day[87] and the Feast of Tabernacles,[88] which now fell together in the seventh month and with which a penitential mood was not in keeping, before then going on immediately to stage the confession, which had been merely delayed.

This same presupposition also means that it is not necessary to go to the trouble of searching out some other original setting for Neh. 10.[89] The obvious dependence of this chapter[90] on Neh. 13.4-31 (Nehemiah Memoir) can be easily explained if Chr. was the author: Chr. wanted to see the abuses which Nehemiah censored as having been, in principle, already corrected as a result of Ezra's reading of the Law. Neh. 10 can only have followed Neh. 9 from the very first because the first person plural which is used here right from the start refers to the assembled congregation, which has been speaking without interruption ever since 9.5b.[91]

The view that Chr. was the author of Neh. 8-10 provides the best explanation for the sudden appearance of this section relating to Ezra in the middle of the history of Nehemiah.[92] There is then no question of a once connected history of Ezra being subsequently divided into two so as to be associated secondarily with the history of Nehemiah; it is simply that from the very first Chr. amalgamated his Ezra narrative with the Nehemiah Memoir which was available to him. All he knew from Ezra 7.12-26 was that Ezra came to Jerusalem during Artaxerxes' reign. On this basis he concluded that Ezra's appearance in Jerusalem was contemporary with Nehemiah's. Thus, although he initially ascribed priority to Ezra, he nevertheless felt he had to have the assembly with Ezra's reading of the Law take place only after Nehemiah's building of the wall had secured Jerusalem's external security. At the same time, he did not proceed straight to the dedication of the wall, but made use of a remark in the Nehemiah Memoir about a summoning of the people to Jerusalem (Neh. 7.5a) in order to introduce at once the long overdue reading of the Law by Ezra. Admittedly this meant that he split into two the passage from the Nehemiah Memoir about the resettlement of the population (Neh. 7.4, 5a + 11.1, 2), but in the end he did at least have the issue of resettlement dealt with by the people whilst they were still assembled together.

For *the remainder of the history of Nehemiah in Neh. 11-13*,[93] Chr. simply followed the Nehemiah Memoir once more as his basis, adding in material of his own at only a few places which were of importance to him. Thus in the account from the Memoir about the dedication of the wall (12:*27, 31, 32, 37-40, 43) he added the priests and Levites with their purifications and music (12.30, 33-36, 41, 42); once again, he created their numerous names from the stock of names that were current in his day. Furthermore at the end he added a bit more about the administration of the dues (vv. 44, 45).

Finally, in the concluding portion of the Memoir which summarizes all manner of arrangements made by Nehemiah (Neh. 13.4-31) he has added a few points on his own account. There are, for instance, several details in vv. 5aβb, 6, 7a concerning the temple chamber which was put at the disposal of the 'Ammonite' Tobiah: he added the remark about the chamber's original use to which it had only to be returned afterwards, so that the sequence of events in the Nehemiah Memoir, whereby a chamber which was originally built for a foreigner came afterwards to be used for sacred purposes, disappeared; then there is the comment about Nehemiah's prolonged absence from Jerusalem, which was evidently made up on the basis of Neh. 5.14 and which had the effect of absolving Nehemiah from responsibility for granting the permission to build that chamber. Next, at v. 22a he introduced the Levites into the guard on the gates of Jerusalem during the Sabbath, as well as the comment in vv. 26, 27 about Solomon's foreign wives. Finally, he added a few words in vv. 29bβ, 30a to emphasize the need for cultic purity on the part of the priests and the Levites.

## Chapter 16

## THE DATE OF COMPOSITION

The *terminus a quo* for the time at which Chr. was formed is naturally determined by the date of the latest events which it records, that is to say the activities of Ezra and Nehemiah in Jerusalem during the reign of Artaxerxes. However, as far as we can see Chr. used nothing but written material for the whole of his work; even in the history of Ezra and Nehemiah he gives no hint of direct knowledge of his own. There exists, therefore, the possibility of lowering this *terminus a quo* at will, until a cut-off point is reached with the development of the Old Testament canon.

Up until now, most attempts to fix the date of Chr. more precisely within this broad framework have relied in the main on the chronological extent of some of the genealogies and priestly lists included in the traditional form of Chr.'s work. In the forefront of this discussion, however, have been precisely those lists which the earlier literary-critical analysis has shown to be secondary additions, so that in reality they are useless for the purpose in hand.[1]

There is only one place where I can envisage the possibility of establishing at least roughly a more precise date for the composition of Chr.—or, strictly speaking, a *terminus a quo*. The account of the temple building in Ezra 4.6–6.18, which was written in Aramaic, was used as a source by Chr., and something can be said about its date of compilation.

This necessitates a brief discussion of the theory of the development of the complex in Ezra 4.7–6.18 which was formerly advanced by A. Klostermann,[2] and which has recently been taken up again and developed comprehensively and in detail by H.H. Schaeder[3] with the support of R. Kittel.[4]

According to this theory, the whole section was a petition by the Tab'el who is mentioned in 4.7. It was addressed to Artaxerxes with the aim of obtaining royal consent for the completion of the building of Jerusalem. With this purpose in view, the petition first included a verbatim transcript of the letter which the opponents of this work had sent to the king (4.8-16) together with the king's reply to this letter in which he gave it his approval (4.17-22); then, however, it supplied documentary evidence of the favourable attitude towards the building of the temple displayed in their own times by the earlier kings Cyrus and Darius (5.3ff.). In this way the apparent chronological confusion of this passage is explained, for it first speaks of (Xerxes and) Artaxerxes and only then refers to Cyrus and Darius.

In fact, however, this ingenious theory cannot be accepted. For the sake of the argument, it may be granted that, as the theory demands, Chr. could have reworked and expanded this passage in Aramaic when he incorporated it into his composition,[5] even though this was shown above on p. 61 (cf. n.64) to be utterly improbable. We may also—though this is considerably harder to do—overlook the fact that 4.6 is not taken into account, since this verse is quite isolated; in fact, however, since it certainly does not belong with 4.5, which Chr. wrote as a conclusion to the preceding section of the narrative, it must be included with what follows,[6] even though the heading to the supposed 'petition of Tab'el' does not come until 4.7. It is therefore necessary to postulate another improbable interference by Chr. in order to explain the present connection of 4.6 with the 'petition'.[7] But even apart from these difficulties, Klostermann's theory comes to grief on the fact that the 'petition' does not include so much as a single word to explain what is intended by its presumed structure, that is to say its starting with the situation in hand and only then following with references to precedents; nor, in addition, is the real purpose of the 'petition' ever expressed. Now, should anyone be tempted to assume that Chr. simply omitted all mention of the logical stages in the process on the ground that what mattered to him was not the actual purpose of the 'petition', but only the information which it contained, then he would actually be accusing Chr. of incomprehensible carelessness: although on the basis of the complete text of the 'petition' with which he was working Chr. must have been quite clear as to the chronological order of the events, he nevertheless retained the order of the various parts of the 'petition' which, without the connecting passages, cannot fail to create the impression that they are intended simply to be in chronological order as they stand. Above all, this applies to 4.24, which constitutes in consequence the most decisive objection to Klostermann's hypothesis. In this verse, it is stated that, after Artaxerxes had forbidden the work of rebuilding to continue, 'then' the work had to be delayed until the second year of Darius. Now, according to the theory, Chr. omitted a reference to the events under Cyrus which stood in front of 4.24. This reference originally stood at this point in the 'petition', and the 'then' at the start of 4.24 originally referred to it; Chr., however, left it out because he had already dealt separately with the course of events from Cyrus to Darius.[8] In the first place, however, this presupposes that Chr. had a correct knowledge of the historical course of events but that for some incomprehensible reason he forced a false understanding upon his readers. More seriously still, we must postulate on the basis of what remains of the 'petition' that the account of events or actions was reported in the form of documents; Chr., however, would hardly have passed these by even if the matters in question had been but recently dealt with in his own presentation. This may be seen by the way in which he has no hesitation in retaining the text of the decree of Cyrus in the 'petition' (6.3-5) even though he had already reported this decree in 1.2-4. In short, the 'petition' theory raises so many difficulties and improbabilities that it cannot be accepted.

It should be further noted that there is an express statement in 5.16 that the work of temple building had proceeded continuously from the time of the decree of Cyrus until the beginning of the reign of Darius but that it had not been completed by that date. This is in flat contradiction to the statement in 4.24 that it was interrupted for a longer or shorter period. This contradiction cannot be resolved by an interpretation based on the Aramaic section alone. In the first place, this demonstrates once more that the 'petition' theory is mistaken, because a petition addressed to the king would scarcely have complicated matters by such contradictions. In the second place, however, this contradiction puts a question mark against the original unity of the Aramaic section, leaving the simplest, face value interpretation of the Aramaic section just as it stands as the most obviously natural and correct one.

A natural interpretation of this sort must start from the observation that the section contains two separate elements. The first is a group of documents in the form of an exchange of correspondence about the building of the city of Jerusalem from the time of Artaxerxes together with a further exchange of correspondence about the

rebuilding of the temple from the time of Darius; the second is a
narrative framework which has been supplied to connect these
documents together. The author of the narrative framework inherited
these documents as a fixed item of tradition. Only so can the factual
tensions between the documents and the narrative framework be
explained. These are, first, the contradiction already discussed
between 4.24 (narrative framework) and 5.16 (document), and,
second, the mistaken relationship between the group of documents in
4.8-22(23), which deals with the building of the city, and the
statement of the narrative framework in 4.24, which speaks of the
building of the temple. If for the moment we presuppose as a
hypothesis the genuine nature of the documents, then the exchange
of correspondence about the building of the city in 4.8-22 (23)
belongs to the time of Artaxerxes I (465-424), because, as we can
now conclude for certain from the Elephantine Papyri,[9] this was a
live issue at that time. At the same time, the exchange of
correspondence about the building of the temple must be dated to the
reign of Darius I (521-485).[10]

Now, as can be seen principally from the way in which 4.24 serves
as a conclusion to the preceding exchange of correspondence, the
narrative framework confused the work of the city and temple
building or else regarded them as part and parcel of the same
undertaking. Consequently, it puts first the exchange of correspondence which resulted in an interruption of this work (4.8-22[23])
and then has it followed by the exchange of correspondence which
led to the completion of the work (5.6-6.12). In doing so, however, it
inverted the historical order in which the events took place.[11] The
possibility of doing so was made all the more easy by the fact that the
Persian kings mentioned in the documents were not more precisely
identified and by the fact that in the Persian royal succession there
were no less than three kings named Darius and three named
Artaxerxes. This means that the author of the narrative framework
must be distanced by quite a substantial chronological interval from
the events touched on in the documents. At the very earliest he is to
be dated to a time when the reign of the first Darius to follow an
Artaxerxes (that would be Darius II, 424-405) already lay so far in
the past that it was no longer common knowledge that the post-exilic
temple had not been completed under Darius II. This would bring us
for preference to the end of the Persian period. More probably,
however, the confusion which the narrative framework displays over

the history of the Persian kings points beyond the Persian period and hence to the start of the Hellenistic period. It would therefore be most appropriate to fix the composition of the Aramaic narrative framework around 300 BC.[12]

Chr. used the Aramaic section with both its documents and its narrative framework as one of the primary sources for his account of the return and the building of the temple.[13] He himself must therefore be dated even later, even though there is no particular reason for dating him substantially later. Furthermore, he added to the chronological confusion. Not only did he follow his source in introducing Xerxes and Artaxerxes between Cyrus and the Darius of the temple-building,[14] but he was also obliged by other relevant sources to speak again later of an Artaxerxes in his account of Ezra and Nehemiah. He can only have regarded this Artaxerxes as being another king of the same name. Even if in this he still had some clear notion of the order of the Persian kings, he must certainly have been thinking in this context of an Artaxerxes II (405–359). The date of this Artaxerxes, however, must have already lain so far in the past that he did not realize that it was not during this king's reign that Ezra and Nehemiah first arrived in Jerusalem. Chr. can hardly have conceived this mistaken presentation earlier than about 300 BC.

This would then bring us to a date around 300 BC as a *terminus a quo* for Chr.; and I am not aware of any counter-argument that would positively favour setting it earlier. On the contrary: should anyone wish to date Chr. even later, there would be no arguments with which to refute him. I grant that it would hardly be advisable to date Chr. significantly later than about 200 BC. We must allow sufficient time between the composition of Chr. and the conclusion of the third division of the Old Testament canon for the growth of the numerous secondary additions to the original text of Chr., especially when it is remembered that in many places we are confronted with a whole series of successive supplements, one added to another. Of course, it can be certainly shown that the third division of the canon was determined only in the first Christian century.[15] The most probable date for the composition of Chr., therefore, remains between 300 and 200 BC, i.e. the period of Ptolemaic rule over Palestine. For the additions, however, and in particular for the numerous supplements to the genealogies, which cannot here be treated in detail, the Maccabean period should be seriously considered. It was at that time that there was a renewed interest in the twelve tribes of Israel as a whole.

# SECTION B : THE CHARACTER OF THE WORK

*Chapter 17*

## THE NATURE OF THE COMPOSITION

We have seen that it is not possible to do justice to Dtr. by regarding him merely as one who reworked books which were to all intents and purposes completed before they reached him; on the contrary, he constructed a major composition on the basis of written sources which were available to him. The situation is similar in the case of Chr.: it would be inappropriate to attempt an appraisal of his work by taking only one side of it into consideration. I refer here to his sifting through older historical accounts, his rearranging of those parts of them which he regarded as important judged by the yardstick of a particular bias and his mixing of them with a few favourite and stereotyped thoughts of his own. In fact, Chr. stands out much more strongly as an independent narrator than is generally supposed.[1] Of course, for the overall shape of the history which he relates he relied upon written sources. Despite this, however, he has gone beyond these by attempting to conjure up in his own mind a lively image of those historical characters and events which were important to him (starting, of course, from the standpoint and concerns of his own day) and then, not without some skill, to convey this portrayal to his readers. Attention has rightly been drawn[2] to the fact that in the books of Chronicles material peculiar to Chr. constitutes nearly half of the total; his work is thus by no means merely a compilation of extracts from sources.[3] At this point there is a very marked difference between Chr. and Dtr., because in the case of the latter the extent of the author's own composition is substantially less in relation to the sources which he cites. In general, a comparison between Dtr. and Chr. can give a particularly clear picture of their individual peculiarities, not only because for some of the time both are working on the same material, but also because of all the literary works in the Old Testament they are the most closely related in their lay-out and style.

In the case of Dtr., it was primarily the systematic planning of the work as a whole which came to the fore in those passages which the author himself contributed. By contrast with this, Chr.'s contribution has been mainly to attempt to enliven and develop the details of the course of history which he is presenting. This can be seen at once in the linguistic style which each employs. In writing his own contributions, Dtr. obviously made conscious use of a simple, stereotyped style. It is found partly in longer speeches made by the characters in question at particular historical turning points and partly in the elements which go to make up a framework which from time to time summarizes a given historical period. It also occurs in shorter remarks which have been introduced here and there to forge connections either backwards or forwards. This style is easily recognizable, and even on a superficial reading it enforces the impression of the unity of the whole work.[4] There is nothing comparable in Chr. His style and use of words are untidy and uneven. This is obviously not only because Chr. wrote at a time when Hebrew was no longer a living and commonly spoken language, so that there was no further feel for the genuine spirit of the language. It was much more because Chr. had no particular concern for the formal tight construction and unity of his work. Admittedly, Chr. had quite distinct interests so far as content was concerned, and the pursuit of these had a decisive influence on the construction of the work as a whole.[5] He did not, however, attempt to impose upon his work any uniformity as regards external form. Instead, by larger and smaller contributions of his own, Chr. attempted to make his historical narrative vivid in matters of detail and to enrich it with concepts that were familiar to him.

In cases where he had a larger, coherent body of tradition in ready and fixed form at his disposal,[6] Dtr. was extremely reticent about interfering with it or adding to it. He preferred to let the sources speak for themselves, even when they did not sit too easily with his presentation of the course of history or with his major theological ideas. Instead, his great concern was with the fixed framework of the work as a whole. It was this which held it all together and determined its meaning. In Chr., however, things are completely different. For the history of the whole of the period of the monarchy, Chr. had Dtr.

available as a large, connected *Vorlage*. There were only a few places where he had the opportunity of adding to this with material from an alternative source for the same period which was apparently still available to him. However, he went way beyond his *Vorlage* by developing on his own account the histories of individual kings who seemed to him to be important; it is accordingly to be expected that he himself was responsible for composing a good deal of the books of Ezra–Nehemiah, where for lengthy passages he was obliged to write the connecting narrative from scratch. The working up of connections was not one of his strong points, as can be seen from the weak and unsatisfactory transitions at 1 Chron. 10.1; Ezra 7.1; Neh. 1.1. Dtr., on the other hand, may be regarded as an absolute master at constructing connections which drew the separate complexes of inherited tradition into an intelligible relationship with each other, or at least made them appear possible.

A characteristic of this difference is the way in which each work handles chronology. Dtr. has furnished his work with a strong chronological backbone. For the history of the monarchy, Chr. simply adopted Dtr.'s chronological framework without showing any concern for how the chronological thread should be traced forwards. Though in 2 Chron. 36.21 he apportions 70 years to the duration of the exile, this figure does not really derive from any great interest in chronology but is included explicitly as an indication of the fulfilment of the prophetic word in Jer. 25.11f.; 29.10. Furthermore, the transition from the account of the building of the post-exilic temple to the history of Ezra is effected with the vague observation, 'after these things' (Ezra 7.1). Admittedly, Chr. did not have any chronological data for the period after the fall of Jerusalem; but apparently he had no particular interest in drawing up an overall chronology. It was therefore only logical that at 2 Chron. 3.2 he should miss out Dtr.'s note which linked the date of the building of Solomon's temple to the Exodus from Egypt (1 Kgs 6.1). In contrast to this, Chr. was generous in supplying information about the dates and times of individual events, even when he had to depend on his own conjectures in order to arrive at these.

So then, if we wish to attempt a brief portrayal of the way in which Chr. has enlivened and graphically developed his historical narrative with details that go beyond his *Vorlage*, we may begin with the notes about dates and times which he himself has introduced. Chr. will certainly have considered it a safe assumption that pious kings could not have shown any hesitation in taking whatever steps were necessary to restore and purify the Jerusalem cult. Thus he had Hezekiah begin to do what was necessary straightaway, in the first month of the first year of his reign (2 Chron. 29.3), and within two periods of eight days each (v. 17) the work of purification was completed, though not soon enough to avoid resorting to the option of not celebrating the Passover, now due, until the fourteenth day of the second month (30.2, 13, 15).[7] The consequential regulating of the cultic levies began straight away, in the third month, so that by the seventh month, the month which included the cultic New Year and autumn festival, everything was arranged and prepared (31.7). Josiah could not very well have waited until the eighteenth year of his reign before beginning his reform (2 Kgs 22.3), but must have embarked as soon as possible on a work that was so pleasing to God. It is true that he was still a minor at the time of his accession, but his sixteenth year could be seen as the time when he must have begun to give serious thought to the correct service of God. Then, after a further four years, it was time to turn his correct insight into action (2 Chron. 34.3).[8]

Chr. gave Jehoshaphat until his third regnal year, however, to set in motion the new arrangements for teaching the Law in the state of Judah, a work for which this king seemed to be predestined by his name (2 Chron. 17.7). In general, the figure three features quite prominently in references to time which Chr. has calculated for himself: God tolerated King Asa's apostasy for three years before he punished him with sickness (2 Chron. 16.1, 12), and this finally afflicted him in the third from last year of his life (v. 13);[9] the work of the commission set up to settle the affair of the mixed marriages lasted three months (Ezra 10.16, 17), ending on a civil New Year's Day; Chr. makes repeated reference to a period of three days (Ezra 8.15; 8.32; 10.9).[10]

On the other hand, the seventh month, being the month of the New Year's Festival and the Autumn Festival, played an important part in Chr.'s calculations: at the dedication of Solomon's temple things worked out exactly so that its celebration fell on the Autumn Festival in the seventh month (2 Chron. 7.10); it was precisely in the seventh month that Hezekiah's cultic reforms were completed (2 Chron. 31.7); after the exile the sacrificial cult was able to be started on the newly erected altar on the first day of the seventh month (Ezra 3.1, 6); and again exactly on the first day of the seventh month the people gathered in Jerusalem in order to listen to Ezra reading the Law (Neh. 8.2). It would certainly be a mistake to assume that Chr. had a particular source for a single one of these time indicators, for they are simply a matter of Chr.'s literary habit.[11]

There is yet another way in which Chr. sought, himself, to enliven his narrative by enlarging the picture offered him by his *Vorlage* with material based on the life and institutions of his own day. Where the old tradition briefly mentioned a celebration of Passover as a conclusion to Josiah's reforming activity (2 Kgs 23.21-23), Chr. considerably amplified the account of this Passover celebration in order to show how one should visualize it in detail (2 Chron. 35.1-19). The laconic note about Hezekiah's cultic measures (2 Kgs 18.4) gave Chr. the opportunity to introduce a very long description of them. Its basic orientation was modelled on Josiah's reform; like that reform it concluded with a Passover celebration and its aim was again to show how one ought to visualize the measures taken by the king (2 Chron. 29.3-31.21).[12] At 2 Chron. 20.1-30 Chr. replaced the account of 2 Kgs 3.4-27 with an extremely graphic narrative showing how, according to his convictions, a campaign waged in the name of God must have turned out; at the same time he was in a position to incorporate very specific details here about the places involved because there was obviously some local tradition known to him.

Chr. also attempted to explain further a number of details in terms of the conceptions of his own time. In 1 Kgs 9.18 he read that amongst other things Solomon had built the city of Tadmor (Palmyra)[13] as a fortress. In his day, Tadmor lay in the province of Hamath-Zobah,[14] and so he thought that he ought to add by way of explanation that Solomon undertook a campaign against Hamath-Zobah. For good measure he added the comment that Solomon also founded yet more store cities 'in Hamath'(2 Chron. 8.3, 4).[15] It was purely in the interests of illustration that the remark about Uzziah's leprosy (2 Kgs 15.5a) was used as a trigger for the account of the reason for and onset of this illness which afflicted the formerly so pious king (2 Chron. 26.16-21a). The same interest led Chr. to give quite concrete personal names to all kinds of people and groups who crop up in the course of his historical narrative. He took these from the stock of personal names current in his own day; a comparison of all the relevant cases[16] shows that in them the same post-exilic names and types of name recur repeatedly. Here too it is a question of literary habit, and it would be as mistaken as in the case of the date and time indicators discussed above to assume that Chr. used some special ancient source for these names.

In all the features of Chr.'s composition discussed so far, no so-called bias (*Tendenz*) is to be perceived. They lead us, rather, to the conclusion that Chr. was always making an effort to go beyond the *Vorlagen* at his disposal by enlivening and giving graphic portrayal to the historical narrative. As is only to be expected, he sought to achieve this aim by making use of the conceptual horizon and interests of his own day, for there was no possibility of his giving a faithful historical picture of those older times which he had in view at any given moment. However, in the interests of an accurate appraisal of Chr.'s work it is also important to appreciate that he deserves recognition as an independent narrator in his own right. His work manifestly displays a purely literary concern, and this concern has influenced the content of his historical presentation in matters of detail.

Beyond this, of course, certain objective goals were also determinative for the way in which Chr. constructed and carried out his work; his aim was not to entertain but to give teaching about various specific consequences which could be drawn from past history and which were of relevance to the present. We have yet to demonstrate in detail the extent to which these aims were decisive for the sifting and arrangement of the sources used;[17] in the same way it will eventually be necessary to examine these aims with regard to their content. For the present our initial inquiry concerns only the form that Chr. used to express those determinative considerations which guided him in the composition of his work. Now, slotted into the narrative we find speeches, and Chr. makes use of these just as Dtr. did. The only difference is that Chr. does not concentrate them at historical turning points but uses any available opportunity to introduce them. As G. von Rad has so well demonstrated, Chr. couched these speeches in the style of the Levitical sermon which was current in his own day.[18]

Reviewing now the more important examples, we find David's speeches to Solomon, to the 'commanders of Israel' and to the assembled people, in which Chr. let expression be given to those matters which he considered important regarding the significance of the Jerusalem temple (1 Chron. 22.7-13 [16]; 28.2-10; 29.1-5); David's prayer in 1 Chron. 29.10-19 also belongs here. Next, there is the speech of King Abijah to Jeroboam and the Israelites; its occasion is the first encounter in battle between the separated states of Judah and Israel, and it is of supreme importance for Chr.'s historical point of view (2 Chron. 13.4-12). Then come Jehoshaphat's prayer before the battle, which gives expression to the principles of God's actions in history (2 Chron. 20.5-12), Hezekiah's speech to the Levites about the significance of the purification of the cult which they are about to undertake (2 Chron. 29.6-12), Hezekiah's letter to the remnant of the population of the state of Israel dealing with God's retributive activity (2 Chron. 30.6-9), and finally the prayer of confession which concentrates on guilt and punishment because of the mixed marriages affair (Ezra 9.6-15) and the long prayer by the community with its historical review which followed Ezra's reading of the Law (Neh 9.6-37).

On a number of occasions, in imitation of some well-known episodes in Kings, Chr. has prophets appear as preachers of repentance. They are primarily made into spokesmen for the doctrine of retribution with reference each time to the situation in hand. Sometimes for this purpose Chr. used prophets who feature in Kings while on other occasions he introduced otherwise unknown characters, no doubt his own creations (2 Chron. 12.5-8;[19] 15.1-7;[20] 16.7-10; 19.2,3;[21] 20.37;[22] 28.9-11[23]). In older tradition, the well-known prophet Elijah was most closely associated with the kings of Israel; Chr., however, managed to involve him at a distance, at least, in the history of Judah by telling of a letter containing a message of judgment, which Elijah sent to Joram, the king of Judah (2 Chron. 21.12-15). In doing so, he made the tacit assumption that Elijah was still alive during the reign of Joram, something not directly stated, of course, in the older tradition. In these ways Chr. went quite a long way beyond Dtr. in emphasizing the prophetic word which accompanied the course of events with words of instruction, warning and punishment. By contrast, in the tradition which Dtr. used this element had been focused predominantly on the history of the *Israelite* kings.

## Chapter 18

## THE HISTORICAL PRESUPPOSITIONS

It was surely inevitable that, like anyone else's, Chr.'s outlook and mental horizon should have been determined by the historically conditioned institutions and conceptions of his own day. They are therefore bound to surface in the way that he gave his historical narrative its general shape. This is so despite the fact that, unlike Dtr., his work was not planned under the fresh and immediate impact of a major historical turn of events but stood at quite a chronological distance from even the latest of the events which it records. The determinative key thoughts of his work, however, naturally grew out of the special concerns of his time, and their intention was precisely to give historical justification to these concerns themselves. Furthermore, the way that Chr. undertook to embellish his historical narrative with numerous individual items of his own making left the door wide open for unintentional anachronisms, whereby elements from the writer's own historical purview were read back into the past which he was describing. A brief consideration of the historical situation at Chr.'s time is therefore indispensable for an accurate assessment of his work. Of course, it is true that we know only very little about the history of the third century BC, during the course of which Chr. presumably composed his work; we must therefore be content with some remarks of a general nature.

The work of Chr. differs from Dtr. in that it developed on the basis of a solidly established institution with traditional forms of life and thought, namely the post-exilic community in Judaea.[1] By that time it had long since adopted a fixed and permanent shape. Now, although Chr. by no means regarded the *external* form of this community's existence as an irrevocable and absolutely final state,[2] yet without doubt the essential elements of the inner life of the community were so obviously familiar to him that in fact he was scarcely able to perceive that in reality they were historically conditioned. We should therefore hardly expect otherwise than that he should assume they also held true for the past which he was describing. This is not a question of catching him pursuing some particular 'bias' but simply of the readily intelligible influence of an author's own times on his historical presentation.

In this category belong the repeated references to the 'Law of Moses'.[3] This law was the constitutive and binding divine charter for the post-exilic community; the individual's membership of the community depended upon his recognition of it. Consequently, Chr. must have reckoned that it was the decisive revelation of the divine will for past history as well. Despite the actual wording of the phrase 'Law of *Moses*', this concept was one of those things which Chr. accepted to such an extent as unquestionably valid that he was able to use the expression without in fact ever introducing the figure of Moses into his historical account at all or even ever offering an explanation of what the 'Law of Moses' was.

This is all quite different from what we find in Dtr. Consideration for the Law led him to begin his historical narrative with Moses and then to include the full text of a 'Law of Moses' in the introduction to his work. That to which Dtr. gave a historical foundation Chr. already accepted as something self-evident and of timeless validity.

Further, it is in this context that the high value placed on the cultic activity conducted in the one single legitimate sanctuary, the Jerusalem temple, belongs. In Dtr. the negative concern for the rejection of all other cult centres came to be even stronger than the positive interest in the conduct of the cult itself. So when Chr. gives much greater prominence to the activity of the cult, he is again showing himself to be simply a child of his time. He gives extensive coverage to sacrificial ceremonies; one has only to think of the descriptions of the celebration of Passover under the kings Hezekiah and Josiah.

The time-conditioned difference between Dtr. and Chr. in this regard becomes especially clear at the dedication of the temple. Here, in the long prayer of Solomon which Dtr. himself composed (1 Kgs 8.23-53), he characterized the temple as the place of the name of Yahweh and as a focal point towards which one might pray. Chr., on the other hand. after having adopted this prayer from Dtr., goes on shortly afterwards in an addition from his own pen characteristically to describe the temple as 'a house of sacrifice' (2 Chron. 7.12bβ; cf.

also 2 Chron. 2.3, 5). Here again there can be no question of detecting a particular 'bias'; it is simply a matter of an element in the way that Chr. usually thought.

The same applies, finally, to Chr.'s concept of holiness. According to this, only cultic personnel who had been specifically designated could gain access to holy places and be involved in holy activities. It is sufficient here to draw attention to the way in which the account of the deposing of Athaliah (2 Kings 11) has been changed around in 2 Chronicles 23, so that instead of officers with their troops Chr. introduces the Levites as soon as the temple becomes the scene of the action (cf. also 2 Chron. 6.13 as a corrective to v. 12=1 Kgs 8.22); or again, take the way in which Chr. develops the story of David's transfer of the ark, according to which the Levites are the only personnel authorized to carry the sacred palladium (1 Chron. 15.2f., 11ff.).[4] The same general considerations apply to the way in which Chr. reserves for the Levites that sacred music about which he so likes to speak, in line with the cultic practice of his own time. None of this justifies us in arguing that Chr. had an especial interest in the Levites or even in including him personally amongst the Levites. The data are adequately explained by the fact that in Chr.'s day no one knew any different; it was taken for granted that the cult conducted in accordance with the 'Law of Moses' was a centralized holy undertaking of supreme importance and that the laity, who were not dedicated to its service, must be scrupulously kept away from all holy activities and every sacred object.[5]

There was probably another problem of current importance which confronted the Judaean community in the third century BC, namely their relationship with the Samaritan cultic community. It would be of material assistance to an understanding of Chr. to have an accurate knowledge about the founding of the cult on Mt Gerizim. Unfortunately, what can be learnt about this from literary sources is extremely sketchy. In *Ant*. 9.8 (§304–347 in Niese's edition) Josephus gives an account of negotiations between Sanballat, the 'satrap'[6] of Samaria, and Alexander the Great and between Jaddua, the high priest in Jerusalem, and Alexander at the time of the latter's appearance in Syria and Palestine in 332 BC. He also tells how Sanballat, having gained permission from Alexander on this occasion so to do, built a sanctuary of his own on Mt Gerizim. But none of this is to be given any historical credence; it is far too naïve and is clearly dependent on apocryphal traditions of the two cultic communities concerning the privileges which it is claimed the great king bestowed upon each of them.[7]

The date implied by all this for the establishment of the Samaritan's own cult on Mt Gerizim, however, will hardly be completely misleading. It is true that from the earliest days of the renewed Jerusalem cult following the decree of Cyrus there was tension between the long-established inhabitants of the province of Samaria and those who were repatriated after the exile.[8] Nevertheless, it does not seem to have reached the point of a completely clean break, that is to say, the point at which the Samaritans constituted a cultic community of their own, at least for the greater part of the Persian period.[9] On the other hand, we have definite information about the existence of a sanctuary on Mt Gerizim from the comment in 2 Macc. 6.2. This mentions the temples in Jerusalem and on Mt Gerizim as being on a par with each other and observes with regard to them both that Antiochus IV Epiphanes wanted to convert them to the cult of the Hellenistic God Zeus. Now, this can hardly come from the time when the Samaritans first began to conduct their own worship. On the contrary, it must certainly have already gained acceptance for some considerable time past as one of the traditional cults of one of the 'nations' which was vested with a limited degree of independence within the Seleucid empire.[10] Only on such a basis can the king's interest in it be explained.[11]

Of course, this still leaves a good deal of latitude when trying to estimate the commencement of this cult, and one is thrown back on personal conjecture in order to establish anything more precise. The greatest weight of probability, however, supports the theory that the 'Samaritans' took advantage of the fall of the Persian empire to cut themselves off from the Jerusalem cult which had been granted such special privileges by Cyrus and later Persian kings. Josephus's story referred to above is therefore not completely wrong when it associates the erection of the temple on Mt Gerizim with the demise of the Persian empire. The only trouble with his story is that he painted the course of events in far too dramatic a light. We must regard it as probable that the cataclysmic events of Alexander's time or at least the start of the period of the Diadochoi gave the 'Samaritans' the opportunity to realize their wish of establishing a cult of their own and that this cult was then recognized as official by the Hellenistic rulers.[12] The cult community which thus established itself, however, never succeeded in encompassing the whole population of the province of Samaria. Rather, several groups remained loyal to their ancient association with the Jerusalem cult; besides the inhabitants of the territory of the Jews who were repatriated at the start of the Persian period,[13] these comprised a section of the inhabitants of the Samarian hill-country[14] together with the long-established population of Galilee.[15]

Chr. could hardly have completely ignored this state of affairs when composing his historical narrative if we are more or less correct in dating him in the third century BC. At that time the separation of the Samaritans from the cult in Jerusalem was only in the recent past and so will have remained fresh in the memory of the Jerusalem community. As such, it will have posed a pressing problem for those who regarded the community gathered round the Jerusalem cult as the direct successors of the ancient people of Israel—and of course Chr. was one of these. This is because with the separation some necessary branches of the Israelite people had been eliminated from the fellowship of the whole and because on Gerizim there had grown up a rival to the temple in Jerusalem which made the same claims to ancient tradition, sanctified by Israelite history. It was inevitable that a presentation of this self-same ancient history in the third century BC would have to take this problem into consideration. We therefore arrive at the proposition that the separation of the Samaritans from the Jerusalem cult constituted one of the historical presuppositions for the work of Chr. and one which must have come to the surface in the construction and formation of his work. It will be shown later that the work of Chr. itself fully endorses this proposition.

*Chapter 19*

# THE ATTITUDE TOWARDS THE INHERITED TRADITIONS

It has already been indicated in another context that to a greater extent than Dtr., Chr. regularly embellished the text of the sources which he took over with additions of his own. Of course, in the cases where he adopted the wording itself of his sources, he retained it as far as possible unchanged; as these sources have been preserved in large part, this conclusion can be precisely established. Exceptions to this rule are that at various points he altered the phrasing to align it in matters of detail with the language and style of his own time[1] or in other ways at his own discretion, that he passed over in silence or altered according to his own opinion those expressions whose wording or substance were unintelligible to him,[2] and that he added various brief remarks by way of explanation or supplementation. He had a perfect right to indulge in these slight formal deviations because he was not setting out to publish his sources in any modern scholarly sense, and so they should not mislead us into doubting that Chr. adopted a basically *positive* attitude towards the sources that he was working with. He used them to determine the basis of his work not only as regards content but also to a substantial degree in terms of its wording. Even in the cases where he reworked his sources on a larger scale than we would consider advisable by our standards he will have believed that in many cases it was only a question of providing a correct understanding of his sources. Chr.'s deviations from his sources have a tendency to colour the way we look at the situation because for the most part we still have in front of us, and are accustomed to making use of, the very sources themselves that he was working with. Even so, a correct assessment will have to accept that Chr. intended basically to be bound by the tradition which he received and that he was broadly successful in this aim. He may not have treated the tradition with such care and respect on this matter as Dtr. certainly did,[3] but that is part and parcel of Chr.'s style which can be seen elsewhere too; Dtr.'s austerity and consistency were foreign to his nature.

Of course, as he had every right to do, Chr. prepared only a *selection* from the material in his sources based upon what he considered important for his own particular purposes. For the introduction to his work he extracted no more than the genealogical skeleton from the Pentateuch. But even when it came to his historical narrative proper he did not adopt everything that his sources offered. For the portrayal of David he selected only that material which led up to the preparation for building the temple and in addition anything which showed up David as a victorious and powerful king; this last point was also an important theme for him.[4] For the period after Solomon, as is well known, he extracted from his source only those portions which dealt with the kings of Judah and for reasons to be discussed later he more or less ignored the history of the state of Israel. Only occasionally, when it was a question of something significant for Judaean history, did he include some material from sections dealing with the Israelite kings, sometimes in a brief summary, as at 2 Chron. 22.7-9, and sometimes in full, as at 2 Chron. 18.2-34. For the history of the post-exilic period, admittedly, he incorporated into his work everything that his sources made available to him; but after all, that was already scanty enough.

When making his selection he was not always aware that he was leaving intact the indications in his source that connected one episode with another. Thus, in 1 Chron. 10.11f. he followed 1 Sam. 31.11-13 in recording the way in which the men of Jabesh took care of the corpses of Saul and his sons but he omitted 2 Sam. 2.4b-7 which is the real climax of that particular episode. In 1 Chron. 15.29b he retained from 2 Sam. 6.16b the note about Michal's attitude at the bringing in of the ark but did not include the appropriate continuation from 2 Sam. 6.20-23. At 2 Chron. 10.15 he included the reference at 1 Kgs 12.15 to the prophetic word of Ahijah the Shilonite even though he had previously passed over the account of the meeting between Ahijah and Jeroboam.[5]

Chr. occasionally indulged in more marked interference when he used his own reasoning to arrange into a *different order*, and thereby to throw a new light on, the elements which made up the narrative of his sources. This applies above all to the structure of the history of David in 1 Chron. 10f., discussed above on pp. 33f. In this passage he portrays what he considered to be David's most important deeds in a highly compacted manner from the chronological point of view. It was pure conjecture which led him to attribute the significance of 'David's heroes' in 2 Sam. 23.8-39 to a role as those who principally worked with David during the period of his rise to kingship over Israel, and this entailed as a consequence that he transfer this list to follow the account of the beginning of David's reign (1 Chron. 11.10ff.). Similarly, the histories of Ezra and Nehemiah are intertwined in the structure of Ezra 7-Nehemiah 13 as we now have it. This too undoubtedly arose from the same characteristic of combining historical events which were separate from each other in the tradition into a closer chronological and material connection. Behind this lay the simple fact that in the sources which Chr. used both men appeared in Jerusalem during the reign of an Artaxerxes.

Alongside such slight formal changes as have already been discussed, Chr. also allowed himself, of course, to make *various minor corrections* to the substance of his sources. Thus he omitted not only statements in his source which he did not understand, but also various matters with whose contents he obviously did not agree. Because of the concept of holiness which was current in his time he ignored Solomon's blessing of the people on the occasion of the dedication of the temple (compare 2 Chron. 7.1 with 1 Kgs 8.54-61).[6] In order to emphasize Solomon's[7] exclusive concern for the sanctuary, he suppressed the passage in 1 Kgs 7.1-12 about Solomon's palace building.[8]

Even more frequently in such circumstances, he quietly changed what his source actually said. According to 2 Sam. 6.17b it was David who offered sacrifice at the transfer of the ark; in 1 Chron. 16.1b, however, Chr. simply refers to the indeterminate subject 'they' instead of David. At 1 Chron. 18.17b he was himself responsible for turning the priestly office of the sons of David (2 Sam. 8.18b) into a position of honour 'beside the king'.[9] The Philistine idols captured by David and his men were not just 'taken away' (so 2 Sam. 5.21b), but 'burnt' (1 Chron. 14.12b). He made the princess Jehosheba of 2 Kgs 11.2f. become the wife of the high priest Jehoiada (2 Chron. 22.11) so as to justify her residence in the temple. By contrast with 2 Sam. 5.17 he cast the anointing of David as king into the passive mood at 1 Chron. 14.8.[10] As is well known, at 1 Chron. 21.1 he substituted Satan for Yahweh (2 Sam. 24.1).

Apart from these minor corrections which touch on the sphere of the cult, when dealing with various kings, he also removed a number of unpleasant features preserved in the tradition.[11] Thus at 1 Chron. 20.1 he had Joab devastate the country of the Ammonites on his own initiative rather than at David's instigation (as at 2 Sam. 11.1). He turned the Israelites from whom Solomon raised a levy of workmen into 'foreigners who dwelt in the land of Israel' (2 Chron. 2.16). King Asa no longer sent '*all* the silver and the gold that were left in the treasuries of the temple and the palace' (1 Kgs 15.18) to support his request to King Benhadad for help, but only 'silver and gold *from* the treasuries' (2 Chron. 16.2), while at the same time Chr. suppressed the word 'bribe' from 1 Kgs 15.19. He reproduced the story of Isaiah from 2 Kgs 20.1-11, 12-19 in a substantially abbreviated version at 2 Chron. 32.24-31, and he did it in such a way as to remove Hezekiah's lack of faith and request for a sign when confronted with Isaiah's word of prophecy, together with Hezekiah's reliance on his treasures and armaments on the occasion of the visit of the Babylonian delegation. Chr. allowed himself very considerable freedom with regard to his source at 2 Chron. 8.1f. Instead of having Solomon cede some Galilean towns to Hiram of Tyre (1 Kgs 9.10-13) he does exactly the opposite: he makes Hiram give some towns to Solomon.

Besides all this, Chr. changed all kinds of details in his sources' statements under the influence of the conceptions of his own time. For instance, his preferred word for the assembled people is 'congregation' (*qāhāl*); at 1 Chron. 19.6 he replaces Aram-Beth-Rehob (2 Sam. 10.6), which he probably found strange, with Aram-Naharaim, a name which was at least familiar to him from the literature, while at 1 Chron. 18.8 he calls the place name Berothai (2 Sam. 8.8) by the name Cun, the Conna of Roman times (=*ras ba'albekk*). Chr. evidently could not make anything of the 'Israelites who were on the other side of the valley and beyond Jordan' (1 Sam. 31.7), and so spoke of the 'Israelites in the valley' (1 Chron. 10.7). Also, in the case of the frequent exaggeration of the traditional numbers for the strength of armies and the like he undoubtedly followed the situation of his own time in which the military levy in the Hellenistic states was on a much larger scale than had formerly been the case.

Even when they are considered cumulatively, Chr.'s deviations from the sources which he inherited, as discussed up to this point, would not have resulted in so wide a difference as we find actually to be the case between the overall view which he sketches of the history of the Judaean monarchy and that of the books of Samuel and Kings. So far, we have really been dealing only with a mass of details where Chr. felt obliged to depart from the wording of his sources; at the very most Chr.'s selectivity in regard to the history of David caused a series of significant traits to disappear from the portrayal of this king and his reign, quite apart from the important difference caused by omitting the description of the pre-history of the Davidic monarchy. What really give Chr.'s historical narrative its different appearance are his *additions*. As already shown,[12] only an infinitely small number of these are based on the use of an alternative ancient source for the period of the monarchy; on the contrary, the additions comprise almost entirely Chr.'s own contributions. Chr.'s intention, it is true, was precisely the reverse. His aim in the use of his sources was, by all kinds of minor omissions and improvements, to correct their presentation without, however, significantly altering their content. In the case of the additions, on the other hand, he entertained the belief that he could offer an appropriate interpretation of his *Vorlage* without having to touch its wording. His method was to develop the historical presentation extensively by using one or another expression in his sources that was important for him as a trigger, or by combining several expressions from his sources together to introduce new elements into them. It was precisely in the course of this procedure, however, that, because he constructed these additions on the basis of the conceptual outlook of his own time, he introduced into his historical presentation those anachronisms which so distort the historical picture preserved in the ancient tradition.

To the extent that this was simply a matter of an author's interest in enlivening his narrative with larger or smaller additions, enough has already been said on pp. 77ff. above. Moreover, attention has already been paid above (on pp. 80f.) to those passages in which Chr. gave expression to his fundamental historical convictions either by speeches which he attributed to historical characters known to him from tradition or by the words of prophets whom he himself introduced *de novo* into his narrative. In the present context our purpose is rather to examine how in different ways Chr. corrected (and partly, indeed, had the intention of correcting) the version in his sources by the additions which he made.

The most important example is the ascription to David of the whole business of preparing for the temple building. This had the effect of making the great king to all intents and purposes into the author of what for Chr. was the most important task of all, the building of the temple. By retaining the actual construction of the building for Solomon, he avoided at least a blatant contradiction of the ancient tradition. On the other hand, Chr. can hardly have overlooked the fact that he differed from the *intention* of this tradition. At the same time, he will have believed that he had hit upon the historical truth; he was simply incapable of thinking that David was not the real founder of the Jerusalem temple.[13]

We find a comparable correction of the tradition in the way that Chr. has Ezra anticipate Nehemiah's reform measures as presented in the Nehemiah Memoir (Neh. 13.4-31). Once again Chr. did not change the wording of the tradition here, but in fact his use of the Ezra narrative distorted the sense of this passage in the Nehemiah Memoir by leaving Nehemiah with no more than the gleanings. As before, so here he certainly thought he was giving an accurate account of the historical situation. In his view there was no alternative: if, as he assumed, Ezra arrived in Jerusalem shortly before Nehemiah, he must himself have already witnessed the same abuses and put a stop to them on the basis of the Law of God which was in his hand (as the tradition which Chr. used at Ezra 7.14b, 25a has it). This would have applied especially to the business of mixed marriages which was so very important to Chr.,[14] and which he therefore had Ezra tackle first with special measures.[15]

Elsewhere he has occasionally constructed additions of his own to the received tradition by combining together various statements of his sources in ways that were necessary in his opinion. Since God could hardly have appeared to Solomon at an illegitimate sanctuary, he concluded on the basis of 1 Kgs 3.4-15 that the tabernacle, which had been erected, in his day, by Moses in the wilderness according to the Pentateuchal narrative, must at that time have stood at Gibeon (2 Chron. 1.2ff.). As a result, Gibeon must have been *the* legitimate sanctuary until such time as the temple was complete (cf. also 1 Chron. 16.39). In this connection, Chr. concluded further from 2 Samuel 24 that as early as David's time Yahweh had settled on Jerusalem as the replacement for Gibeon as the place of sacrifice for the future, and this is just what he says in his addition at 1 Chron. 21.26b-22.1.[16] In a similar manner Chr. put together the edict of

Cyrus as it came down to him (Ezra 6.3-5) and the list of those who returned (Ezra 2.1-67), which he also inherited,[17] and deduced from this combination that in addition to the rebuilding of the temple Cyrus had also ordered a general return; consequently, on his own account he made up what he thought the wording of the edict of Cyrus must have been (Ezra 1.2-4). In these cases we find in Chr. the typical procedures of authors of works containing traditional material who do not sift the information of their sources critically, but add to them.[18]

Thus despite his intentions, Chr. changed the presentation of history offered by his sources to a far greater extent than did Dtr., for Dtr. gave expression to his own viewpoint primarily in the framework to his composition but interfered only relatively slightly in the wording of his sources.

*Chapter 20*

## THE CENTRAL THEOLOGICAL IDEAS

Since G. von Rad has devoted a detailed and first-rate monograph to a treatment of the Chronicler's theology,[1] the following discussion can be kept short. It will be limited to the main points and in addition will give particular attention to those matters where von Rad's exposition must be corrected and expanded as a consequence of the literary-critical results achieved above.

Von Rad has demonstrated persuasively in numerous matters of detail that Chr.'s overall outlook is not so closely related to P as to Dtr. In actual fact, we should hardly have expected anything different. Even if it can be proved that Chr. both knew and occasionally made use of the Pentateuch, and the P narrative within it that formed its literary basis, still his principal source and, moreover, the real pattern for his composition was the work of Dtr. In any case, because of the literary stages through which it passed the Pentateuch is a unique phenomenon. Because they are both works of historical tradition, however, the works of Dtr. and Chr. are closely related to each other within the literature of the Old Testament. The earlier familiar reconstruction of a simple linear development Dtr.–P–Chr. took no account of this difference in type but inappropriately interpreted every step of chronological succession in terms of the younger being always directly dependent on the one immediately older than it.

Chr.'s purpose was to present the history of the formation of the post-exilic community in which he lived. It is, to say the least, inexact, misleading, and a pointless exercise to try to 'excuse' Chr.'s distortion of the traditional picture of his people's history by arguing that he did not have the *intention* of writing *history*.[2] It is, of course, certain that he could not have done this in any modern, scientific sense, and it is equally certain that his interests in history were determined by the situation in the post-exilic period. But that in no way contradicts his clear intention of giving information about what really happened. He believed (and here he was undoubtedly right) that only in this way would he be able to serve the concerns of his own time. So far as the subject-matter of his presentation is concerned, he saw in the institutions of his own time something which had developed historically.[3] Dtr. regarded his time—a very different one from Chr.'s—in the same way; in this respect the historical writings of the Old Testament represent a unique phenomenon in the whole of the ancient orient.

Naturally, as they saw things (and hence this goes for Chr. too) history was the arena of *God's dealings with men*. An understanding of this developed for Chr., as earlier for Dtr., into the so-called doctrine of retribution. It was a presupposition of this doctrine that God's will was known to man, and within Israel, at least, this was revealed in the Law. Chr. goes even further than Dtr. in constantly directing attention to this will of God by means of prophetic words of warning and admonition. As von Rad (1930: 10ff.) has shown, there is a difference between Dtr. and Chr.: in Dtr. the collective application of this doctrine to the people of Israel stands in the forefront[4] whilst in Chr. it seems to be directed more pointedly towards the individual and the particular phases of his life.[5] King Asa, for instance, was given a positive assessment by Dtr. (1 Kgs 15.11=2 Chron. 14.1), but it is stated that 'in the time of his old age he was diseased in his feet' (1 Kgs 15.23b; cf. 2 Chron. 16.12a). Chr. therefore assumed that his reign fell into two parts, each of which could be exactly dated (cf. 2 Chron. 15.19; 16.1), and that these two parts were separated by the king's apostasy from his initial piety. Similarly, according to Chr. the pious king Uzziah (2 Kgs 15.3=2 Chron. 26.4) must have committed some blatant sin which was punished by God on the spot with leprosy, because according to 2 Kgs 15.5a he became a leper towards the end of his life; thus it was that Chr. came himself to compose the story in 2 Chron. 26.16-21a. These examples show that, as in Dtr. so also here in Chr. inferences are drawn on the basis of the doctrine of retribution, namely that blessing or misfortune must have followed innocence or guilt respectively, and this presupposes the absolute validity of the doctrine.

Another related difference between Dtr. and Chr. is that Dtr.'s collective application of the doctrine of retribution has had a decisive impact on the plan of the work as a whole whereas in Chr. it is applied more to numerous individual instances. It thus emerges clearly that, unlike Dtr., Chr. was not really concerned with establishing guilt and punishment in the history of Israel. Again unlike Dtr., he was not working at the close of an historical epoch with the aim of considering retrospectively the net results of what had happened. Rather, he was part of a current institution which had arisen in the meantime, an institution whose meaning and significance within the framework of God's activity should be determined for him by a consideration of the way in which it developed historically.

Without any doubt, the relationship between God and Israel as regulated by the Law and the pattern of service which it offered was not a problem for him but rather a reality of unquestionable validity. He speaks not a word about the formation of this relationship. In fact there is a remarkable gap at this point in his presentation, a presentation which stretches from Adam to Ezra/Nehemiah: he passes without a ripple over the whole conquest and Sinai tradition which had always been taken as the foundation for the relationship between God and people. This cannot be explained away with the observation that these matters were included in the Pentateuch, that by his time this had long since gained authoritative recognition and that therefore he had no need to repeat them; if that were the case he would certainly have included at least a reference to them. The reason why he did not speak about these things is rather that at this point there was quite simply no problem either for him or, apparently, for those to whom his work was addressed. In his view, rather, this was a relationship whose validity was quite without precondition and which therefore needed no historical justification.

It follows at the same time that he had no concern to discuss the question of Israel's position within the family of nations. This can be seen from the strange fact that his real historical presentation starts with David, something quite unmotivated by his primary source (Dtr.) but which has to be the most secure and important starting point for an understanding of what really concerned him. It shows that his historical presentation was intended to explain problems that were *internal* to Israel alone, for, as the work of Dtr. had already made clear, the Davidic kingdom only arose long after the separate history of the Israelite people within the family of nations had unfolded, in its essential features.

Now there is a consensus of opinion that Chr.'s primary interest concerned an internal affair, namely the justification of Levitical

claims to certain new and important roles in the temple cult.[6] I
cannot help but regard this view as *unquestionably mistaken*. This
conclusion follows partly from the fact that the long Levitical
genealogies and lists in Chronicles have been shown on literary-
critical grounds to be secondary additions to Chr.'s work.[7] Furthermore, the role which the Levites play in the basic text of Chr. does
not go beyond what is to be expected once it is realized that Chr.
projected back into the past which he was describing the relationships
which prevailed at the time he was writing.[8] But the principal reason
for my negative judgment derives from the overall plan of Chr.'s
work. If someone wanted to validate and give historical justification
to new Levitical claims to special roles in the temple cult at the
expense of the priests' privileges (and the priests were the only
possible opponents of such claims), he could not possibly have based
these claims to new rights on arrangements which David made
without exposing himself to the obvious objection that these more
recent arrangements of David's could not make any headway against
the older pronouncements of Moses. In a period when the privileged
position of the Aaronite priests could claim firm and sacred
legitimation in the accepted authority of the Pentateuch, such a
hypothetical reformer would have had to expand the tradition about
Moses to conform it to his purpose, for in the cultic sphere the age of
an ordinance is always a valid legitimation: the older carries greater
weight than the more recent. But Chr. remained completely silent
about Moses. As a consequence it is clear that any intention to
change or expand the Mosaic ordinances lay completely outside the
realm of his interests.

If we pay due regard to the striking fact that Chr.'s historical
recital proper begins with David, and if at the same time we survey
what Chr. omitted from the content of the books of Samuel and
Kings which he used and what he added to them, then we can come
to no other conclusion than that Chr.'s central concern was to
demonstrate the legitimacy of the Davidic dynasty and of the
Jerusalem temple as Yahweh's valid cult centre.[9] If we then go on to
take the concluding part of the work into account, we must conclude
further that Chr. aimed to demonstrate that the Jerusalem cultic
community was the genuine successor of this ancient and legitimate
'Israel'. The opposition whom Chr. had in view can only have been
the Samaritan community with a cult of their own on Mt Gerizim.[10]
This insight affords so clear an explanation of the structure overall

and the content in detail that there can hardly be any doubt that this is the correct understanding of Chr.[11] The fact that 'in this work the author gives expression to the whole of his religious estate as it touches both past and future'[12] does not rule out that it was nevertheless a particular purpose which governed the unique construction and the peculiar choice of content.

Accordingly, Chr. omitted the traditions which were common to the Jerusalem and the Samaritan communities; naturally, they could contribute nothing to the dispute between them. This applies to the material in the Pentateuch in its entirety, for this was also the Samaritans' sacred scripture.[13] Why, then, did Chr. borrow from the Pentateuch the genealogical skeleton which served to introduce and lead up to the twelve tribes of Israel? His only intention in this was to indicate that the people of the twelve tribes, who in effect constituted a self-contained whole, belonged within the framework of humanity as created by God. The traditions of the conquest and judges period too, at least as mediated through Dtr., provided no argument to use in the dispute between the two later cult communities, and nor did the reign of Saul. All this was to change only when David emerged as the founder of the Davidic kingdom in Jerusalem. Consequently, and from his point of view quite correctly, Chr. began his historical account proper with David and emphasized very heavily from the start of his narrative the divine establishment of this kingdom.[14] This can be most impressively seen in two apparently quite insignificant deviations from the wording of Dtr.; at 1 Chron. 17.14 Chr. simply changes the suffix of 2 Sam. 7.16a but thereby turns the dynasty and kingdom of David into the dynasty and kingdom of God; again, by a slight textual alteration he transforms the 'throne of Israel' in 1 Kgs 10.9 into a throne of God at 2 Chron. 9.8.[15] Thus Chr. vested the Davidic kingdom with quite exceptional authority as a kingdom of God on earth. On the occasion of the first military encounter between a Davidide and the tribes who had 'fallen away' from the Davidic dynasty after the death of Solomon, Chr. most emphatically underlined this thought once again in the speech which he attributed to King Abijah. He makes Abijah speak not only about the kingship over 'Israel' which was given for ever to David by Yahweh, the God of Israel (2 Chron. 13.5), but above all of 'the kingdom of Yahweh in the hand of the sons of David' (v.8).[16] Finally, whereas in Dtr. the people of Israel were the object of election, in Chr. this concept is applied to the kingdom of the Judaean dynasty of David (1 Chron. 28.4).[17]

It is on this basis too that the complete neglect of the history of the state of Israel in the framework of the history of the monarchy is to be explained. It is not that Chr. had no particular interest in the kings of Israel; it is rather that alongside the Davidic kingdom this kingdom simply had no right to exist, in his view. Consequently, he took it upon himself to omit the passages in Dtr. which dealt with the Israelite kings. In Dtr. a gradual difference emerges between the two kingdoms: measured by the yardstick which Dtr. applied, the Israelite kings were judged in a wholly negative way whilst the Judaean kings were judged negatively only for the most part; consequently, the Israelite kingdom came to an end earlier than the Judaean. For Chr., however, the issue at this point was the black and white question of a fundamental difference between what is legitimate and what is illegitimate.

In the post-exilic cult community of Jerusalem, however, the Davidic kingdom no longer existed; despite this, Chr. regarded this community as the substratum of the former legitimate kingdom whilst he could look upon the Samaritan community as no more than the successor of the tribes who 'fell away' after Solomon's death together with their illegitimate kingdom. That is why Chr. was so concerned to clarify the connection between the Judaeans of the pre-exilic period and the post-exilic Jerusalem cult community. He achieved this by joining the edict of Cyrus, which Chr. expanded to include the order to return, directly on to the history of the end of the state of Judah (Ezra 1.2-4) and by the designation which Chr. readily used for the post-exilic community, namely 'Judah and Benjamin' (Ezra 1.5, etc.; cf. 2 Chron. 11.1, 3 =1 Kgs 12.21, 23).

The idea that the Jerusalem cult community stood in succession to the ancient and legitimate 'Israel' comes to expression with particular clarity in the great communal prayer of Neh. 9.6-37, which derives from Chr. For Chr., therefore, the legitimate line ran exclusively through the Judaeans who had been deported to Babylon. The Samaritans, on the other hand, even excluding from consideration those amongst them who had been deported from other countries (Ezra 4.2b), could only trace their origins back to the 'apostate' old tribes and therefore could not, in Chr.'s view, be the heirs of a genuine tradition.[18]

For the related question of the legitimate cult centre Chr. needed only to carry on the line already plotted by Dtr. Basing himself on Deuteronomy, Dtr. had already established that Jerusalem was the only possibility. According to Chr. the destruction of the temple by Nebuchadnezzar was followed by the edict of Cyrus, which ordered its rebuilding (and in this case Chr. could appeal to the genuine content of the edict of Cyrus, Ezra 6.3-5), and the restoration of the valuable temple vessels which Nebuchadnezzar had removed. The rebuilding of the temple started directly after this—at least, this is how Chr. presents it, though it does not conform completely with historical reality—and finally, after all kinds of obstacles had been overcome, it was brought to a successful conclusion. Here too, then, the close association of the Jerusalem cult community with what had been legitimate in the past was granted.

For Chr.'s understanding of this past, however, the association of this sanctuary with the Davidic kingdom (itself quite correct historically) was so important that he really could not imagine that the founder of the dynasty did not regard concern for the building of the sanctuary to be his most important task. The 'apostate' tribes (and here again Chr. will certainly have been thinking of their successors, the Samaritans of his own day) had renounced the sole legitimate cult.[19] This had already been stated by Dtr. (cf. 1 Kgs 12.26ff.); in Chr.'s case it was above all Abijah once again who in his speech, which comes at an important point in the narrative (2 Chron. 13.4b-12), gave expression to the view that the 'apostates' had driven out the legitimate priests and Levites (v. 9a) and that they had installed 'priests after the manner of the heathen' for their 'no-gods' (v. 9b) and golden calves (v. 8b) The result was that the true cult with its true personnnel were confined to Jerusalem and Judah alone (vv. 10-11a). Prior to this, however, Chr. had introduced an addition of his own (2 Chron. 11.13-17) to the effect that following the establishment of the apostate Israelite kingdom the genuine priests and Levites who lived in its territory had left everything behind in order to come over to Jerusalem and Judah. At the same time, even the pious lay people who adhered to the true service of God are said to have left the territory of the state of Israel in order to settle in Jerusalem.[20] According to Chr., therefore, there was a clean and clear break right from the start, so that there could be no doubt as to where one should look for legitimacy. But in view of what has been said, Chr.'s interest in these historical events was a thoroughly topical interest in his day.

It is also against the background of the particular interests of his own time that we can understand the frequent remarks which Chr.

himself added about relations between the inhabitants of Samaria and Galilee and the kingdom and cult of Jerusalem. It was not unimportant for the Jerusalem cult's claim to general validity for the whole of 'Israel' that there should have been circles even within Samaria itself who did not adhere to the new cult on Mt Gerizim but who continued to maintain cultic ties with Jerusalem.[21] Chr. transferred this circumstance of his day back into the past which he was describing, and so presented the phenomenon as something which was known to have existed from a long time back. Examples of this are when he makes numerous people from 'Ephraim, Manasseh and Simeon'[22] desert to King Asa (2 Chron. 15.9),[23] when after the fall of the state of Israel he has King Hezekiah invite not only Ephraim and Manasseh, but 'all Israel from Beer-sheba to Dan' to celebrate the Passover in Jerusalem (2 Chron. 30.1, 5) and many members of the Samarian and Galilean tribes also accept this invitation (2 Chron. 30.10, 11, 18, 25), and finally when in Josiah's reign he has people visit the temple not only from 'Judah and Benjamin' but also from 'Manasseh, Ephraim and all the remnant of Israel' (2 Chron. 34.9).

In fact, Chr. seems even to have been of the opinion that the Davidides had always ruled the hill-country of Samaria too, at least in part. According to 2 Chron. 19.4 Jehoshaphat had undertaken his task of converting the people throughout the territory 'from Beer-sheba as far as the hill-country of Ephraim', and according to 2 Chron. 31.1 Hezekiah had pursued his radical purification of the cult in 'all Judah and Benjamin and in Ephraim and Manasseh'. That Josiah extended his politico-cultic measures to 'the towns of Manasseh and Ephraim and Simeon and as far as Naphtali' (2 Chron. 34.6) is, of course, based on the ancient statement from the annals as recorded in 2 Kgs 23.19, and it may be asked whether this piece of information about Josiah was not the basis for Chr.'s assumption of a similar extension of the sphere of authority exercised already by earlier kings of Judah.[24] At any rate this point must have been a matter of topical interest to Chr. Even as early as his day the province of Judah, the territory of the 'people of Judah', was presumably laying claim to at least the southern part of the hill-country of Samaria on the ground that its inhabitants were loyal to the cult of Jerusalem. Eventually, in the Maccabean period this claim was to be realized in fact by the edict of the Seleucid Demetrius II in 145 BC.[25]

In developing his special interest in the legitimate kingdom and the legitimate cult, Chr.'s attention to the cult inevitably turned him against the Samaritan cult community. In the case of the kingdom, however, he was left equally inevitably with an open question regarding the future. Since this kingdom had once arisen on the stage of history as an institution that should last 'for ever' (1 Chron. 17.14; cf. 2 Sam. 7.16), the consequence of its demise in 587 BC had to be the hope that one day in the future it would once again be renewed by God; and Chr. clearly shared this expectation, even though he did not speak about it openly. In the two prayers of Ezra 9.7-9 and Neh. 9.36f. Chr. voiced his judgment of his own period[26] as a time of slavery under foreign overlords. Rather clearly included here was the conviction that this condition was indeed a justified punishment by God (Dtr. had held the same conviction), but that this was not yet the end of God's dealings with his people. Similarly, it was not for nothing that at 2 Chron. 6.40-42 Chr. provided an alternative conclusion to Solomon's prayer at the dedication of the temple (1 Kgs 8.50αb-53). In it, he not only cited Ps. 132 (vv. 8-9), a Psalm for the dedication of the temple which deals with the divine promise made to David and Zion, but he also referred to the words of Deutero-Isaiah (Isa. 55.3) concerning God's 'sure mercies' to David (despite the fall of the Davidic dynasty) and he alluded to the introduction of Ps. 89, a Psalm of lament which requests the restoration of the Davidic monarchy. Evidently, therefore, Chr. shared the hope for a future renewal of the throne of David.

It is from this standpoint that Chr.'s interest in the Judaean kings' development of the externals of power should be understood. This interest is expressed partly in the way that in his section about David Chr. included from his source the stories about the king's exploits in war alongside the elements in the tradition which led up to the preparations for building the temple. The main point in this connection, however, is the information which he supplied in addition to Dtr. for the more important characters in the history of the Judaean monarchy about fortifications, weapons etc. A small part of this material was drawn from another ancient source which stood at his disposal alongside the books of Samuel and Kings. Most of it, however, was his own composition. These references were intended to hold up before his readers' eyes a counterpart to the miserable political situation of his own time and at the same time to indicate what a future renewal of the Davidic kingdom would look like. In this respect, therefore, Chr. differed quite markedly from Dtr., who did not dare so much as to cast a glance in the direction of the future. Probably in this respect we should regard Dtr. and Chr. as being generally representative of the widespread opinion of their respective times.

Not so long after Chr.'s time, a good part of his concerns were temporarily fulfilled in the Maccabean period. An independent kingdom arose once more in Jerusalem; this kingdom eventually brought the whole of the ancient area of settlement of the twelve tribes of Israel under its sway, it integrated its inhabitants into the Jerusalem cult community and it paved the way towards the end of the Samaritan cult on Mt Gerizim. One can well imagine that at this time the work of Chr. would have been read with particular interest and understanding.

# THE 'PRIESTLY WRITING' AND THE REDACTION OF THE PENTATEUCH

## Chapter 21

### THE 'HEXATEUCH' IN THE LIGHT OF THE DEUTERONOMISTIC WORK

The opening of the great Deuteronomistic historical work, which starts at Deuteronomy 1 and finishes at 2 Kings 25, overlaps with the 'Hexateuch'; the establishment of the fact that it exists, therefore, has a bearing on the question of the literary development of the 'Hexateuch'. The task should thus not be avoided of developing and undergirding the results achieved in Chapter 1 from the point of view of 'Hexateuchal' criticism. At first sight, certainly, the question of a serious conflict does not seem to arise at the most important points. Rather, it is possible to allow for the mutually peaceful co-existence of the sources of the 'Hexateuch' on the one side and of the work of Dtr. on the other.[1]

For the book of Deuteronomy, especially, the situation is quite straightforward. The major section Deuteronomy 1–30, which comprises the start of the work of Dtr., has always been recognized as a discrete element within the framework of the 'Hexateuch', whilst amongst the 'Hexateuchal' sources which have been reintroduced in Deuteronomy 31–34 it is possible to separate out quite easily and cleanly those few short portions which make up the continuing thread of Dtr.'s narrative.[2]

The situation is more complicated in the book of Joshua. Its basic shape is determined by its Deuteronomistic framework, and this has proved to be an important and necessary element in the work of Dtr.

At the same time, however, it is generally reckoned to result from the working together of the usual sources of the 'Hexateuch'. Despite this, there would be no fundamental objection to the supposition that the ancient conquest tradition which Dtr. took up and worked into his composition derived either from one of the sources of the 'Hexateuch' or from more than one of them already woven together, especially since it undoubtedly comprised a major narrative complex which already lay at Dtr.'s disposal. Indeed, one would have to make such an assumption were it the case that the analysis of the sources of the 'Hexateuch' from Genesis to Joshua had in every respect led to illuminating and assured results. Such, however, is not the case.[3] The question must therefore be raised whether the discovery of the work of Dtr. should not be capable of shedding new light on various 'Hexateuchal' questions, and thereby, because it has resulted in a broadly-based conclusion which has proved to be illuminating, not only advancing the literary analysis of the books of Deuteronomy and Joshua, but more especially contributing something towards the solution of the question of the 'Hexateuch'.

Starting out from this vantage point, therefore, the question certainly arises about the relationship between the conquest tradition as taken over by Dtr. in the book of Joshua and the sources of the 'Hexateuch'. What happens if one sets out by studying this tradition (as well as the pre-deuteronomistic core of Joshua 24) not in the light of the presupposition of 'Hexateuchal' criticism but from the standpoint of the particular themes which it deals with? The result is that no special connections of a literary or factual nature can be established with the agreed sources of the 'Hexateuch' in Genesis–Numbers (Deuteronomy). Indeed, most surprisingly of all, in those few cases in which reference is made to one of the events related in these sources, this happens in a way which from the point of view of both form and content has no connection with the form of narrative present in any of these sources.[4] This fact can be established without as yet any consideration for the existence of the great work of Dtr.[5] However, once it is established that the book of Joshua belonged to this great work of tradition, which originally had not the least literary connection with the 'Hexateuch', then the conclusion can and must be drawn that this lack of association between the conquest tradition which Dtr. used and the sources of the 'Hexateuch' is no accident. Rather, we must conclude that this conquest tradition no more derives from one or more of the interwoven sources of the

'Hexateuch' than do the many other ancient sources which lay at Dtr.'s disposal and which he was able to use as building blocks for his great work of tradition. In this way the existence of Dtr. explains and confirms a literary state of affairs which was discovered first on the basis of an analysis of the book of Joshua on its own.[6]

This conclusion, of course, will affect 'Hexateuchal' criticism at a far from insignificant point. At the same time it should not be overlooked that the state of affairs in the book of Joshua is not to be divorced from various curious features, primarily in the book of Numbers, which have been a source of difficulty for the criticism of the 'Hexateuch'. We are therefore confronted with the task of broaching the question of the 'Hexateuch' from the standpoint of Dtr. and of taking a closer look at some of its aspects.[7]

## Chapter 22

# THE PRIESTLY WRITING IN THE BOOK OF JOSHUA

Even if we have eliminated the ancient 'Hexateuchal' sources from the book of Joshua, there still remains the possibility that the 'Priestly Writing' (P), which is generally regarded as more recent than Dtr., may have had its conquest narrative subsequently worked into this part of the work of Dtr. The first task is simply to undertake a literary-critical analysis of the book of Joshua to inquire whether a P-narrative is included in it or not. As will be seen, however, this is a question which has quite far-reaching consequences.

As far as Joshua 1–12 is concerned, Smend[1] and Eissfeldt[2] have already disputed the presence of traces of a P-narrative and explained away the fragments which are generally claimed for it as secondary insertions into the ancient core. Despite the inadequacy of their reasoning they are, in fact, undoubtedly correct. The following passages might fall to be considered as parts of P: Josh. 4.15-17;[3] 4.19; 5.10-12; 9.14, 15b, 17-21. These would admittedly be but scanty fragments of a P-narrative, but it would be possible to appeal to the assumption that the P-narrative had been 'overlaid almost beyond the point of recognition by other sources',[4] even though on the whole the reverse is the case: as the youngest literary layer P has usually 'overlaid' the older layers. The passages listed, however, are actually not elements of a once-independent P-narrative at all. Josh. 4.15-17 is an addition to the secondary reworking which introduced the priests as bearers of the ark throughout Joshua 3–4.[5] Containing as it does the first reference to Gilgal as a camping place, Josh. 4.19 is indispensable to the basic form of the history of the crossing of the Jordan; only the date has been added subsequently, and this by reference to Josh. 5.10-12. This latter passage is admittedly integrated only very poorly into the context of the conquest narrative, but it certainly cannot be traced back to P. As Exod. 12.1ff. shows, P would not have used the extremely peculiar expression 'unleavened cakes and parched grain';[6] nor, quite certainly, would it have attributed the eating of unleavened cakes in connection with the Passover to the opportunity afforded the Israelite tribes of eating the corn which had recently ripened at Passover time once they had crossed over into the cultivated land on the west side of the Jordan—it would have attributed it rather to a divine command. The only elements to have been added subsequently to this passage are the various chronological notices;[7] they are derived from the later stipulations about the dates for the feast of Passover and Unleavened Bread which we come across for the first time in the Holiness Code (Lev. 23.4ff.).[8] P seems most clearly to be present in Josh. 9.14, 15b, 17-21 because of the occurrence of the 'leaders' ($n^e\acute{s}\hat{\imath}$' $\hat{\imath}m$) and of the 'congregation' ('$\bar{e}d\hat{a}$), familiar from elsewhere in the P-narrative. However, the office of the 'leader' already appears in the Covenant Code (Exod. 22.27), while in Joshua 9 the 'leaders' are mentioned expressly in the specific and central statement of v. 14. It thus looks as though they belonged rather in the oldest core of this chapter, though it is admittedly very difficult to analyse.[9] Of course, some further supplements were subsequently added; these will have had the occurrence of the 'leaders' in the P-narrative in mind and will therefore have made use of its usual formulations.[10] It may be concluded, therefore, that in Joshua 1–12 there is not the slightest trace of an independent P-narrative.

P is also lacking in Joshua 13–19, however. Admittedly there is a consensus of opinion that P at least provides the literary structure of Joshua 13–19 and that it constitutes a significant portion of the material; some, indeed, believe that, with the exception of a few insertions, the section should be attributed to P in its entirety.[11] It is possible, however, to prove that this is mistaken with a certainty that is rare in literary-critical discussions. When examined closely, the positive arguments in favour of an ascription to P are weak enough. Apart from the general and very vague argument from the probability that compilations of lists in the 'Hexateuch' belong to P, pride of place is given to the formulation of the stereotyped titles and conclusions of the individual sections, for they are supposed to betray the 'linguistic usage' or 'style' of P.[12] But that proves absolutely nothing. One simply cannot talk of 'linguistic usage' or 'style' in connection with these brief and regularly repeated titles and conclusions. Even the use of the word $ma\underline{t}\underline{t}ae$ for the constantly recurring idea of 'tribe' would only be an indication of authorship by P if one could assume that P had been the first to use *maṭṭae* with this meaning; but probability is all against this. It is much more likely that this is a case of a more general use of this word having developed in the exilic and post-exilic period. We come across *genuine* indications of P only in Josh. 14.1b; 19.51a. Here the division of the land is undertaken by a body at whose head there stands Eleazar the son of Aaron (cf. Num. 20.28 P) and to which, besides Joshua, there also belong 'the heads of the fathers' houses of the tribes of Israel' (cf. Exod. 6.25 and frequently, P). Josh. 18.1 should also be included, since here 'the congregation of the children of Israel' and the *'ohael mō'ēd* appear. As will be discussed below, however, precisely these sentences prove to be additions which can be isolated without difficulty. They only go to demonstrate, therefore, that elsewhere in Joshua 13–19 we are not dealing with P. The hypothesis that the whole or a specific part of Joshua 13–19 should be ascribed to P has already been basically refuted by the positive results of the literary and material analysis of this section as set out in detail in M. Noth, *Das Buch Josua* (1938), pp. ixf. and 47ff. However, since this matter is of particular importance in the present context, let us here explicitly develop the negative consequences of these conclusions, namely the exclusion of P from Joshua 13–19.

The description of the territories settled by the Israelite tribes in the cultivated land of Palestine as presented in Joshua 13–19 rests on two sources which were originally independent of one another. The one lays down the borders of the tribal territories; it will have existed originally in the form of an enumeration of boundary points.[13] The other is a list of towns for a part of the Israelite territory, organized on the basis of smaller districts. In order for the book of Joshua to achieve its purpose of supplying an overview of the cultivated land settled by *all twelve* of the Israelite tribes, it is possible to assert with complete confidence that *only* a combination of both these sources together would do. There was not a single case in which the lists of towns on their own could serve for the presentation of tribal geography and hence be taken up for this purpose in some conquest narrative. These lists of towns were not originally arranged according to tribal territories, and their existence can be established only in connection with the quite small southern portion of the country. Even in the most favourable cases, therefore, they could only be used as a secondary supplement to the system of boundary descriptions.[14]

This system in turn, however, *required* just such an expansion if it was to furnish a complete picture of the division of the inheritance of the cultivated land which was supposed to have been given to the twelve tribes of Israel by Joshua. This was so because it was only with the help of the list of towns that the territory of Simeon could be determined (since Simeon was not provided with a separate district in the system of boundary descriptions) and because only so could the territory of the tribe of Dan be fixed;[15] according to the system of boundary descriptions Dan was already established in the region of the source of the Jordan whereas in Joshua's time it was still located on the western edge of the Judean hill-country.[16] As a matter of fact, the present literary condition of the territorial descriptions of the Galilean tribes also shows that the reworking of the system of boundary descriptions was clearly carried out only in connection with the simultaneous inclusion of the list of towns relating to the southern part of the country. The goal of all this activity was a generally intelligible presentation of the division of the cultivated land between the twelve Israelite tribes after the conquest. This involved primarily the provision of a consecutive text for the 'system of fixed boundary points' which had come down from ancient times in the form of sparse lists. The literary condition of the territorial descriptions of the Galilean tribes shows this because they present us with a tangle which can no longer be sorted out but which is made up of material both in the boundary-description style and, apparently, the town-lists style. This tangle is to be explained by the fact that the redactor was sometimes no longer in a position of knowing how to arrange his text on the basis of actual circumstances and therefore simply allowed the fixed boundary points to stand together, in the style of the list of towns.[17] The result of this was that at some time[18] this literary construction developed which is certainly of great value because of its many precise historical-geographical details but which has ended up with such formal unevenness in its various parts.[19] The finished product is so *sui generis* that neither from its content nor from its form can it be deduced for what broader literary context it was originally created or in what wider composition it was originally included.

This question can only be resolved on the basis of the remarks which frame the whole at its introduction and conclusion; and there can be no doubt that this whole is presented to us in a *Deuteronomistic* framework. The introductory sentence of Josh. 13.1 begins with a verbal anticipation of a remark drawn from the Deuteronomistic chapter Joshua 23 (23.1b) while at the end there comes the Deuteronomistic passage Josh. 21.43-45.[20] This in turn is then followed by the equally Deuteronomistic narrative about how Joshua sent the Transjordanian tribes away into their tribal territories. There is only one conclusion that can be drawn from this: the overarching literary whole in which the description of the tribal territories was first included was the work of Dtr. and not one of the sources of the 'Hexateuch'. Now of course at various other points we have some further notices which are indicative of a framework and which show that the arrangement of the whole has occasionally been altered. We must take an even closer look at these in order to confirm our conclusion.

The framework of the section about the geography of the tribes is in three layers.[21] What is obviously the oldest layer speaks of 'the Israelites' (*bᵉnê yiśrā'ēl*) 'inheriting' (qal of *nḥl*) their territory. We find this formula in Josh. 14.1a and 19.49a.[22] The occurrence of the introductory formula as late as the start of Joshua 14 demonstrates clearly enough that this layer of the framework represents a stage (undoubtedly the initial stage) in the literary development of the section about the geography of the tribes in which the west-Jordanian territories (presumably arranged from south to north)[23] came at the beginning and the Transjordanian tribes came only at the end. What nucleus did this layer of the framework enclose? As a minimum, of course, the system of fixed boundary points which forms the factual basis of the whole. In all probability, however, it also already included the *mixtum compositum* which we now find formed by the amalgamation of the boundary descriptions and the town lists. As will be readily apparent from what follows below, this stage is pre-Deuteronomistic. The way in which the framework is phrased gives no hint of a wider literary context;[24] most probably, therefore, the section about the geography of the tribes was still an independent literary unit at that time.[25]

The next, second layer of the framework has made Joshua the subject throughout and has him 'divide up' the land (pi'el of *ḥlq*). We find it occurring in Josh. 13.1, 7a and in 18.*2-10.[26] It represents a stage in which the older summary of the tribal *possessions* in the cultivated land has now been turned into an account about how the tribes *took possession* of the cultivated land; in consequence, the arrangement of the whole has been altered somewhat, as the positioning of the framework's components already makes clear. The Transjordanian tribes are dealt with first in the form of an anticipatory supplement, whilst of the west-Jordanian tribes Joseph is singled out first alongside Judah (cf. 18.5b).[27] The rest are then treated in summary fashion. This results in the arrangement which we find now. All this is probably a question only of a rearrangement and fresh encasing of material which was already present beforehand in its complete extent. However, if the view is taken that in the first stage, as represented by the oldest layer of the framework, the nucleus comprised only the system of fixed border points, then at any event the town lists must have been added at this second stage. Either way, by the conclusion of this second stage the basic shape of the corpus which we now have in the book of Joshua will have been reached. This can be seen from the observation that in the second layer of the framework there is an explicit emphasis on the number of tribes being twelve (13.7b, 8abα and especially 18.6). As already noted, however, the number twelve can only be arrived at by the combination of the system of boundary descriptions with the town lists. Furthermore, the broader literary context of this stage is clear: as is shown by the connection of Josh. 13.1a with 23.1b already discussed, the process in question is that of the inclusion of the section dealing with the geography of the tribes into the *Deuteronomistic* work.[28]

The third layer of the framework comprises the sentences written in the 'style' of P: Josh. 14.1b and 19.51a, with which Josh. 18.1 also belongs. Here those responsible for the division of the land are the commission discussed above on p. 113, who 'gave' the individual territories 'as an inheritance' (pi'el of *nḥl*). Now at no point does this layer have recourse to any part of the section on tribal geography to which it might have originally belonged. It must, therefore, be merely a matter of additions to the older text of the framework, made primarily at those points where the oldest layer of the framework still gave the impression that the Israelites had divided up the inheritance themselves. Their purpose at these points was to lay a special emphasis on the sacral and official manner in which the division of the land was handled. The relevant sentences, moreover, are in part explicitly phrased as additions to an already existing text. In no way, therefore, can they be fragments drawn from a literary work that was *independent* of the older layers in the way that the 'Hexateuchal' source P certainly was from a formal point of view. This applies in particular to Josh. 14.1b, which is simply attached to what precedes as a relative clause;[29] being the second of two relative clauses that are dependent on the same noun, it can be seen quite clearly to be a secondary addition. The same is true too for Josh. 18.1. Without its sequel it would be left hanging completely in the air. It has in view the paragraph in 18.2-10, which it presupposes. The situation is similar in the case of the references to Shiloh in vv. 8, 9 and 10, which refer back to v. 1: they are obviously additions which nevertheless presuppose the remaining shape of these verses. Only 19.51a has been added as an independently worded sentence. We conclude, therefore, that the only elements in Joshua 13-19 which refer to P are isolated additions made to material which was already in existence;[30] the situation is just like the 'P'-styled additions in 1 Kgs 8.1-11 (namely vv. 1aβ, 4a, 10, 11) which, quite rightly, have not caused anybody to assume that there was a P-narrative for the books of Kings.

Some, however, may find themselves unable to agree with the comments made above about the way in which the section dealing with tribal geography developed. They may prefer to regard the boundary descriptions and the town lists as two quite separate and independent sources relating to the land settlement of the twelve tribes of Israel. If so, they will not only believe they may to this end expand the system of boundary descriptions beyond its original extent but they will have in particular to postulate off their own bat that there were town lists for the territories of all twelve tribes, and all this without regard to what can be proved about the actual extent of the town lists and the question of their original significance. Even so, such people will have to admit that alongside the *two* layers in the nucleus of the passage which are accounted for in this way we find *three* layers in the framework and that since the most recent layer in the framework is the one formulated in conformity with P there is in any case no layer left in the nucleus of the passage which can belong to it. This conclusion imposes itself all the more in view of the fact that the parts which make up this third layer of the framework are in the main phrased as obvious additions to material which was already in existence beforehand. Thus whichever way one prefers to look at the matter one will in any case arrive at the conclusion that *in Joshua 13-19 there is no consecutive material from the priestly writing.*

It is also a fundamental mistake to attribute Joshua 20 to P. What we have here rather is the notice of a designation of six cities of refuge furnished with a *Deuteronomistic* introduction, orientated towards Deut. 19.1-13. Accordingly it is Joshua who in v. 1 undertakes the selection of the cities of refuge and not the body which was described in Josh. 14.1b and 19.51a. By contrast, the individual points in this chapter which demonstrate agreement in form and content with Num. 35.9ff.[31] can easily be shown to have been added secondarily to the Deuteronomistic material which was already in existence beforehand; they cannot, therefore, be regarded as evidence for an independent P-version. The situation is different in the case of Josh. 21.1-42. Here, right in the introduction we come up against this self-same body; it is they who respond to the request of the Levitical family heads by designating the 43 priestly and Levitical cities.[32] This passage is linked to Josh. 14.1b and 19.51a by the naming of that body, and it is linked to Josh. 18.1 by the reference to Shiloh as the scene of the action (v. 2). It is thus linked to places which have been shown not to be parts of an independent P-narrative but to be isolated additions to the Deuteronomistic book of Joshua. The passage is thus itself seen to have the character of a later isolated addition.[33] There is no need to add anything further on this, because nowadays other scholars too do not generally attribute this passage to the basic P material but regard it as a secondary addition.[34]

Nor in Josh. 22.9-34,[35] finally, do we have a part of the 'Hexateuchal' source P, even though the people who act here are not Joshua but Phinehas the son of Eleazar the priest, known to us from Josh. 14.1b; 19.51a and 21.1, and the *nᵉśî'îm* of the ten west-Jordanian tribes, and even though the role of the 'congregation' (*'ēdâ*) and the occurrence of such expressions as 'the land of Canaan' are reminiscent of P. On the other hand, however, there are such clear deviations in language and content from P that this peculiar passage, whose factual basis has become quite unrecognizable because of the evident gaps in vv. 26 and 34, is no longer ascribed by anyone to the 'Hexateuchal' source P.[36] It must obviously be a very late isolated supplement to the book of Joshua.

The clear result of all this is: *the 'Hexateuchal' source P is completely lacking in the book of Joshua.* The first consequence of this conclusion is that the book of Joshua is found to have no literary connection with the 'Hexateuch'. It developed as part and parcel of the work of Dtr.; leaving aside the various later supplements of greater or lesser extent, it presents the ancient traditions of the conquest narrative and the passage about the tribal geography in a Deuteronomistic framework and redaction. On the other hand, the question now arises of the original extent of the P source; the fact that we no longer have its report of the conquest may indicate that it never actually had one. There remains the possibility, however, that a P report of the conquest has simply been lost to us, especially since in the book of Numbers P seems to speak in quite some detail about preparations for the forthcoming conquest. We must therefore turn to examine carefully this latter circumstance.

## Chapter 23

# THE PRIESTLY WRITING
## IN NUM. 10–36 AND DEUT. 31–34

Before the account of the death of Moses in Deut. 34.*1, 7-9, P represents Moses as receiving God's command to survey the promised land from the vantage point of the highlands on the borders of Transjordan—that promised land which he himself was never to enter. Linked with this command comes the announcement of his impending death. This incident actually comes twice in P, at Num. 27.12-14 and at Deut. 32.48-52. The wording of these two passages is so closely related that one can only have arisen on the basis of the other.[1] As von Rad 1934b: 125ff. has already shown, the content and wording of Num. 27.12-14 have clearly and intentionally been joined on to the P-portion in Num. 20.1-13; in Deut. 32.48-52, on the other hand, precisely these delicate links with Numbers 20 seem to have been obliterated whilst at the same time various other additions come to the surface.[2] It is certain, therefore, that Num. 27.12-14 should be regarded as an original element in the P-narrative and that Deut. 32.48-52 is a secondary repetition. The latter was deemed necessary once the account of Moses' death in Deuteronomy 34 had become so widely separated from the announcement of his death in Num. 27.12-14 by numerous later passages which intervened between them.

In close, factual connection with Num. 27.12-14, Num. 27.15-23 represents the P-narrative of Joshua's installation as Moses' successor,[3] and this is distinguished in an extremely characteristic manner from its parallels in other literary layers. In Deut. 3.23-28[4] Dtr. has Moses receive instruction that he is to commission Joshua to lead the 'people' over the Jordan after his death and to apportion the land on the west side of the Jordan, whilst in Deut. 31.1, 2, 7 and 8 Dtr. recounts how this instruction was carried out. In this way renewed emphasis is laid on the fact that it is Joshua's task to take possession of the land on the other side of the Jordan which Moses may view only from afar, and to divide it up. The situation is similar in Deut. 31.14, 15 and 23,[5] a passage which derives from one of the ancient 'Hexateuchal' sources. According to this account, shortly before his death and in full view of the manifestation of the divine presence, Moses executes God's command to lay upon Joshua the charge of completing the work which he himself has left unfinished and of leading the Israelites into the land promised to them by God. It is thus all the more striking that when P speaks of Joshua's future role in Num. 27.15-23 he is quite deliberately silent about the occupation and division of the land to the west of the Jordan. All he says, rather, is that Joshua will 'go in and out' before the people and that he is to 'lead' the people 'in and out' (vv. 17 and 21b). According to 1 Sam. 18.16 and 2 Sam. 5.2 (also 1 Sam. 29.6), this language can only refer to leadership in war. Precisely at that point, there was every reason to say something, at least, about the task of leadership in war which was inevitably imminent on account of the present historical circumstances. The fact that both here and at Deut. 34.9 P so strangely avoids all such talk can lead to only one conclusion: *the conquest theme lay outside the purview of the material which he took into account in the preparation of his work*. This is also the simplest and best explanation for the lack of a P-narrative in the book of Joshua.

In the book of Numbers, however, we find various passages which look as though they ought to belong to P and whose subject-matter consists of instructions or preparations for the forthcoming conquest. Taken individually, nearly each one of these has at some time or another been attributed to secondary parts of the P-source. In the case of some of them, there is virtual unanimity in this regard today. In the context of our present discussion, however, this question must be subjected to a comprehensive analysis. A further reason for this is that the passages in question come for the most part after Num. 27.12-14; they therefore separate the announcement of Moses' death from the account of it and so fall under suspicion of having come in secondarily.

We shall deal in the first place with Numbers 32-35.[6] It displays the same arrangement as Joshua 13-21, dealing first with the apportionment of land tenure in Transjordan, and then with instructions for the division of the land to the west of the Jordan and for the selection of the priestly and Levitical towns and the cities of refuge.[7] The most important part of this is Num. 33.50–34.29, and so far as I can see it is almost universally ascribed to the original P-narrative. The core of this passage is the precise description of the boundaries of the territory to the west of the Jordan which is to be divided up between the tribes. This description proceeds in a quite similar manner to the descriptions of the tribal boundaries in Joshua 13–19. What is more, it is based on the same system of fixed boundary points as that which lies behind the passage in Joshua. The fixed points along the southern border of the southernmost tribe, Judah (cf. Josh. 15.2-4), serve to determine the southern border in Num. 34.3b-5.[8] Although the fixed points used to determine the northern border and the northern part of the eastern border in Num. 34.7b-11 are not mentioned anywhere in Joshua 13–19, that is to be explained by the fact that in the book of Joshua the description of the boundaries of the northernmost tribe, Dan, has been quite deliberately omitted.[9] There is, therefore, a strong presumption in favour of the view that what we have in Num. 34.7b-11 is the relevant part of the old description of the borders of Dan.[10] Even the wording of the text which has been added to join together the lists of fixed boundary points does not generally differ to any significant extent from what we find, for instance, in Joshua 15. Naturally, it has been tailored to make it appropriate to the context of Numbers 34 which is dealing with instructions for the division of the land which still lies in the future. Even this, however, is achieved only very loosely: in stereotyped manner the entirely vague formula 'it shall be for you' is added to the introductions and conclusions of the individual sections of the boundary descriptions (seven times in all, in vv. 3, 6, 7, 9, 12), whilst at the start of v. 4 an additional 'for you' has crept in. This apart, the text of vv.3bβ,*4, 5, 8b, 9a, 10b, 11 and 12a (i.e. the real substance of the boundary description) could equally well stand, without the slightest alteration, in Joshua 13–19, in which case it would have to be ascribed to the most complete form of the boundary descriptions, with their connecting text. Furthermore, the verbs which are usually used in this connecting material in Joshua 13–19 appear also throughout Numbers 34, and they even alternate in the quite regular manner familiar to us from Joshua. Quite exceptionally and without parallel Num. 34.7b-8a uses the imperative of a verb which occurs only here in the Old Testament ('to mark out').[11] This, however, seems to be tied up with the fact that this passage is in any case quite out of the ordinary and gives the impression of being an alien element.[12] It is not, therefore, sufficient to cast doubt on the conclusion that even as regards the wording of the connecting material there is a striking agreement between Numbers 34 and Joshua 13–19. There are some points of detail at which the description of the southern boundary of the territory as a whole in Num. 34.3bβ-5 has a different connecting text from the description of the identical southern boundary of Judah in Josh. 15.2aβb-4a; however, there is an exact parallel for this situation in the two other cases where an identical border is described twice over (northern boundary of Judah, Josh. 15.5b-11 = southern boundary of Benjamin, Josh. 18.15-19; northern boundary of Benjamin, Josh. 18.12, 13= southern boundary of Joseph, Josh. 16.1-3).[13] Even the factual difference between Num. 34.4bα and Josh. 13.3bα has an analogy in the description of the common border between Judah and Benjamin (cf. Josh. 15.8b and 18.15b).[14]

Now, it is scarcely possible to assume that the old system of fixed boundary points was provided with a connecting text in a quite similar manner on two completely separate and independent occasions.[15] It must, therefore, be maintained that there is an original literary connection between Num. 34.3-12 and Joshua 13–19. All the more is this so in view of our demonstration that the basis of Num. 34.3-12 was certainly not phrased with its present context in view but was only worked into its present context by means of a rather loose-fitting framework. If it is true that Joshua 13ff. is a passage which has been inserted into the work of Dtr. and which therefore has nothing whatsoever to do with the 'Hexateuchal' source P, then it must follow that the passage in Numbers 34 does not come from P either, since from a literary point of view they belong so closely together. It must, rather, have been subsequently moved to its present position from an original setting within Joshua 13ff.; it was thought appropriate to include here a pointer towards the future division of the land to the west of the Jordan. It will have once stood, therefore, in connection with Josh. 14.1-5. The only question which remains is: to which stage in the development of the passage dealing with the geography of the tribes should it be attributed? Because Num. 34.3-12 is concerned with the possession of cultivated land on the west side of the Jordan alone, one thinks inevitably of the second stage in the development of the framework as outlined on pp. 115f. above. It was during this stage that the Transjordanian tribes came to be included

by way of anticipation, after which a brief description of the land
which was yet to be distributed on the west of the Jordan was not
inappropriate. That the sea marked the western border and Jordan
the eastern would have been obvious. For the southern border,
however, this description would have appropriately made use of the
southern border of the southernmost tribe extracted from the system
of boundary descriptions, and *mutatis mutandis* for the north. With
appropriate connecting comments this could have stood at some
point after Josh. 14.2bβ, 3a.[16] Consequently, Num. 34.3-12 will have
been put into its present position only at the time when the
Pentateuch was joined to the work of Dtr. In addition to the
framework which has been adapted to its present context and which
we have already discussed, it will also have been provided with a few
introductory words in Num. 34.1-2 in the style of P. Besides this,
Num. 33.50, 51 and 54 were added as a pronouncement made in the
same style,[17] whereby God instructed the Israelites through Moses to
'distribute' the land to the west of the Jordan 'as an inheritance'.[18] In
Num. 34.13-15 a comment has been added on about the number of
tribes who have yet to be provided with land to the west of the
Jordan; in v.13 this comment again displays the style of P,[19] while in
vv. 14 and 15 it follows rather the phraseology of Josh. 13.7, 8abα,
15ff. (Dtr.). Finally, in Num. 34.16-29 information has been added
about the establishment at God's command of the commission
mentioned in Josh. 14.1b, 19.51a and 21.1, whose task it was to divide
up the land;[20] unlike the passages in Joshua where the tribal
representatives are called 'heads of the families of the tribes of Israel',
however, they are here termed *neśî'îm*. These last two passages are
not generally attributed to the basic text of P. In fact, however, *all* the
passages discussed above have so little in the way of content and are
of so little consequence, at least from a literary-critical point of view,
that they simply stand or fall with the central unit, Num. 34.3-12. If
this latter proves not to derive from P but to have been transferred
subsequently to its present position from the section in Dtr. which
deals with the geography of the tribes, then none of the rest of Num.
33.50-34.29 should be attributed to the 'Hexateuchal' source P
either.

The only paragraph in Numbers 35 that can seriously be
considered in relation to P is vv. 9-15.[22] The first section, vv. 1-8,
which records the divine command for the future selection of the
Levitical cities, is usually and quite rightly regarded as a considerably

later addition. Even if we regard v. 6 as a secondary explanation to v. 7 and one which has been added clumsily to the present context, there can still be no doubt that this passage presupposes the already late chapter, Josh. 21.1-42,[23] in the even later form which it acquired after it had been expanded by the addition of the cities of refuge in Joshua 20; the mention of the number 48 in v. 7 demonstrates that, to go no further. There is thus no question of its having belonged to the primary material of P. The paragraph in vv. 9-15, by contrast, appears to be older. In general it displays the distinguishing linguistic features of P. On the other hand, however, there can be no doubt that it has Joshua 20 in view, for the only thing it contains are instructions for what according to Joshua 20 was carried out later. Moreover, it lays its chief emphasis on the fact that there were to be six cities of refuge and that they were to be divided equally between the east and west sides of the Jordan. This emphasis is central to the tradition in Joshua 20 whereas in Deut. 19.1-13, by contrast, it is the fact of asylum as such which is central. On this latter point Num. 35.9-15 is defective; it says no more than was necessary for the setting up of the cities of refuge themselves—and this, of course, it does with the use of words and concepts which deviate from Deuteronomy 19 and which belong to a later period as may be seen from the fact of their occurrence in the post-Deuteronomistic additions to Joshua 20.[24] Without Joshua 20, Num. 35.9-15 would thus be left hanging completely in the air. Consequently, it must be assumed that it was composed with Joshua 20 already in view. Joshua 20, however, does not derive from the 'Hexateuchal' source P but is Deuteronomistic; it is part of the section in the work of Dtr. which dealt with the geography of the tribes. It follows that Num. 35.9-15 cannot be ascribed to P either. It is another passage which belongs rather to that late stage when the Pentateuch and the work of Dtr. were amalgamated.

Things are somewhat different in the case of Numbers 32, for it is clear that the older 'Hexateuchal' sources have had a hand in this chapter; this can be seen especially at the beginning and the end. It was principally the information which they supplied at this point about the settlement of the Transjordanian region by various Israelite tribes and clans which opened up the opportunity for the detailed but secondary treatment of the theme of the conquest in Numbers 32-35. Since the analysis of the older sources is not our immediate concern here, a brief statement must suffice: there are two literary layers in vv. 39-42.[25] According to vv. 39, 41 and 42, certain clans of Manasseh[26] moved off and each one conquered for itself a portion of cultivated land in central Transjordan, whereas according to v. 40 Moses acted on his own initiative to 'give' the land of Gilead[27] to the clan of Machir.[28] In view of the fact that in v. 39 the pre-Israelite inhabitants are called 'Amorites', vv. 39, 41 and 42 can be assigned to E[29] and hence v. 40 should presumably be reckoned as J.[30] We find this same duality of literary layers in the opening of the chapter. In vv. 2abα and 5[31] it is assumed that it is Moses who apportions the land, and so the Gadites and Reubenites[32] come to him to ask him to 'give' them 'this land' in Transjordan and to allow them not to cross the Jordan.[33] This is obviously the same layer as in v. 40, and so belongs to J. According to this source Moses apportioned possession of the cultivated land in Transjordan as desired, apparently granting the Gadites and Reubenites a territory on the south side of the Jabbok and Machir one on the north.[34] Verse 1, on the other hand, clearly introduces an account in which some of the tribes took upon themselves the initiative for taking possession of the land. According to v. 1 the Reubenites and Gadites[35] decided to take possession of 'the land of Jazer and the land of Gilead'[36] because it would be suitable for them as wealthy cattle owners. Verse 16a (//vv. 2abα and 5) is probably the immediate continuation of v. 1 and it tells how they informed Moses of this decision of theirs. Verses 39, 41 and 42 will then also have belonged to this layer, telling, in similar fashion, how various Israelite clans also acted off their own bat.[37]

Everything else in Numbers 32 comprises secondary growth on the basic stem which is represented by the older sources in the shape just described. It does not contain any elements of a narrative layer which is independent of them. In essence all that is dealt with here are secondary questions relating to the participation of the Transjordanians in the conquest of the land to the west of the Jordan; it has nothing more to say about the actual theme of the annexation of territory in Transjordan. First, there are a few pieces which are clearly dependent on Dtr. and the section about the geography of the tribes which is included in the work of Dtr. This applies to v. 17, according to which the Transjordanians voluntarily declare themselves willing to take part in the conquest of the land on the west side of the Jordan;[38] it applies further to v. 24, in which Moses consequently promises them a possession in Transjordan,[39] and finally to vv. 33-38, in which, in complete conformity with Dtr.'s outlook, the whole of the land taken in Transjordan is identified with the former territories of the kings Sihon and Og,[40] and in which the Gadite and Reubenite cities are enumerated in dependence upon Josh. 13.15ff.[41] The remainder grew up even later. Verses 6-15 make up a paragraph which is generally rightly regarded as a very late and isolated addition. It unites together in a most curious manner various occurrences which are not strictly comparable and besides that it appears to be independent not only of Num. 13.14 but even of Josh. 14.6aβb. There is some material which might be considered in relation to P in vv. 18-32. However, in working through this passage we find that vv. 18-19[42] are related to v. 17 and therefore cannot be considered as part of an independent narrative.[43] In vv. 20-23[44] we again find at the very outset a formal and factual dependence on v. 17,[45] which is where the theme of the Transjordanians' participation in the campaign to the west of the Jordan is mentioned for the first time. It is the section comprising vv. 25-32 that gives the strongest impression of containing an independent piece of narrative, provided vv. 25b and 27b are set aside as secondary links with what precedes. Against this, however, must be set its clear literary ties with the latest layer of the framework of Joshua 13.ff.,[46] a layer which does not derive from a consecutive P-narrative but is simply made up of isolated additions. We must, therefore, conclude that it is itself an isolated addition which has clearly been influenced by this material in Joshua. We thus have no option but to agree with the view of Smend[47] and Eissfeldt[48] that the P-narrative is not represented in Numbers 32.[49]

The clear and important result of all this is that *the 'Hexateuchal' source P is completely lacking in the literary complex Numbers 32–35.* What we have here rather is material relating to the theme of preparation for the conquest which has been attached to various brief items of information in the older sources dealing with the settlement of Israelite tribes and clans in Transjordan (32.*1-5, 16a, 39-42). This material was the result of editorial activity brought about by the amalgamation of the Pentateuch and the work of Dtr. This was without any doubt done primarily in dependence upon the conquest tradition in the work of Dtr., but partly also by the transposition of items of tradition which had their original setting in Dtr.; all this accounts for 32.16b, 17, 24, 33-38; *33.50–34.29; 35.9-15. Finally, there ensued what was probably a quite lengthy process in which the text as it then stood was expanded by all manner of amplifications.

These are admittedly reminiscent of the language and style of P but they do not represent this language and style in its pure form. Above all, they are so clearly dependent, from a literary point of view, on the older text that they cannot be regarded as elements of a once independent narrative account.

Now, once the usual opinion is accepted that neither the brief corpus of legal specifications in Numbers 28–30[50] nor the discussion of a particular precedent in Numbers 36[51] belongs to the basic core of the P-narrative, then of the last quarter of the book of Numbers only ch. 31 remains to be investigated. This chapter, which recounts a war of revenge against the Midianites and describes the division of the spoil in excessive detail, has nothing directly to do with the theme of the conquest and is therefore of lesser importance for the issue here under discussion. If it belongs to any source, then it must be to P. It is more than questionable, however, whether it does belong to a source. The details about the division of the spoil in vv. 13-54, at any rate, comprise a complex of later expansions which lacks unity. The only question, therefore, is whether to regard vv. 1-12 as an original element of the P-narrative, as von Rad (1934b: 132ff.) does, or whether to follow the majority of others[52] in explaining the whole chapter as a supplement to the Pentateuchal narrative which has developed in successive stages. The latter opinion appears to me to be the correct one. This is so in particular because of v. 2b, which takes account of the announcement of Moses' death but which does it in such a way that the campaign against Midian appears to interpose a hitherto unforeseen delay before the death of Moses. This is a clear pointer to the fact that Num. 31.1ff. was only slotted in subsequently, following Num. 27.12-23.[53] (The body of material in Numbers 28–30 must consequently have come in even later.) It can no longer be determined for certain why exactly this should have occurred at this seemingly unsuitable point. Probably this account of the Midianite campaign was added in as a postscript at the latest possible place: before the Pentateuch was amalgamated with the work of Dtr. the theme of the conquest was taken up immediately after this story.

The result of the discussion to date is as follows: *between Num. 27.12-23* (the announcement of the death of Moses and the command to appoint Joshua) *and Deut. 34.\*1ff.* (the death of Moses and the installation of Joshua as his successor) *there is no trace of the original P narrative.* Consequently, these two passages originally stood side by side in the original P-narrative. *All the references to the*

*forthcoming conquest which now appear between these two passages
are material of secondary and tertiary origin.* This result does not
require any further confirmation; it is desirable, however, to round it
off with an examination of the passages in the middle section of the
book of Numbers which belong to P.

We shall deal first with the section which comes between P's
account of the death of Aaron and the installation of his successor in
Num. 20.22-29 on the one hand and the passage in Num. 27.12-23,
which we have already dealt with, on the other. P certainly had no
part in Numbers 21.[54] Furthermore, P is also lacking in the Balaam
story, Num. 22.2-24.25. Thus, apart from the brief itinerary note
in Num. 22.1, which undoubtedly belongs to the basic core of the
P-narrative, the only material which has to be seriously considered in
relation to P is the body of material comprising Num. 25.6-27.11.
A decision about this revolves chiefly around Num. 25.6-18. This
passage is not completely self-contained but depends on the story in
Num. 25.1-5 which derives from the older sources. Wellhausen
postulated that originally Num. 25.6ff. had its own introduction
which had since been lost, and he attributed the whole of this original
account to P.[55] Since Holzinger's analysis,[56] however, it has been
usual to regard Num. 25.6ff. as a post-exilic supplement to Num.
25.1-5 phrased in a not very pure form of the P style. In view of the
careless manner in which we generally find that such individual
supplements have been introduced, it is not surprising that in this
case too there is only an inadequate join with what precedes. The
important item in this addition from the point of view of the post-
exilic period was the high-priestly office of Phinehas and his
successors (vv. 6-13); verses 14, 15 and 16-18 will then have followed
in succession as yet further supplements. More recently, however,
von Rad (1934b: 131) has reverted to an explanation of Num. 25.6ff.
in terms of a fragment of a P-narrative which was once complete. His
reason is not fully intelligible, but it seems to be that the redactor
who worked the older stories into the P-framework could have
introduced 'half a story', but that a later redactor could not. For that
argument to work, however, it would be necessary to prove that what
we have here is in fact 'half a story' and not rather a supplement to
the already existing text of Num. 25.1-5. And besides, the assumption
that a significant item of the P-narrative was dropped contradicts
everything that we know from elsewhere about the way in which the
'Hexateuch' was edited. Finally, since on linguistic grounds vv. 10-13

cannot be ascribed to P,[57] von Rad has to delete them as a later 'expansion'. In doing so, however, he sacrifices the real goal of the whole of the story about Phinehas.[58] This only goes to show that there is no way in which Num. 25.6ff. can be ascribed to the basic P material.

Turning next to the long genealogy in Num. 26.1-56,[59] we find that it is attached to Num. 25.6ff. by 25.19. In origin, it is probably a very ancient piece of tradition.[60] According to the heading in v. 4bβ it will once have been reckoned as a list of those Israelites who came out of Egypt, whilst in its traditional form it serves as a way of presenting the results of a census. According to the concluding remark in vv. 52-54,[61] this census will in turn have formed the basis for a fair division of the cultivated land which was to be taken into possession, and it is at this point that the opinion of those who set the list in its present context comes to expression. It is probable that not too much weight need be attached to the formal connection with what precedes by way of 25.19; after all, this comment could easily have been added in secondarily. Of more significance is the fact that this list follows on a whole series of supplements and that it comes at a point in the overall narrative which was particularly suitable for the addition of supplements. It must be remembered that before the Pentateuch was amalgamated with the work of Dtr. this passage was followed immediately by the brief concluding episode concerning the final arrangements and death of Moses. It is above all, however, the concluding remarks in vv. 52-54 which tell against the list belonging to the basic text of P. These remarks expressly state the purpose of the census which is presented in this list; but according to everything that we have seen up until now, P took no account whatever of the forthcoming conquest. We must, therefore, agree with those who have long declared that it is not possible to ascribe Numbers 26 to any source, even if we do not have to agree with all their individual arguments in favour of this conclusion.[62] Finally, it hardly requires further demonstration that along with Numbers 26, Num. 27.1-11 also drops out as a candidate for P. It depends on Numbers 26 and at the same time looks forward to the forthcoming conquest. Moreover, it does not tell a proper story but rather imparts a legal ruling in the guise of an historical account.

We are thus presented in Num. 25.6-27.11 with a whole series of supplements. They were probably added to the older text in the order in which we now find them. More precisely, it may be asserted that the list in Num. 26.1-54 was incorporated prior to the time when the Pentateuch was amalgamated with the work of Dtr. Otherwise, it would have been included somewhere in Numbers 32–35 which deals so expressly with the theme of the future conquest.[63] Thus between Num. 20.22-29 and Num. 27.12-23 only the brief remark in 22.1 belonged to the original text of P.

Finally, we need to take a brief look at the situation regarding the P-narrative in Numbers 10–20. Opinion about this has been relatively stable for some time, and we have nothing of any great significance to add to this. Our only aim is to draw attention to a few facts of particular significance within the context of our present discussion. In P the brief account of the departure from Sinai and the migration to the wilderness of Paran in Num. 10.11-12[64] was followed by the story of the spies. This is also located in the wilderness of Paran, and it provided the literary basis for the combination of sources which we now find in the text of Numbers 13–14.[65] Because of its subject, this story necessarily touches upon the theme of the conquest.[66] It is very noteworthy, however, and scarcely accidental, that P has taken the greatest pains to avoid any positive reference to the conquest despite the fact that it must have been more than tempting to do so. Thus it is that he passes in total silence over the real point of this story even though it still appears clearly in the structure of the older stories (14.24), namely that because of his good conduct Caleb received the promise that he would be allowed to keep as his future possession that part of the territory which he and the other spies had traversed.[67] Furthermore, P intentionally makes nothing whatever of the comment about the next generation taking possession of the land instead of the present generation who were condemned to die in the wilderness,[68] even though one would have thought that it could scarcely be avoided once it had been decided to make use of this story within the broader context of the Israelites' wilderness wanderings. Ever since Wellhausen (1899: 101) Num. 14.30-33, which gives expression to this idea, has rightly been regarded on linguistic and stylistic grounds as a later insertion into the P context of 14.29 + 34-38.[69] The very existence of this addition, however, shows the extent to which it must have been, and was, regarded as extraordinary that there should be no mention in this context of the conquest which the following generation was to accomplish. As far as P was concerned, the whole episode ended in a completely negative fashion with the judgment that the sinful people should die in the wilderness and with the death of all the spies apart from Joshua and Caleb. Thus as far as possible P eliminated every reference to a future conquest from his account of the spies.

The next episode that P recounted[70] was the story of Korah and its various consequences in Numbers 16–18. After the material deriving from the older sources has been set aside, there remains for P a juxtaposition of two separate layers together with all manner of secondary material besides. It deals in historical guise with disagreements which clearly arose in the post-exilic period about the respective privileges of the Aaronites and the Levites. In the present context we do not need to bother about the details. The only point which requires comment is that the extensive descriptions of the Aaronide and Levitical revenues in 18.8-32, at any rate, are to be regarded as a secondary appendix.[71] That being so, the reference to the future division of the land in 18.20 is not part of P.[72]

P's share in Num. 20.1-13 is also relatively easy to fix. As is usual elsewhere, it forms the literary basis for the passage and comes in vv. 1a, 2, 3b, 4, 6, 7, 8aβ bβ, 10 . . . 11b, 12 and 13. Von Rad (1934b: 117ff.) has successfully shown how P has introduced the theme of Moses' and Aaron's blameworthy lack of faith into a traditional account which he received about the murmuring of the people, and how he has laid particular emphasis on this new theme. What really mattered to P was an explanation of the deaths of Moses and Aaron, because, as was shown above, these were the only two events which it still remained for him to relate (Num. 20.22-29 and Num. 27.12-23 + Deut. 34.*1, 7-9). In this context P was obliged once again to make a negative reference to the future conquest. After all, death itself could not constitute a divine punishment of Moses and Aaron; it had to be a premature death. In view of the tradition about Moses' age, however,—and P has then simply set Aaron alongside Moses—there was no way in which this point could be made except by the negative statement that Moses and Aaron would not be permitted to enter the promised land. In these particular circumstances, therefore, we find that at Num. 20.12b P has in fact made another reference to the future conquest.

If we now review the literary-critical results which we have achieved in this chapter, then it must be concluded that the literary situation in the second half of the book of Numbers is very different from that in the part of the 'Hexateuchal' narrative which precedes the Sinai pericope. That, however, is just the impression which anyone would receive if they moved from the results of a literary-critical analysis of the primeval and patriarchal histories to a closer study of the literary make-up of the second half of the book of Numbers. One quickly realizes that at this point little progress can be made on the basis of the simple question as to which of the familiar sources of Genesis and Exodus the particular passages or their smaller and even smallest elements belong to. On the contrary, passages which cannot be ascribed to any particular source occupy quite a lot of space. Because these passages are partly composed in a post-exilic linguistic style which is reminiscent of P and are at any rate grounded in the mental horizons of the post-exilic period, it is customary to lump them together under the siglum P and to attribute most of them to this source's secondary material (P$^s$). In reality, however, as we have shown, the traces of the P-narrative become fainter and fainter in the second half of Numbers, just as the older sources too become more and more sparsely represented. The secondary material which we find instead is hardly ever to be regarded as the direct development of P as a source. It should therefore not be labelled P$^s$. It has, rather, grown up around the narrative which had already been compiled from the various sources.[73] The reason why it is piled up so markedly at this point in the narrative is that at one time it was followed immediately by the conclusion of the narrative as a whole with only a brief treatment of the theme of Moses' death. Every supplement to the history of Moses had therefore to be accommodated here.[74] Then later on the Pentateuch was amalgamated with the work of Dtr., a process which remains to be discussed. When this happened, the opening of Dtr. with its introductory address by Moses as well as its proclamation of the Deuteronomic law had also to be fitted in immediately before the death of Moses (Deuteronomy 1ff.). As a consequence, the secondary passages which prepare the way for Dtr.'s account of the conquest and which are now presupposed by Dtr.'s presentation within the larger narrative work which emerged at this time also had to take their place in the last part of the book of Numbers.[75] This situation may appear to be very complicated. It becomes clear without much difficulty, however, if one keeps in mind the major stages of the literary process, the detailed outworkings of which we have been concerned with.[76]

## Chapter 24

# THE PRIESTLY WRITING AS THE LITERARY BASIS
# OF THE PENTATEUCH

At various points the conclusions of the previous two chapters make for a rather different picture of the source P from that which has generally been portrayed hitherto. It may now be maintained with confidence that P did not include an account of the conquest. Because of this, furthermore, he avoided as far as possible making any reference to the future conquest in the story of Moses,[1] even though this had been the aim of the wilderness wanderings of the Israelite tribes according to the older tradition. He concluded his presentation, rather, with the death of Moses, and he was totally consistent in directing the last part of his narrative towards this goal. The premature deaths of Moses and of Aaron were announced by God as a punishment for their lack of faith in the incident at Kadesh concerning the procurement of drinking-water from the rock (Num. 20.*1-13). Once that had happened, the scene of the action shifted from Kadesh to Mount Hor (20.22), and that is where Aaron dies (evidently following some older tradition)[2] after his son Eleazar has been consecrated as his successor by Moses (20.23-29). After that the scene shifts yet again, this time to the 'arbōth Mō'āb (22.1). It was in this area, again according to ancient tradition, that Moses met his death, a death which occurred, once again, on a mountain peak, following the installation of Joshua as his successor (Num. 27.12-23 + Deut. 34.*1, 7-9). These two narratives, the one about the death of Aaron and the other about the death of Moses, have clearly been constructed in parallel to one another; the only reason why their close relationship is not so immediately obvious and striking is that they have been separated quite far apart from each other by the mass of material which came in later. It must be agreed without further ado that in their original close association together they would not have provided a bad end to P, for in the bulk of it they play an absolutely central role. However, in order to make this point fully clear, it is necessary to cast a glance over P as a whole.

No one will deny that the object of P's special interest was the national and cultic community of Israel as constituted at Sinai with all its attendant statutes and ordinances. The very extent of the treatment given to this theme shows how prominent it was for P alone, and everything which P narrates before it has the particular purpose of leading up to this theme. Any analysis of P from the point of view of either literature or content has, therefore, to start out by taking this part of his work into account.[3] Viewed from this standpoint, it would be intelligible if, because of his creative treatment of this theme, P had regarded his work as basically self-contained. All he needed to do, since he was writing a historical narrative, was to round off his account with the report of the death of those two men who mediated so decisively between God and the congregation of the people during the events at Mount Sinai. At the same time the question cannot be avoided whether a narrative work which prefaces its central section with a treatment of the primeval and patriarchal histories can end suitably with the death of Aaron and Moses without giving some sort of conclusion, however brief, to the account of the wider history of the Israelite community; after all, there seem to be constant hints in the patriarchal history which presuppose this. Now of course we must not tailor our literary findings by a particular preconception of P, but rather our conception of P by the literary findings; and the literary findings are clear that P ended with the accounts of the death of Aaron and the death of Moses. The question, therefore, is whether this situation, contrasting as it does with the usual opinion which has prevailed hitherto, cannot be understood on the basis of the work of P as a whole.

The most important point to grasp, in my opinion, is that in terms of the overall structure of his narrative P unmistakably follows older tradition just as we have it in fixed literary form, primarily in J. This does not mean that J has to have been used by P as a literary *Vorlage*. The situation is rather that the structure of the tradition concerning the pre-history of Israel as we encounter it in J[4] was undoubtedly determinative for P as he shaped his work. The reason for this is presumably that by P's time the tradition had long since assumed a generally binding form. On this matter, therefore, P could not act with complete freedom, and so we cannot look in this direction for the specific nature of his intentions. Indeed, it is conceivable that his own concerns did not entirely dovetail with the structure of the whole which he had to adopt willy nilly. This at least would fit with the fact that that sense for design and order which is often so prominent in the individual parts of his work is not noticeable to the same degree at all in the plan of the whole. At all events, the attempts which have been made to demonstrate that some specific system lies behind the plan of P as a whole must be deemed to have failed. Von Rad[5] was quite right to reject as unsuccessful Wellhausen's hypothesis[6] of 'the book of the four covenants', as well as subsequent attempts to retain it in a moderated form.[7] But then von Rad had a proposal of his own to make, namely that we should conceive of the progress of P's thought and presentation as three concentric circles, the circles relating to the world, to Noah, and to Abraham. This proposal in turn, however, does not really emerge naturally from the text of P's work but rather forces the latter into a scheme which is not entirely suitable for it. Why?—because it takes insufficient account of the fact that P's primary emphasis is on the constitution of the national and cultic community at Sinai and the fact that this has shaped both the centre and the goal of the work as a whole. It has to be said, rather, that although P was driving at this theme, he did at the same time provide a setting for the events at Sinai within the broad context of human history as itself a part of God's creation. Added to this was the fact that for a long time the incident at Sinai had formed part of a tradition which located the history of Israel within this broad framework. For these reasons, then, P followed the outline of this tradition down as far as the events at Sinai. Once he had then given expression to his own concerns, however, he regarded his work as complete and so brought it to a close. In doing so, he left out a part of the tradition which belonged originally to it, namely the history of the conquest.[8] All he did to round off his narrative was to introduce the stories of the death of Aaron and the death of Moses; in the process he was obliged by ancient tradition to lead the Israelite tribes to within close range of the land which they were later to occupy. At this point, however, he concluded his work, without tracing the history of Israel any further.

It cannot be denied that this introduces an element of conflict into the work of P. The reason is that the tradition for which P had regard was not tailor-made to fit P's particular concerns. Admittedly, as we have shown, P did all that was possible to avoid making reference to the future conquest even when it could scarcely be avoided. Nevertheless, in the first place he was not able to pursue this policy with absolute consistency (cf. Num. 13.2; 20.12b) whilst in the second place and most significantly, even without explicit reference to it, the theme of the conquest was the inevitable goal of the narrative thread, at least from the departure from Sinai onwards. If in spite of this P concluded his narrative before the conquest and thus to our way of thinking broke it off inorganically at a point that was unsuitable in the light of the whole,[9] then we can only draw the conclusion that P really did not have any historical presentation of his own in view and that as far as the course of history was concerned he merely reproduced a section of inherited tradition in his own way. There is another way too in which we can see that his interests did not lie in the course of events themselves, but rather in the formulation of binding statutes and ordinances[10]—binding in his sense of the word meaning, basically, unconditionally and eternally valid. For him, this was simply a question of the institutions and statutes for the national and cultic community of Israel which according to ancient tradition had been given at Sinai; the question of in which land or under what historical conditions Israel would have to live by them was no longer of any concern. Viewing the situation in this light, we have no difficulty in understanding why P's work concluded after the Sinai pericope with the stories of the death of Aaron and Moses,[11] in line with the conclusions reached on the basis of our literary investigation.

As things eventually turned out, P became the literary basis for that larger whole which we find in the books of Genesis–Deuteronomy. By this is meant that the older sources were incorporated into the literary framework which was offered by the P-narrative. One of the most secure results of a literary-critical analysis of these books is that both in general and in matters of detail the redactor took the P-narrative as his starting point and worked the older sources into it. Whenever possible, this was done without anything being cut out, but if the need arose the older sources were cut and rearranged in favour of the P-narrative which was being used as the basis. This method of the redactor, which is too well known to require any more precise exposition, was not only determinative for the combination of the sources in individual cases of greater or lesser significance. By extension, it was also responsible for the delimitation of the larger whole which emerged from this redactional process. Because of this our earlier remarks about the extent of the P-narrative lead to a really major conclusion. The larger literary whole which resulted from the inclusion of the older sources within the framework of P and which we now have in the books of Genesis–Deuteronomy, quite naturally came to be co-extensive with the P-narrative and thus concluded with the death of Moses. *That is how the Pentateuch came into being.* Its introductory chapter is provided by the first part of the P-narrative and its final words are the concluding sentences of the P-narrative.[12] Thus exactly the same situation obtains here in regard to the whole as has long been determined for many individual passages. This hypothesis is not based on a general consequence drawn from particular premises but on our literary findings themselves. Once one gets past Deuteronomy 34, the narrative threads of the older sources cannot really be traced any more than they can for P.[13] Though it has hitherto been the unanimous verdict of the literary critics that they can be traced, at least so far as the book of Joshua is concerned, this has not so often been the result of an independent literary-critical analysis of the book of Joshua. On the contrary, it has been based in the first place on the recognition that the older sources must have culminated in an account of the conquest (and that this is actually correct will be shown immediately below) and in the second place on the equally correct recognition that the book of Joshua was not initially an independent literary unit but belonged rather to a larger literary whole. This quite easily resulted, however, in the presupposition that the book of Joshua belonged with the Pentateuch. No longer, therefore, was it the question *whether* the older literary layers of the Pentateuch could be traced in the pre-Deuteronomistic text of the book of Joshua but rather *to which* of these layers the individual elements of the old Joshua narrative should be ascribed. As a matter of fact, however, the basic text of Joshua does not display any positive connections with any one of these layers.[14] What is more, the larger literary whole in which the book of Joshua was once integrated has proved beyond doubt to be the work of Dtr., a work which originally had nothing whatever to do with the Pentateuch.

The older sources of the Pentateuch, however, must have been cut short when their editing was undertaken on the basis of the framework of the P-narrative. Because their account of the conquest extended beyond this framework it must have simply gone by the board at the time when the Pentateuch was redacted. For there can be no doubt, on the other side, that they did once include a conquest narrative of whatever shape and form. This may be concluded first from the fact that one of the larger tradition complexes which they included was specifically directed towards the theme of the conquest,[15] and secondly from the observation that within their overall structure the future conquest is purposely alluded to as the climax of the narrative by the promises concerning the land in the patriarchal history. The most telling argument, however, is that even before their account of the death of Moses they included various matters to do with the conquest theme. Then, because of their position within the narrative as a whole, they came to be included in the Pentateuch. They thus demonstrate that the occupation of the land by Israelite tribes and clans was included in the author's plan. Thus we find that in Num. 14.24 there is a reference forward to Caleb's occupation of the land whilst in Num. 14.23[16] the general prospect is held out of the next generation entering into the promised land. In particular, however, there is the account of the conquering of Sihon, the king of Heshbon, in Num. 21.21-32, with its reference to 'Israel's' settlement in his land (vv. 25b and 31), and the two separate layers in Num. 32.*1-5, 16a and 39-42 which tell of the occupation of Transjordan by some of the Israelite tribes and clans. In line with what we know of him from elsewhere, the redactor of the Pentateuch worked here in a completely mechanical way. As far as he could he included everything from the older sources within the framework of the P-narrative up as far as the account of Moses' death and then left out everything else after it. In so doing, however, he paid no regard to the fact that he thereby cut off the older sources' treatment of the conquest in the middle whereas it would have been more consistent if he had also omitted those references to the conquest and the conquest narratives themselves which occurred before the account of Moses' death in the older sources.

It is idle to speculate on how exactly the conquest sequence might have been presented in the older sources. We really cannot derive a full picture from the brief accounts of the settlement in Transjordan. Nor is it possible now to give a clear answer to the question whether some of the ancient narratives subsequently added into the work of Dtr. are actually scattered fragments of the conquest narratives that belonged originally to the ancient Pentateuchal sources. Josh. 15.13-19 and the various paragraphs in Judges 1 could be considered, and the possibility cannot be denied. All the same, the probability is not very great. At the most it would be a matter of various isolated and particular traditions.

The major conclusion at which we have arrived can now be formulated as follows: *there never was a 'Hexateuch' in the sense that it is usually understood, i.e. that the books of Genesis to Joshua once formed a literary unity in roughly the shape that we have them now.* The older sources admittedly culminated in the theme of the conquest. However, when they were fitted into the framework provided by the P-narrative it was the *Pentateuch* which emerged, with the theme of the conquest of the land to the west of the Jordan dropping away completely. The conquest narrative in the book of Joshua, on the other hand, was part of the work of Dtr. from the start, and this developed completely independently of the Pentateuch.

*Chapter 25*

# THE PENTATEUCH AND THE DEUTERONOMISTIC
# HISTORY

The Pentateuch and the Deuteronomistic History were only joined together at a relatively late stage in their literary development. It was quite an obvious move to make since the end of the Pentateuchal narrative, which dealt with Moses' final arrangements and his death, overlapped with the introduction to Dtr's narrative. What is more, Moses' retrospective speech in Deuteronomy 1–3 was but a further recapitulation of the events following the departure from Sinai (Horeb) as described in the final part of the Pentateuch. Links on the basis of content thus already lay to hand. It was, moreover, very much in line with the way these two great works developed at the literary level that a secondary join between them should be effected by the interweaving of those parts whose contents overlapped, namely the end of the one and the beginning of the other. These writings had long since adopted the carefully thought-out procedure of combining every possible item of inherited tradition. It would thus have been extremely odd if this culminating step had not also been taken. Thus there finally emerged at the end of the whole process that all-embracing literary complex which traces the course of affairs apparently without a break from the creation of the world till the demise of the states of Israel and Judah.

It might be thought that this combination was effected in direct connection with the major work of Pentateuchal redaction and that therefore the incorporation of the first part of Dtr. was undertaken *simultaneously* with the fitting of the older sources into the framework of the P-narrative. So far as I can see, however, there are three factors which tell against this possibility. They show that the Pentateuch must have first existed on its own as a work drawn up on the basis of the P-narrative and that only later was the link made with the work of Dtr. It was demonstrated above on pp. 131f. that the additions to the Pentateuchal narrative which we find in Num. 25.6–27.11 were obviously made prior to the time of the insertion of the basic material of Numbers 32–35 (36) which points towards Dtr.'s account of the conquest. If that were not so the list in Num. 26.1-56, which is linked to the future conquest by its conclusion, would certainly have been placed in the context of this later passage. Now Num. 25.6ff. was grafted in stages on to the combined Pentateuchal narrative; there is no question of its having been an addition to the source P whilst the latter still existed independently, because the actual jumping-off point for the addition is provided by a section which comes from the older sources (Num. 25.1-5). At the time that all this was happening, therefore, it looks as though the Pentateuch was in existence but still without any association with the work of Dtr.

Secondly, attention should be drawn to the nature of the redactional activity in Deuteronomy 34. This chapter, which records the death of Moses, is the one passage where the elements deriving from the Pentateuch and from Dtr. could not simply be placed side by side, as they are elsewhere. Rather, the two brief narratives,[1] which dealt with the same theme, had to be woven together in just the same way as happened often enough when the Pentateuchal sources were combined together. Now it can easily be demonstrated that the method used in the combination of Deuteronomy 34 is different from what we find elsewhere in the Pentateuch. It follows from this that the combination of Dtr. with the Pentateuch is to be distinguished from the composition of the Pentateuch and hence is also without doubt to be separated from it chronologically. In the process of Pentateuchal redaction the P-narrative was generally used as the literary basis even in matters of detail. In Deuteronomy 34, however, that is not the case. Here the decisive passage—the account of Moses' death—comes not from P but from Dtr., for vv. 4-6 are undoubtedly Deuteronomistic.[2] The only items to come from P are one of the place names in v. 1[3] and the passage comprising vv. 7-9. Later, and certainly after the combination of the Pentateuch and Dtr. had been achieved, the closing paragraph (vv. 10-12) was added secondarily to this latter passage. The basis for the combined text was thus probably provided by Dtr.; at any rate it was not provided by P.

There is a third consideration that needs to be added. Even after the amalgamation with Dtr. meant that Joshua–Kings now joined smoothly on to it, the Pentateuch nevertheless continued as a distinctive unit with its extent determined by the P-narrative. Being the basic scripture of the post-exilic community, it was first accorded canonical status on its own, as its adoption by the Samaritan community amply demonstrates. This only makes sense, however, if it was already in existence earlier in the basic shape determined by the P-narrative and as such was already especially highly valued. From this angle too is to be explained the fact that the combining of Dtr. and the Pentateuch did not really lead to the emergence of a single whole uniting both works. What happened, rather, was that the Pentateuch was already established on its own as a literary whole; then, when the beginning of Dtr. was absorbed into it, it left the rest of Dtr. as a sort of appendix to it, something which seemed to be of lesser importance. There was yet another consequence of the inclusion of the first part of Dtr. into a Pentateuch which had already been completed: once the external unity of the work of Dtr. was lost by these means, the way was clear for the division of the continuation of this work into individual 'books' in which the continuation of the history following the death of Moses could be pursued in sections divided up on the basis of content.[4] We may thus conclude that the literary amalgamation of the Pentateuch and Dtr. was a separate and late stage in the process by which the tradition came to acquire the shape in which we have it today.

It was, furthermore, a relatively easy process to introduce the beginning of Dtr. into the final part of the Pentateuch up to and including the account of the death of Moses. After all, it really only involves a long speech by Moses (historical retrospect and proclamation of the Deuteronomic law with its framework) which he delivered immediately before his death. Its setting before the Pentateuchal narrative about the death of Moses was thus obvious.[5] In the Pentateuch the immediately preceding material had been the reports taken from the older sources about the settlement of the Trans-jordanian region by various Israelite tribes and clans (Numbers *32). At the same time it must be remembered that the same theme is handled later in connection with Dtr.'s broader presentation of the division of the land. In view of this fact, either at the time of the amalgamation of Dtr. with the Pentateuch or in the immediate wake of this process the opportunity arose of expanding the brief reports of the older sources in Numbers 32 with various items of information from Joshua 13. Furthermore, by making use of this same passage to bring forward some of the material from Joshua 13ff., it was possible to anticipate the theme of the conquest as a whole and to prepare for the later detailed presentation in Dtr. Thus a further consequence of the amalgamation of Dtr. with the Pentateuch was the gradual growth into its present shape of the complex which now comprises Numbers 32–35 (36).

In connection with this, the long speech of Moses with which Dtr. commenced his work could have been accepted unchanged into the Pentateuch (Deuteronomy 1–30). Only in the case of the following section of Deuteronomistic narrative concerning Moses' last words and instructions would the need have arisen for some careful splicing with the corresponding items in the Pentateuchal narrative. Along with that we shall need to bear in mind that according to our earlier analysis of Dtr. (Noth 1981: 34f.) the text of Deut. 31.1-13, 24–30 + 32.1-47, which developed only gradually, was already in place when the beginning of Dtr. was worked into the Pentateuchal narrative. Consequently the narrative material which was attached to the long speech of Moses in Dtr. was left more or less intact and in its original place when it was absorbed into the Pentateuch. It was only interrupted at one place, namely by the secondary addition (from a literary point of view) of Deut. 31.14, 15 + 23.[6] It looks as though this passage should be attributed to one of the older sources; it must, therefore, derive from the Pentateuchal narrative. Its traditional setting points to its having once stood in the Pentateuch between Numbers *32 and Deuteronomy *34. In the case of the older sources on their own, it would have been quite appropriate that the installation of Joshua as leader of the occupation of the promised land (Deut. 31.23) should have followed straight on from the accounts in Numbers *32 of the settlement of various tribes and clans in Transjordan. Again, at the level of the redaction of the Pentateuch it would have been quite understandable that P's account of the appointment of Joshua as Moses' successor, an account which said nothing about Joshua's role in the future conquest, should have been prefaced to these accounts (Num. 27.15-23). Thus within the Pentateuch as a whole, Deut. 31.14, 15 + 23 could be understood without any violence being done to it as the entrusting of a particular task to Joshua who had already been appointed in a general way as Moses' successor. When Dtr. was worked into the Pentateuch, however, it was essential to move that part of the older sources which we now find in Deut. 31.14, 15 + 23 to a position following the long speech of Moses in Deuteronomy 1–30 because in this speech (Deut.

3.28) Moses refers to the prior divine command that he should commission Joshua to lead Israel into the promised land. It was thus quite self-evidently appropriate to place it after the account of the proclamation of the law by Moses with its attendant instructions but before Moses' final exhortations. Since a result of this was that the Dtr. account of how Moses commissioned Joshua to lead the people into the promised land (Deut. 31.7-8) now stood in front of Deut. 31.14, 15 + 23, the latter must, in its new context, have been understood as divine confirmation[7] of Moses' words to Joshua.[8]

Finally, a repetition of Num. 27.12-14 was added at Deut. 32.48-52 in between the large Dtr. interpolation of Deut. 1.1–32.47 and the account in Deuteronomy 34 of the death of Moses which combines material from both the Pentateuch and Dtr. This can certainly have happened only after Deuteronomy 34 became separated so far from Num. 27.12-14 by the inclusion of the first part of Dtr. Admittedly, there are also references to the imminent death of Moses in Deut. 31.2 and 14a, but they lack the specific command to climb the mountain and to view the promised land (Deut. 3.27 lay too far back to be taken into account at this point). Thus the first announcement to Moses that he was going to die was repeated secondarily once more in Deut. 32.48-52 along with all kinds of changes and expansions shortly before the account of the death of Moses itself.[9]

Thus it came about that a single work developed from the Pentateuch and Dtr. in the last quarter of the book of Numbers and in the book of Deuteronomy. Of course it could not completely obliterate the traces of its manifold seams, especially since here, as elsewhere, it was the redactor's policy to include as many as possible of the items from the material at his disposal. Despite this, however, he succeeded in general in conveying the impression of a fairly well-arranged composition.

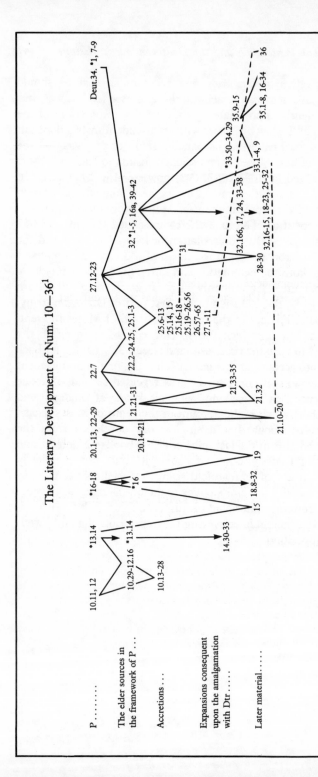

The Literary Development of Num. 10—36[1]

| | | | | | | | | | | |
|---|---|---|---|---|---|---|---|---|---|---|
| P . . . . . . . | 10.11, 12 | *13.14 | *16–18 | 20.1–13, 22–29 | 22.7 | 27.12–23 | 32.*1–5, 16a, 39–42 | | | Deut.34. *1, 7–9 |

The elder sources in
the framework of P . . . . 10.29–12.16 *13.14 *16 20.14–21 21.21–31 22.2–24.25, 25.1–3

Accretions . . . 10.13–28

25.6–13
25.14, 15
25.16–18 *31
25.19–26.56
26.57–65
27.1–11

Expansions consequent
upon the amalgamation
with Dtr . . . . . . 14.30–33 32.16b, 17, 24, 33–38 *33.50–34.29 35.9–15

Later material. . . . . . 15 18.8–32 19 21.32 28–30 32.16–15, 18–23, 25–32 33.1–4, 9 35.1–8, 16–34

21.33–35

21.10–20

1. On Num. 21.1.9, a passage which cannot be classified with any degree of certainty, cf. Noth 1940/41: 175ff.

# NOTES TO THE CHRONICLER'S HISTORY

## Notes to Chapter 14
### The Original Form of the Work

1. At the beginning of 28.1 the author of the oldest layer of the massive insertion has repeated 23.2a (except that he has used a different verb) in order to pick up again the interrupted narrative thread.

2. Whether 22.14-16 is a later supplement remains an open question. 22.17, at any rate, is an anticipatory addition, and, *a fortiori*, so is the quite unexpected installation passage in 22.18, 19 with its strange command that 'the princes of Israel' should build the temple.

3. Chr. uses 'princes' with the same sense as 'elders' in the older sources, and pays no attention to the fact that the word originally meant royal officials; apart from cases where he is quoting from sources, he uses 'elders' only at 1 Chron. 15.25 and 21.16.

4. Since 28.18b is certainly a later expansion, 28.19 should also be regarded as an addition, tracing the plan for the temple back to a 'writing from the hand of the Lord'. It can be integrated into its present context only on the basis of textual emendation.

5. In 23.2b a necessary connection is forged by adding 'the priests and the Levites' to the 'princes' who are summoned to the assembly.

6. Only a very few secondary additions take account of chs. 23-27: they include the expansion of the object in 28.1 and of the subject in 29.6, together with 28.21a, a sentence which is not well integrated into its context.

7. However unsuitable the place chosen for the insertion of the lists may seem to be, there was in fact hardly any other available setting for working the arrangement of the varied classes of temple personnel into the account of David's preparatory activities.

8. So Benzinger 1901: 61f.; Kittel 1902: 79f.; Rothstein 1923: 606f. Later on, Rothstein (Rothstein-Hänel 1927: 395ff.) correctly attributed the account of the preparations for the building of the temple to what he regarded as the original composition of the Chronicler, but then confused the issue again in another way by the assumption that there were one or more later 'Chroniclers'. It is true that Goettsberger 1939: 165 and 191 speaks

of 23.3–27:34 as an 'insertion', but rather than drawing any literary-critical conclusions from this he merely attributes it all to Chr.

9. On this use of 'Biblical' citations by Chr., cf. von Rad 1934a: 115ff.

10. The following remarks may be briefly added simply by way of annotation: the basic core of the addition comprises the Levitical genealogy in 23.3-5, 6b, 7-24aα. It agrees basically with Num. 3.17ff. Into this context 23.6a, 24aβ, 25, 26, 28-32 were added (vv. 24b and 27 are yet later additions). In 24.20-30 we have a later appendix to this genealogy (v. 31 being a connecting link). 26.20-32 is apparently a further appendix. The passages which come in between must then be even more recent, viz. the list of the 24 priestly classes (24.1-19), whose position *following* the Levitical genealogy is in any case disturbing, the 24 classes of temple singers (25.1-31) and the statement about the gatekeepers and their duties (26.1-19). Finally, the various lists in ch. 27 have absolutely nothing to do with the theme of preparations for the building of the temple. They were added only after a collection of lists had already been accumulated at this point.

11. On the date of Chr. and thereby the *terminus a quo* for the admission of this list into Chr.'s work, see below pp. 69-73.

12. In 13.2 it is quite unequivocally presupposed that the assembly of Israel which elevated David to be king and then immediately conquered Jerusalem with him is still acting with him.

13. Further additions have in turn been made to this list; cf. Rothstein's analysis in Rothstein-Hänel 1927: 232ff.

14. Rothstein (1927: 307ff.) has undertaken a generally convincing literary-critical analysis of chs. 15 and 16.

15. Note the accusative marker, which is quite out of place in the present context.

16. In the final form of the text the verb of v. 37 must also be reckoned to govern v. 39, but that is completely unsuitable. Rothstein (1927) mistakenly attributes v. 4, and hence vv. 39 and 40 as well, to the secondary material.

17. The cult centre of Gibeon, which is here introduced quite unexpectedly (like so much else in Chr.), plays a certain part again later in 1 Chron. 21.29; 2 Chron. 1.3, 13, all based on 1 Kgs 3.5 and 9.2. The absence of Abiathar from 16.4, 39 and 40 tells in favour of Rothstein's conjecture (1927: 274) that this name is secondary in 15.11.

18. 16.5 and 6 and 16.37 and 38 hardly belong to the same layer either; 16.5 and 6 may be a later supplement to 16.37 and 38.

19. This relates primarily to Codex Vaticanus.

20. It is precisely the section between the name Arpachshad in v. 17 and the same name in v. 24 which has fallen out. This perfectly clear situation is presented in a strangely inexact fashion in the commentaries of Benzinger, Kittel and Rothstein-Hänel, and even in the text-critical apparatus of *Biblia Hebraica* (3rd edn). Goettsberger's comments on the passage (1939: *ad loc.*), are correct.

21. The fact that in v. 34b the Septuagint changes the name 'Israel' into the name 'Jacob' shows how little reliance can be put upon it for 1 Chron. 1; the name 'Israel' undoubtedly represents the original reading because of its link with 2.1.

22. The next generation of Benjamin, which is also reviewed in Num. 26.40, is omitted in 1 Chron. 7.12.

23. The peculiar position of the name of Dan is probably due to no more than a copyist's error; cf. Rothstein–Hänel (1927: 13, n. a).

24. There is no reason to regard these statements as secondary, as Rothstein–Hänel (1927) do (*ad loc.*); v. 3b is the only part which may be an addition, drawn word for word from Gen. 38.7; there is no corresponding remark about Onan.

25. Verses 6-8, which rest basically on a combination of Josh. 7.1 with 1 Kgs 5.11, are certainly an addition.

26. Grammatically, v. 9 is very strangely phrased (cf. Rothstein–Hänel 1927: 15); there has clearly been some later interference here. Two formulations have apparently been combined with each other. Chr. presumably wrote, 'Hezron begat Ram', and vv. 10ff. join smoothly on to this. The heading which originally belonged with vv. 18ff. and 25ff. was subsequently amalgamated with this: 'The sons of Hezron were Jerahmeel and Caleb'.

27. The genealogy of David in Ruth 4.18-22 comes from Chr. (not the other way about), not least because Chr. has a fuller text than Ruth, since it also includes the names of David's brothers. It is not difficult to suppose that even in the late post-exilic period a genealogy of David was known—whether genuine or at least partly fictitious—and that Chr. could have made use of this. The name of David's father and three eldest brothers (cf. 1 Sam. 17.13) had long been known.

28. The material in 2.16f. is probably also a later addition, based on passages like 2 Sam. 2.18; 17.25. In what follows the genealogy of the Davidides in ch. 3, which from a formal point of view could quite well be joined to 2.15, must be considered secondary, because in the introduction to his own subsequent account Chr. would hardly have anticipated chronologically to such an extent.

29. On the whole Chr. here follows in detail the form of names as handed down in Numbers 26, not those of Gen. 46.10, which diverge in various ways.

30. It is unlikely that the remarks about the order of priority amongst the sons of Israel (5.1-2, picking up from Gen. 49.4 and 26) derive from Chr. He would hardly on his own account have attributed the right of the firstborn to Joseph.

31. Similarly there can be no doubt that originally Chr. included a notice about Zebulun and that this was then completely lost as a consequence of the subsequent expansions and alterations in the introductory genealogical

section.

32. Subsequently vv. 7-13 were further confused by the introduction of a genealogy of Samuel based in part on 1 Sam. 1.1; 8.2. This was presumably placed here because one name or other in the Kohathite line agreed with a name in the genealogy of Samuel (whether genuine or artificial) which had been handed down.

33. Could this have been done on the basis of Gen. 49 by the person who introduced the remark about the order of the tribes in 5.1f., since this depends on Gen. 49?

34. The grandchildren of Benjamin in Num. 26.40 have been added into the list of the sons of Benjamin in Gen. 46, and this in turn has subsequently influenced 1 Chron. 8.2f.

35. The whole section about Zebulun has fallen victim to the subsequent alterations to this passage; so too have the headings which once introduced Manasseh and Ephraim.

36. In vv. 30f. the tradition of Gen. 46 has been preferred to that of Numbers 26. Perhaps, as in the case of the consideration paid to the generation of the grandchildren, which does not appear to be usual with Chr., it is only a case of a secondary filling out of the original material on the basis of Gen. 46.17.

37. The concluding remark here, 'the sons of Bilhah', is an addition based on Gen. 46.25. Chr. certainly did not arrange the tribes in precise dependence on the order of their mothers.

38. These two enlargements would thus be the only two parts of the genealogical introductory section which Chr. has not created on the basis of the Pentateuch.

39. Cf. Hölscher 1923.

40. Similarly Hölscher 1923.

41. On the question of the original text, see in detail Kittel 1918: 6ff., and also Schaeder 1930a: 19. The versions (LXX and Pesh.) still preserve to some extent the missing, but necessary, words, 'in Jerusalem'; on the other hand the words 'and the singers, and the doorkeepers and the temple slaves in their towns' can be seen on the basis of their positioning to be an addition based on the preceding main list. Consequently, the original text ran: 'The priests and the Levites and some of the people settled in Jerusalem, (the rest of) all Israel, however, in their towns'.

42. In fact this addition is not present in Neh. 7.70. This favours the hypothesis advanced above, regardless of how we otherwise settle the issue of the relationship between Ezra 2 and Neh. 7.

43. On the original form of 35.15, see above, p. 36.

44. It was only a pedantic supplementer who felt the need in 2.70 to add in the separate classes of cultic personnel mentioned in the list *alongside* the Levites.

45. These two crop up earlier in 2.2. This is probably not an original

introduction to the long list, but one which nevertheless already lay in front of the author of the narrative framework. It was doubtless intended that they should be regarded as leaders of those returning in a capacity subordinate to Sheshbazzar.

46. Until there is any demonstration to the contrary, we must hold to the view that the use of Aramaic shows that we are dealing here with a self-contained unit which is separate from the Hebrew narrative. It is true that the Aramaic only starts in 4.8; but 4.7 was demonstrably written originally in Aramaic and was only subsequently translated into Hebrew (cf. Schaeder 1930b:16f.), and since v. 6 belongs with it, as its content shows, we must assume the same in its case too.

47. On 7.1b-5, see below, pp. 62f.

48. So correctly Hölscher 1923: *ad loc.*

49. The abbreviated repetition of v. 6b in v. 9bβ may be taken as an indication that vv. (7) 8 and 9 have been added.

50. It is striking that in the subsequent course of the narrative no exact dates are given, but only vague chronological references. 8.31 is an exception, but it is uncertain whether the reference to a date there is original.

51. It is contested by Hölscher (1923: 517f.). At all events, it is inadmissible to conclude that it is not genuine on the basis of historical considerations, as Hölscher does. Whether or not it belonged to the work of Chr. does not in any way prejudge the question whether it is a genuine or a fabricated list.

52. The names ascribed to them presumably derive from the stock of common personal names current at the time of the author.

53. Verse 20 is an even later addition.

54. At most the last three words of v. 18b could belong with v. 18a.

55. The words 'After these things had been done' (cf. 2 Chron. 7.1; 29.29; 31.1) do not at all demand the previous mention of major events; the matters which have already been mentioned (delivery of the votive offerings to the temple, the offering of sacrifices, handing over of the royal decrees to the Persian officials) are completely sufficient to explain the expression.

56. So correctly Hölscher (1923: 522).

57. See most recently Hölscher (1923: 529).

58. The explanation that 3.33-38 is an addition by the Chronicler (Torrey 1910: 225f.) is not soundly based in terms of the arguments from language and style which have been advanced to support it. At most, 3.36-37 might be regarded as an addition by Chr.

59. Torrey (1896: 37ff.) tries to prove that the list was fabricated by Chr., but he advances only a few isolated and completely unsatisfactory linguistic arguments.

60. Torrey (1910: 226) regards 6.16-19 as being also an addition by Chr., but without offering detailed reasons.

61. See above p. 44.

62. That these elements once stood together cannot be proved by reference

to 3 Esra (= Esdras *a* in the Septuagint [and 1 Esdras in the English Apocrypha—Tr.]) because this book has demonstrably recorded the material which it inherited for reasons of its own (e.g. the material in Ezra 1-6).

63. It is worth noting explicitly that there is naturally no question of the introduction of a new law in Neh. 8-10; we are dealing here with the old law of Moses. What is more, these chapters do not speak either of a new general commitment to the old law: all that is said is that certain specific, hitherto neglected regulations will henceforth be implemented. The usual view of Ezra as the one who brought the law which was to serve as the founding force of the post-exilic community can be based only on Ezra's official title (Ezra 7.12, 21) and the phrase 'the law of God in the hand of Ezra' in the Aramaic decree (Ezra 7.14; cf. vv. 25, 26).

64. Schaeder 1930a: 26 defends the originality of the list in both places by arguing that Chr. first completed the book of Nehemiah on its own and only wrote his whole work afterwards. This theory is contradicted, however, by the fact that the composition of the book of Nehemiah can only be understood in the light of the purpose of the complete work. In particular, without the book of Ezra Neh. 8-10 would be left hanging totally in the air.

65. In the case of Ezra 2.68f. (cf. Neh. 7.69-71) it was not possible to decide for certain whether these verses belong to the list or the narrative (see above p. 43). Unfortunately, the differences between Ezra 2.68f. and Neh. 7.69-71 do not allow us to draw any certain conclusions about the original wording. It is equally possible that variation has been subsequently introduced into Neh. 7.69-71 (so Hölscher 1923: 539) as that Ezra 2.68f. represents a secondary simplification.

66. The repetition in Neh. 7.72 of the statement about the settlement of those named in the list as having returned is quite unsuitable (and is in any case already based on the interpolated text of Ezra 2.70). To associate this statement with those who returned with *Ezra* (so Schaeder 1930a: 22f.) is a scarcely possible and extremely remote way of establishing the originality of Neh. 7. The reference to the seventh month in Neh. 7.72 (= Ezra 3.1a) is certainly suitable up to a point, because the subsequent account in Neh. 8ff. is similarly set in the seventh month (cf. 8.2b etc.). However, as the seventh month, being the month of the new year, is suitable for all kinds of ceremonial occasions, no particular significance need be attributed to this coincidence. In any case, it cannot be maintained that the date in Neh. 8.2b *had* to be prepared for by Neh. 7.72b.

67. The phrase 'that they might be reckoned by genealogy' in Neh. 7.5a is best considered an integral part of the Nehemiah memoir since it was this which gave the opportunity for the repetitious insertion of the long list from Ezra 2.

68. The fact that the list in Neh. 10.2-28 is certainly an artificial composition, and therefore not 'genuine' (cf. Hölscher 1923: 544f.),

would not of itself point decisively away from its belonging to Chr.

69. The remainder of the verse is a very defective and obviously interpolated addition.

70. The next two words have third-person suffixes; coming in the middle of a speech cast in the first-person plural these are obviously an addition.

71. Elsewhere, with his peculiar inconsistency, Chr. refers to Ezra as *either* 'the priest' (Ezra 10.10, 16; Neh. 8.2) *or* 'the scribe' (Neh. 8.1, 4, 13; [12.36]), except where he uses the name on its own.

72. 3 Esra (1 Esdras) 9.49 is of no text-critical value; the traditional Hebrew text is clearly presupposed here and the name Nehemiah omitted because 3 Esra joined Neh. 8-10 on to the history of Ezra and in the process either remodelled or mistranslated the text of Neh. 8.9. In I/II Esra (= the Septuagint translation of Ezra–Nehemiah—Tr.), however, the addition to the name of Nehemiah is lacking at 8.9 in the great majority of the manuscripts.

73. In Neh. 9.5b, disregarding a few other necessary small emendations, the verbal form should undoubtedly be read as an imperfect consecutive.

74. Generally, it is held that 1 Chron. 9 is dependent on Neh. 11. Hölscher (1923: 551f.), however, has tried to uphold the reverse relationship. If he were right, it would prove without a doubt that Neh. 11.3-19 is an addition to Chr. In reality, however, neither view can be demonstrated with any degree of certainty.

75. The list can certainly not be attributed to the Nehemiah memoir because as its contents show there is no way in which it can be a 'genuine' document relating to Nehemiah's resettlement. The only possibilities are to ascribe it to Chr., who, if he had reworked the list for his own purposes would certainly have included the gatekeepers with the Levites, or to some later redactor, who simply left his parent text unchanged in this regard.

76. Within this catalogue vv. 21-24 represent a miscellaneous collection which interrupts the surrounding context and is therefore an even later addition.

77. The first three words of v. 27 may possibly have belonged to Nehemiah's account of the dedication of the wall as reworked by Chr.

78. Characteristically, the singers in this passage again stand independently alongside the Levites. Not until we reach one group of Septuagint manuscripts do we find that by an addition at the beginning of v. 28 the singers have subsequently been made into Levites.

79. The secondary character of vv. 46-47 is clear from the fact that they are reflected in the words 'the singers and gatekeepers' in v. 45, words which, however, have obviously been added secondarily as a gloss.

*Notes to Chapter 15*
*The Sources which have been Used*

1. It is customary to assume that all specific information which does not come from the sources known to us derives from an ancient, more or less authentic report.

2. Rothstein–Hänel 1927: xliv ff.

3. Anyone feeling the need to stake a greater claim in favour of the unity of this introductory section might conclude that the list of the sons of Keturah (1.32-33) and the list of Edomite kings (1.43-54) have been borrowed secondarily from the Pentateuch, because neither of these two elements is particularly well embedded in its context; but even then we still have not arrived at the minimal text required for Rothstein–Hänel's hypothesis.

4. It must be strongly emphasized here once again that the Septuagint's minus with regard to the Hebrew text does *not* take us closer to a text favourable to Rothstein–Hänel's thesis. Neither the gap in Shem's genealogy at 1.17ff. (caused by homoioteleuton) nor the omission in the list of the sons of Ham in 1.9ff. coincides with the material not derived from P.

5. Rothstein–Hänel (1927) advance as an important argument the observation that the basic text of 1 Chron. 4.28-33 makes use exclusively of the P section of Josh. 19.1-9. This is unacceptable, however, because 1 Chron. 4.28ff. does not belong to Chr. (see above, p. 39), and Josh. 19.1ff. does not belong to P (see below pp. 112ff.).

6. 2.10 makes use of Num. 1.7, and 2.13 makes use of 1 Sam. 17.13. 6.35 uses a passage like Exod. 6.25 while 6.37b-38 obviously uses the corrupt text of 2 Sam. 8.17 (contrast 1 Sam. 22.20).

7. This agrees exactly with the fact that Chr. knew the Pentateuch in its completed form. It is shown more particularly at p. 145 below that the division of the Deuteronomic history into 'books', which is presupposed by the accumulation of supplements to the book of Samuel, is diretly linked to the redaction of the Pentateuch.

8. On this, see more particularly Chapter 19 below.

9. Chr.'s characteristic inconsistency may be seen at once from the fact that, although he deals only with the succession of Judaean kings, he refers sometimes to the annals of the kings of Israel and sometimes to the annals of the kings of Judah and Israel (or the like). This shows very clearly the extent to which, without detailed consideration, he simply imitates his Deuteronomic exemplar.

10. For a comprehensive collection of these 'source'-citations, cf. Steuernagel 1912: 386f.

11. In most cases this is quite clear. 2 Chron. 20.34 mentions Jehu ben Hanani in connection with Jehoshaphat. He, of course, derives from 1 Kgs

16.1, 7, where admittedly he is associated with Jehoshaphat's somewhat older colleague, Baasha. However, tradition did not supply Chr. with a Judaean prophet for this period, so he associated Jehu with the Judaean king Jehoshaphat (2 Chron. 19.2) and even linked Jehu's father, Hanani, with Jehoshaphat's father and predecessor, Asa (2 Chron. 16.7). Uncertainty surrounds only the origin of Jedo in the concluding notice about Solomon (2 Chron. 9.29). He is usually identified with the Iddo mentioned in the concluding notices for Rehoboam and Abijah (2 Chron. 12.15; 13.22), and this is undoubtedly correct. The later tradition (cf. Josephus, *Ant.* 8.231 in Niese's edition) which identified this Jedo-Iddo with the unnamed prophet of 1 Kings 13 could very well also have been Chr.'s opinion. If we consider further that Chr. calls the father of a prophet not known in Samuel–Kings Oded (2 Chron. 15.1) and calls another prophet who equally does not appear in Samuel–Kings Oded (2 Chron. 28.9—and 2 Chron. 20.37 is the only other place where a prophet who does not come from Samuel–Kings occurs in Chr.), then the conclusion seems obvious that Chr. formed names for those prophets whose names were not supplied for him by tradition from the root '*dd* (— '*wd*, 'to bear witness'?). In the light of 1 Kgs 15.1, 9, Chr. could in the last resort have considered that the prophet of 1 Kings 13 was still contemporary with the Judaean kings Rehoboam and Abijah, and the formula Chr. uses in 2 Chron. 9.29 to describe Jedo-Iddo is strongly suggestive of the prophet of 1 Kings 13. It is therefore not likely that Chr. had any special tradition for the character of Jedo-Iddo the prophet.

12.   To be absolutely precise we should also include the Pentateuch as part of his *Vorlage*, because there is a brief allusion to Exod. 38.1ff. at 2 Chron. 1.5 and because Exod. 40.34f. and Lev. 9.24 served as a pattern for 2 Chron. 7.1-3a.

13.   Additions that can be easily recognized as characteristic of Chr. would be 5.11b-13a (cf. pp. 35f. above); 7.6; 7.9; 7.12b-15 (a reference to the prayer at the dedication of the temple); 8.11b. The remarks in 4.8-9 should also be reckoned as additions by Chr. on the basis of furnishings of the post-exilic temple.

14.   For the original form of this section, see above pp. 31ff.

15.   The introduction to the history of the ark in 1 Chron. 13.1-5 is, of course, also to be attributed to Chr.

16.   See especially the commentary of Rothstein-Hänel 1927: *ad loc.*

17.   No significance should be attached to the various changes in wording nor to the substitution of 'all Israel' for 'David's men' (2 Sam. 5.6); not knowing of the real historical circumstances, Chr. presupposed that this was the situation because of his overall point of view.

18.   There are other examples of places where Chr. did not understand the wording or meaning of expressions in his source and so simply omitted them (1 Sam. 31.12bβ in 1 Chron. 10.12; 2 Sam. 8.2aβ in 1 Chron. 18.2; 2 Sam. 12.31aβ in 1 Chron. 20.3) or else changed them at his own discretion (2 Sam.

5.17bβ, 24aβ in 1 Chron. 14.8, 15; 2 Sam. 8.1b in 1 Chron. 18.1).

19. Verse 8b may be a free addition by Chr. It will have suggested itself once Joab had been mentioned, and in view of the implication that the city of Jerusalem was completely destroyed at the time of David's conquest.

20. Rothstein–Hänel (1927: 240f.) consider this possibility. They in fact favour the hypothesis that Chr. had in front of him an older form of the complete book of Samuel, but this view should certainly be rejected; see below, pp. 56f.

21. It would be possible to suppose in this connection that the longer original list was broken off in 2 Samuel 23 after the thirtieth name (since v. 36 deals with only *one* name we in fact have exactly 30 names in vv. 24-39). Although the original list was known as a roster of the 'Thirty', it could in fact have included more names, because the 'Thirty' was a traditional institution with a traditional designation (cf. Elliger 1935: 66ff.) and did not have to be comprised of exactly thirty members.

22. Cf. Noth 1981: 124f. n. 3.

23. On this, see further p. 145 below.

24. Rothstein–Hänel 1927: 241.

25. Cf. Gray 1896: 229f. The first name of all belongs to the group of names formed from the root *zbd* which became very common in the post-exilic period; cf. Noth 1928: 47. Admittedly it is also attested earlier with an example in each of 2 Kgs 12.22 and 23.36 (the example in 1 Kgs 4.5 is textually uncertain).

26. The text of 1 Chron. 11.35b, 36a and 38 should be corrected to agree with 2 Samuel 23 and, conversely, 2 Sam. 23.32b and 33a to agree with 1 Chronicles 11.

27. We may imagine that underlying this secondary lengthening was the fact that some post-exilic families traced their ancestry back to one of David's thirty heroes. The fictitious names of these presumed ancestors would then have been added to the list in 1 Chronicles 11. Only the reference to a 'Moabite' in v. 46b fails to fit this suggestion.

28. Rothstein–Hänel (1927: 385ff.) above all follow the older commentators in this, but with the strange twist (the reasons for which are not fully clear) that Chr. reproduced this *Vorlage* of his from memory.

29. Presumably, therefore, Chr. read the text in the same damaged state that we do today. For Chr.'s omission of passages in his *Vorlage* which he could not understand, cf. above, n. 18.

30. In this connection an investigation ought to be undertaken to see whether the differences in numbers are not often to be explained by the use of numerical notations in ancient manuscripts. [Noth's suspicion here was later confirmed by H.L. Allrick, 'The Lists of Zerubbabel (Nehemiah 7 and Ezra 2) and the Hebrew Numeral Notation', *BASOR* 136 (1954), pp. 21-27—Tr.]

31. Only Chr. states that the threshing-floor of Araunah (Ornan) became

the site of the later temple. However, granted the tacit presupposition that there could be only one legitimate cult centre, this was so obvious a consequence to be drawn from 2 Samuel 24 that there is no need to assume that Chr. must have derived it from some special tradition.

32. In this way the site of the future temple was designated by God in an especially clear manner. In the same way fire again fell from heaven to ignite the sacrifice on the occasion of the dedication of the temple itself (2 Chron. 7.1). For the wording of 1 Chron. 21.26, cf. 1 Kgs 18.24; for the subject matter, cf. (besides Lev. 9.24) 1 Kgs 18.38.

33. The idea that Yahweh's desert tabernacle was at Gibeon (see too 1 Chron. 16.39) will have been worked out by Chr. from a simple combination of Exodus 25ff. with 1 Kgs 3.4ff. In this, he presupposed that Solomon could only have offered his sacrifice at Gibeon (1 Kgs 3.4) at the single legitimate cult centre at the time, and that this was the 'tabernacle of Yahweh' which Moses had erected. In 1 Chron. 21.28–22.1 it is carefully explained that David could not go to Gibeon at that time, and then comes the solemn declaration that Yahweh himself has decided that Jerusalem shall in future serve as the place for offering sacrifices. It is certainly no accident that in 1 Chron. 15.26b; 16.1b-2a Chr. followed his *Vorlage* (2 Sam. 6) in speaking of sacrifices at the celebration of the transfer of the ark, but then in 16.4 + 39-40 (cf. above p. 35) mentioned the arrangements for a permanent sacrificial cult only at Gibeon while at first there was to be nothing but cultic singing in front of the ark. This arrangement lasts until the place where the ark is stationed is made into the legitimate site for sacrifices by the history recounted in 1 Chronicles 21 and as David explicitly decrees in 22.1. Two further points should be made in connection with 1 Chronicles 21. The name Ornan (instead of Araunah in 2 Samuel 24) hardly points to the presence of a special tradition though it represents the form in which the foreign name Araunah was subsequently pronounced. It is uncertain whether Chr. coined this form himself or whether he derived it somehow from a local Jerusalem tradition. Verse 6 is presumably an addition (Rothstein–Hänel [1927: *ad loc.*] agree) to ensure that Levi and Benjamin are not included in the census. This is because of their association with the city of Jerusalem, the place where the divine punishment stopped.

34. Steuernagel's supposition (1912: 400) seems to me to be quite mistaken. He thinks that the three 'sources' named in 1 Chron. 29.29 refer to the traditional book of Samuel, to a special source which comes to light in 1 Chronicles 21 (in reality, this never existed) and finally to the basic text of 1 Chronicles 23–27 (but this was not even a part of the original work of Chr.).

35. It is not difficult to imagine that Chr. would, by an obvious analogy, have composed such a statement about 'sources' for David's reign, even though there is no basis for it in Dtr.

36. One of these variations involves the occasional use of the word

'midrash' (2 Chron. 13.22; 24.27). It has played—and continues to play—a role of quite unjustified prominence in discussions of Chr.'s sources.

37. This idea certainly rested on the frequent occurrence of prophetic narratives in Samuel-Kings, although Dtr.'s statements about sources do not actually refer to them. It was current amongst the Rabbis, as, for instance, the naming of this part of the canon shows. It first appears, however, as early as Chr., and he in turn was probably only following the common assumption of his day, which was invoked to increase the value placed upon these books.

38. Rothstein-Hänel 1927: xlvi ff.

39. Underlying this, moreover, there is a mistaken notion of the literary development of the books of Samuel-Kings. It assumes that Dtr. already knew of an older version of the whole of David's reign and that he merely reworked it. On this, see in more detail Noth 1981: 54-74.

40. To this category belongs, *inter alia*, the secondary alteration of names compounded with *ba'al*, which have survived unchanged in Chr. (e.g. Beeliada in 1 Chron. 14.7 against Eliada in 2 Sam. 5.16, where, however, the Septuagint still reads the original form). Further, the divergence between 1 Chron. 20.5 and 2 Sam. 21.19 rests on quite obvious and simple textual corruption. It is therefore impossible to trace it back to a separate source (*contra* Rothstein-Hänel 1927: xlvii, n. 3).

41. I here pass over points which do not concern the original form of Chr. but only secondary additions.

42. The 'stopping of the upper spring', the 'bringing down' and the leading 'to the west side of the city of David' are all quite accurate statements.

43. So E. Junge 1937: 92, n. 4.

44. Cf. Gadd 1923.

45. The statement that Necho was taking to the field '*against* the king of Assyria' is wrong.

46. Cf. Hjelt 1925: 142-47.

47. It must be presumed that Chr.'s phrasing of the whole of v. 5 has been influenced by 1 Kgs 12.25 (cf. Junge 1937: 75). This would explain the inelegant repetition of the verb at the start of v. 6. Nevertheless, it is clear that Chr. borrowed the phrase quoted above from his source.

48. See especially Beyer 1931.

49. Junge's objections (1937: 73ff.) to associating the list with Rehoboam are hardly convincing, being based on too rigid an application of an otherwise correct presentation of the history of the Judaean army. Of course, we should not entertain an exaggerated conception of the equipment of these 'fortresses'. There is not much to be said for associating the list with Josiah.

50. In the four passages mentioned so far, the juxtaposition of 'Judah and Benjamin' is typical of Chr.; it is thus Chr. who characterized the Benjamites as having a special role as archers in the Judaean army in 14.7

51. We may wonder whether 26.10aα does not also belong to the source

quoted in 26.9 and whether this was not then developed by Chr. himself in 26.10aβb.

52. Chr. has also prefaced the material from his source about Hezekiah's tunnel in 2 Chron. 32.29 with some general information (of which he is so fond) about building cities.

53. Junge 1937: 37ff. has dealt with the passages discussed above. He regards them as giving ancient and reliable information about the time of Josiah, but thinks that Chr. has distributed them over the whole period of the Judaean kings. This assumption is totally forced and rests on the presupposition that all OT notices about fortifications and the associated troop dispositions must be genuine accounts of Josiah's time and that Chr. must have taken these things over from somewhere else because he himself can have had no interest in them (against this latter assertion, see below, p. 105).

54. Admittedly, this brief notice has clearly been worked over by Chr. (compare v. 6b and the phrasing of v. 7).

55. It might be objected that Jotham could not have waged war against the Ammonites because Judah and Ammon did not have a common border at that time. This cannot be maintained for certain, however; we do not know whether the Ammonites did not take advantage of the weakness of the nation of Israel in decline to expand their border towards the west as we know for certain that they did in later times.—The last three words of v. 5 cannot be construed with what precedes. It would not just be a case of bad Hebrew; it would not be Hebrew at all. They must be the start of another notice which has subsequently been lost by a textual accident.

56. Of course, the other possibility cannot be absolutely excluded that, in the last two passages discussed, battles of the author's own time or recent past have been projected back into the past. An example of this kind of thing is the appearance of Maccabean campaigns in Jubilees' presentation of the history of Jacob and his sons (cf. Klein 1934: 16ff.). In the present case, however, this is not probable, because there is no obvious reason why it should be specifically the insignificant kings Abijah and Asa who are singled out for description as forerunners of later battles.—The way in which 2 Chron. 20.1-30 more or less turns 2 Kgs 3.4-27 on its head remains curious. 2 Chron. 20.1ff. is a typically chronistic description of a battle. Its precise geographical information in vv. 2, 16, 20 and 26 is dependent on local knowledge of the way from Engedi northwestwards up into the hill-country. One can hardly postulate here the use of an ancient historical source; it might be preferable, rather, to detect the traces of a local tradition from Chr.'s own area. [Noth later developed this suggestion more fully in 'Eine palästinische Lokalüberlieferung in 2 Chr. 20', *ZDPV* 67 (1944-45), pp. 45-71—Tr.]

57. The passage about the wives and sons of Rehoboam in 2 Chron. 11.18-23, with which the history of the sons of Jehoshaphat in 2 Chron. 21.2-4

belongs, can scarcely go back to an old source; the names which crop up in
these passages and which are not derived from the old tradition belong to the
post-exilic type, as Gray 1896: 231f. has already shown for 21.2. The
question must be asked whether these two passages were an original part of
Chr. at all or whether they are not rather secondary additions. 21.2-4 comes
at an unsuitable place and would be better placed after v. 5. Moreover, it tells
against 11.18-23 that Chr. then includes a different statement about Abijah's
mother in 13.2. The statement in 13.2 is certainly correct from a factual
point of view, even in preference to 1 Kgs 15.2, where the name of the
mother has obviously arisen secondarily under the influence of v. 10 (the
Abishalom of 1 Kgs 15.10 is scarcely the same as Absalom, the son of David).
The passage in 2 Chron. 11.18-23, however, presupposes the textual
corruption of 1 Kgs 15.2. Since this was not yet the case in the form of Kings
which Chr. followed, it is presumably more recent than Chr. The only
question which remains unresolved is what the purpose of the passages in
2 Chron. 11.18-23 and 21.2-4 was and where their content came from.—
There are also various items of information about the burial places of some
of the Davidides which do not come from Dtr. (2 Chron. 16.14; 21.20; 24.25;
26.23; 32.33). These too do not go back to a separate source used by Chr., but
are his own free conjectures. Perhaps they are partly to be explained by the
fact that late into post-exilic times there continued to be apocryphal
Jerusalem traditions about the sites of the graves of the former kings. This is
demonstrated by the tombstone dating from roughly the time of Christ's
birth which speaks about a new burial of King Uzziah's bones (cf. Sukenik
1931).

58.  Cf. especially 2 Chron. 26.9; 32.30.

59.  It may be possible to assume that this source had a brief chronological
framework. This may account for the statement about the length of
Jehoiachin's reign in 2 Chron. 36.9, which is more accurate than 2 Kgs 24.8.
For other differences in the numerals included in the chronological
framework one must always allow for the possibility of an alternative
tradition or even textual corruption. The dates which do not come from Dtr.
are undoubtedly Chr.'s free conjecture for the most part (thus 2 Chron 7.10;
15.19; 16.1; 12, 13; 17.7; 24.15; 29.3, 17; 30.2, 13, 15; 31.7). Similarly, the
rearrangement of the tradition about Josiah's reform and the introduction of
a new date into 34.3 is secondary by comparison with 2 Kgs 22.23. It is based
on the presupposition that the pious king must have begun his work for God
as soon as possible.

60.  Cf. Galling 1937.

61.  So too Galling 1937: 179f.

62.  For discussion of the conclusion of this list, see p. 43 above.

63.  For the inclusion of 4.6, 7 in this section, see above p. 153, n. 46.

64.  If the use of Aramaic had been reserved for the documents alone, this
would have emphasized their official character especially well. In view of the

repeated changes of language elsewhere in Ezra, there would then have been no reason subsequently to translate the narrative parts. These must therefore have been written in Aramaic from the start and combined with the documents at some time into a single literary unit.

65. For the most recent, detailed discussion, cf. Schaeder 1930a: 27ff.

66. For the appearance of these two names earlier in Ezra 2.2, see above p. 152, n. 45.

67. To make a start by setting up the altar for burnt offerings is perfectly understandable. Schaeder's suggested special explanation (1930a: 32f.) is thus not absolutely necessary.

68. For the date of Chr., see below pp. 69ff.

69. The start of v. 6 was altered slightly at a later date in order to take account of the genealogy which had been inserted; on the secondary character of vv. 8-9 and v. 7, see above, p. 44.

70. At this stage, the question whether this decree is genuine or fictitious can be left on one side.

71. It can be seen that this list was not simply invented by the author of the basic text because in a way that is not usual for him the wording of the basic text in 7.28bβ takes the list which follows into account.

72. So Schaeder 1930a: 6ff.; Eissfeldt 1934: 586 (ET pp. 543f.), *et al.*

73. Cf. Driver 1913: 535ff.

74. Torrey 1896: 16-20.

75. I find no reason for treating Ezra 10 separately and then deriving it from yet another source (Eissfeldt 1934).

76. Other examples of a similar change from the first to the third person are advanced by Torrey 1910: 244f.; see especially Dan. 3.31–4.34.

77. This dependence on Neh. 13.23 can be seen in the adoption of the unusual use of the expression for 'to marry', which is employed regularly in Ezra 10 (vv. 2, 10, 14, 17f.). In addition, the word *sāgān*, which is especially frequent in the Nehemiah Memoir, is used in the introduction to the account of the mixed marriages (Ezra 9.2). This too favours the view that Chr. used the Nehemiah Memoir as a pattern for Ezra 9 and 10.

78. Cf. above p. 162, n. 59.

79. The date in 8.31 is probably an addition (see above, p. 45). Otherwise it would also have to be understood as Chr.'s chronological calculation.

80. Steuernagel 1912: 422 has also drawn attention to the expression 'evening oblation' in 9.4f., which he finds 'incomprehensible in the Chronicler'. Now this expression is also used as here to designate the time of day in Dan. 9.21, so that it was hardly unusual in the post-exilic period. Admittedly Chr. speaks elsewhere of 'the morning (or evening) burnt offerings' (2 Chron. 2.3; 31.3; also 1 Chron. 16.40), but this is in contexts which are dealing not only with the daily sacrifices but also with all other kinds of sacrifices; only in 2 Chron. 13.11 and Ezra 3.3 is there the thought of the daily offerings alone. In no case, therefore, is it a question of the time of

day as at Ezra 9.4f. So even if we did not have to reckon with Chr.'s notorious inconsistency in such matters, there would still be no decisive objection to be raised against this expression itself. There is therefore no difficulty either in attributing to Chr. Neh. 10.34, which speaks of 'the continual meal offering and the continual burnt offering' and other burnt offerings.

81. On this, see more particularly pp. 76ff. below.

82. There is in Chr. a similarly abrupt transition at 1 Chron. 10.1, while at Ezra 7.1 it is only lightly veiled by a technical device; for the whole of the history of the monarchy Chr. was able to use the connected work of Dtr.

83. For the subsequent insertion of Neh. 7.6-72 (with 7.5b as its introduction), cf. above, p. 48.

84. Cf. Torrey 1896: 23ff.

85. The people's first reaction to hearing the Law read and explained was actually mourning and weeping, as 8.9 indicates, until Nehemiah and the Levites pointed out to the people that on New Year's Day such a reaction was not *yet* appropriate (for the textual question about the original subject in v. 9, see pp. 48f. above); then on the following day (v. 13) the preparations for the celebration of the Feast of Tabernacles in a new way (v. 17) had to be undertaken, which had the consequence of staving off mourning and weeping. Thus in 8.9-12 Chr. already prepares the way for a penitential mood to come to expression in 9.1ff. and therefore must have had the connection between chs. 8 and 9 in mind from the outset.

86. The Levites who explain the Law are one of Chr.'s favourite topics (cf. 2 Chron. 17:7-9; 30.22; 35.3). Chr. has described the scene in Neh. 8.1-12 in a very lively and evocative manner. The Levitical names in 8.4, 7, like those in 9.4f., derive from Chr.'s common stock of names.

87. The last preceding date in the Nehemiah Memoir was 25 Elul (= the sixth month) in 6.15; it was therefore simple to conclude that what followed took place in the seventh month.

88. On the substance, though not the wording, of the description of this festival, compare Lev. 23.40ff. Chr. simply proceeds on the basis of the usual manner in which the Feast of Tabernacles was celebrated in his own day.

89. So Schaeder 1930a: 8.

90. On the original form which Chr. gave this chapter and the later supplements to it, cf. p. 48 above.

91. This too shows the secondary nature of the Septuagint's addition at the start of 9.6; on the text of 9.5b see above, p. 155, n. 73.

92. For evidence that this was the situation in Chr.'s own work, see pp. 47f. above.

93. For the original state of this section in Chr., see pp. 49f. above.

## Notes to Chapter 16
### *The Date of Composition*

1. The passages concerned are the Davidic genealogy in 1 Chron. 3.15-24 and the list of high priests in Neh. 12.10f.; in any case they could supply only a *terminus a quo*.

2. Klostermann 1896: 216f.

3. Schaeder 1930b: 14ff.

4. Kittel 1929: 602f.

5. Cf. Schaeder's summary (1930b: 25), according to which it is assumed that 4.6, 7; 5.1, 2; 6.14, 16-18 represent Chr.'s redactional activity.

6. 4.6 must originally have been in Aramaic, as is demonstrably the case with 4.7. The way in which the expression 'at the beginning of his reign' is phrased is striking, since elsewhere the technical term in Hebrew for the incomplete accession year of a king when reckoning by the post-dating system is *rēšīt* (cf. Jer 26.1 and frequently); presumably Chr. has here supplied a loose Hebrew translation of an original Aramaic *rēš malkūtā* (cf. Akkadian *rēš šarrūti*).

7. Schaeder's attempted explanation (1930b: 24) is not clear to me.

8. So Schaeder 1930b: 23.

9. The Cowley Papyrus no. 30, which dates from 408 BC, mentions the sons of Sanballat, the governor of Samaria (line 29), who was a contemporary of Nehemiah; consequently, Nehemiah's Artaxerxes is undoubtedly Artaxerxes I. The work of building the walls of Jerusalem was current at that time, as the Nehemiah Memoir shows, and it is with this that the exchange of correspondence in Ezra 4.8-22 (23) is concerned.

10. There is general agreement that the Darius mentioned in the books of Haggai and Zechariah is Darius I. This is clear from Hag. 2.3, to go no further. Chr. made use of this passage at Ezra 3.12, without allowing for the fact that according to the book of Haggai the incident in question took place in the second year of Darius.

11. The same conclusion would follow even if we did not accept the authenticity of the documents. Quite apart from the documents the temple-building can be securely dated in the time of Darius I and the wall-building in the time of Artaxerxes I. Either way, therefore, the Aramaic narrative framework is chronologically confused.

12. The analysis of the Aramaic section which was common in earlier times (cf. Steuernagel 1912: 417f.) was therefore basically correct.—I have avoided attempting to date the Aramaic section on linguistic grounds. Baumgartner (1927) has recently undertaken another detailed investigation of the history of the Aramaic language with this question in mind, and on this basis he believes it possible to show that this section comes 'at the earliest from around 300' (pp. 122f.). At the same time he established that there is no linguistic difference between the documents and the surrounding

narrative. This can be explained, however. Even if the documents date from
an earlier time, they were modernized by the author of the narrative
framework under the influence of the orthography of his own time—and for
the most part the relevant diagnostic criteria concern orthographic details
alone. In fact, however, the Aramaic of the Persian period and the beginning
of the Hellenistic period can by no means be certainly classified as a single
whole with a simple, unilinear development. Thus Schaeder (1930b: 27-56)
is able to empty Baumgartner's linguistic arguments of much of their force
by appealing to the tension between historical writing and spoken language.

13.   In 4.6 and 7 it is clear that there remain the headings of two letters.
They were included in full in Chr.'s Aramaic *Vorlage*, but he omitted them
as of less significance to his own purposes. In fact, he seems generally to have
abbreviated the start of his Aramaic *Vorlage*. The juxtaposition of 4.6 and 7
tells against linking 4.7 with what follows. 4.8-11 as we have it includes
various additions to the original text. Schaeder (1930b: 22f.) advances a
possible explanation of the origin of this passage.

14.   The claim that in Ezra 4.5-7 Chr. has the quite correct order of
succession, Cyrus–Darius–Xerxes–Artaxerxes (so Schaeder 1930b: 23) is
only apparently true, however, because these verses are not part of a single,
unified passage. The situation rather is that a new paragraph begins after
v. 5, with the last words of v. 5 quite clearly anticipating 4.24ff. Verse 6,
however, marks the beginning of the extract from the Aramaic source. The
words at the end of v. 5, 'all the days of Cyrus, king of Persia and (further)
until the reign of Darius king of Persia' leave all kinds of possibilities open,
including the thought of as long a succession of kings as one wishes between
Cyrus and Darius. Chr.'s concern in 4.5 is with Darius, and is not to point to
events which transpired after Darius only then finally to return to Darius
again (4.24ff.). He himself understood his Aramaic *Vorlage* to imply that the
exchange of correspondence in 4.6-23 took place before Darius. The
appearance of a correct succession of kings in vv. 5-7 is thus purely
fortuitous.

15.   Allusions which Chr. makes to the historical situation of his own day
(cf. p. 105 below) show that he must certainly be placed prior to the
nationalistic uprising in the Maccabean period. On the other hand, it seems
to me to be incorrect to say that the book of Jesus Sirach, which was written
around 190 BC, betrays knowledge of the Chronicler's work. The great hymn
in praise of the fathers in this book speaks of David having 'appointed
stringed instruments for the singing before the altar' (47.9) and of his having
'ordered the chanting of Psalms to the accompaniment of harps' (*ibid.*), while
in this connection it further speaks of the cultic celebrations under David
which were accompanied with hymns and songs. But none of this proves
dependence on Chr. or on the supplements to Chr. in which Levitical singing
is so strongly emphasized. The tradition of David's association with the
music of the cult also existed independently of Chr., as the Psalter in its

present form shows. The statement in Sir. 48.17 about Hezekiah's tunnel derives from 2 Kgs 20.20, not 2 Chron. 32.30. Above all else, however, the fact that Sir. 49.13 mentions only Nehemiah, while there is no reference to Ezra anywhere in the hymn in praise of the fathers, shows clearly that Jesus Sirach knew nothing of Chr., in which Ezra and Nehemiah appear in such close association with each other; Jesus Sirach, on the other hand, still knew the Nehemiah Memoir as a separate document. None of this proves, of course, that Chr. was not yet in existence in the time of Jesus Sirach.

### Notes to Chapter 17
### *The Nature of the Composition*

1. So far as I know, only Torrey (1910: 231ff.) has studied and given emphasis to this side of Chr.

2. Torrey 1910: 227.

3. If this is true for the books of Chronicles, it is presumably also true for Ezra–Nehemiah; we may couple with this the literary-critical conclusions arrived at above, pp. 62ff., which showed that Chr. was personally responsible for a not inconsiderable proportion of Ezra–Nehemiah.

4. On this, see the description of the nature of the composition of Dtr. in Noth 1981: 76f.

5. For fuller details, see below, pp. 98ff.

6. This applies above all to the account of the conquest and then to the history of Saul and David.

7. In the manner of official dating formulae, the notice in 29.3 should refer to the first *full* calendar year of the king's reign. Presumably, however, Chr. meant the start of the king's reign. He thereby overlooked that he was working on the highly improbable presupposition that Hezekiah ascended the throne precisely on the civil New Year's Day.

8. The suggestion that for these dates and for his presentation of Josiah's reform generally Chr. had access to an alternative source other than the book of Kings (so Oestreicher 1923: 60ff.) is incorrect. Chr. presupposes the presentation of Josiah's reform in the traditional book of Kings, including its arrangement of the story of the finding of the Law and its annalistic report. This is shown by the fact that in 2 Chron. 34.32b, 33 he reproduces a quite short extract from the annalistic report in exactly the same place as in the book of Kings. All he has done in 2 Chron. 34.3b-7 is to bring up earlier an equally abbreviated extract from the annalistic report, being convinced that even without knowledge of the Book of the Law Josiah would have already had inducement enough for the measures here reported. In doing so, Chr. evidently hit the historical nail on the head, but this was based on no more than his own, quite intelligible, considerations. This fact cannot therefore be adduced as an argument in favour of the view that for Josiah's reform he had

at his disposal another old and authentic source besides the book of Kings.

9. The only point which Chr. could use in working this out was the observation in 1 Kgs 15.23b that Asa 'was diseased in his feet in the time of his old age'.

10. We should regard the period of ten days which Chr. set aside for the formation of the mixed marriages commission (Ezra 10.9, 16) in a similar light.

11. Chr. was not particularly consistent in this matter either; thus at 2 Chron. 18.2 he replaced the specific chronological indicator of 1 Kgs 22.2a with a completely vague transitional formula, no doubt doing so because in his version it followed on from something different than in Kings.

12. Chr. follows basically the same procedure when he goes his own way to give vivid and concrete shape to the account of the handling of the mixed marriage affair in Ezra 9–10 and Ezra's reading of the Law in Nehemiah 8–10.

13. In the original text the name of another town was mentioned here.

14. On this, cf. Noth 1937: 40ff.

15. The use of Hamath as a territorial designation is also to be explained in terms of Chr.'s own day, because again it must be referring to the province of Hamath.—It is possible that the addition of vv. 16 + 17aα to 1 Kings 9 (see Noth 1981, p. 129, n. 54) was not yet present in the text which Chr. was following; Chr. selected at random only some of the towns named in the list in vv. 15b + 17aβb-18. Amongst these he selected Tadmor in particular because he thought it appropriate to pass some special comment on this name.

16. They do not need to be presented here in detail; the following passages are involved: 1 Chron. 15.11; 2 Chron. 17.7, 8; 20.14; 23.1; 24.20; 26.5, 11, 17, 20; 28.7, 12; 29.12-14; 31.10, 12-15; 34.8, 12; 35.8, 9; Ezra 8.16, 33; 10.2, 15; Neh. 8.4, 7; 9.4, 5; 12.33-36, 41, 42.

17. See below, pp. 100ff.

18. Von Rad 1934a.

19. Here Chr. has the prophet Shemaiah, mentioned in 1 Kgs 12.22 (= 2 Chron. 11.2), appear once more under Rehoboam.

20. The prophet who speaks here, Azariah the son of Oded, is otherwise unknown; his name is a common one; for the name of his father, see p. 156, n. 11 above.

21. In both of these passages Chr. has made use of the prophet Jehu the son of Hanani from 1 Kgs 16.1, 7 (12); see above, p. 156, n. 11.

22. The prophet Eliezer the son of Dodavahu, about whom Chr. knows enough also to be able to give Mareshah as his place of origin, is otherwise unknown. His name is not particularly common, however, and Chr. probably knew of him from some local tradition.

23. For the name Oded, see p. 156, n. 11 above.

## Notes to Chapter 18
### The Historical Presuppositions

1. Quite rightly nobody has ever doubted that Chr. should be located in Judaea and not somewhere in the Diaspora.

2. For Chr.'s assessment of the historical situation of the post-exilic community, see p. 105 below.

3. The formulaic use of this expression is not in itself sufficient to enable us to say what exactly Chr. understood 'the Law of Moses' to contain. Nor can we learn anything certain about what Chr. considered to be the content of the law which Ezra read and which in his view can have been none other than what he elsewhere calls 'the Law of Moses' (cf. Ezra 7.6). Though we might have turned to Neh. 10.31ff. for guidance, its dependence on Neh. 13.4ff. leaves the issue uncertain. We may well consider it probable that he had in mind the completed Pentateuch as then known to him; however, should anyone insist on maintaining that Chr. intended a collection of laws of unknown character but still separate from the Pentateuch, we should not be in a position decisively to refute him.

4. It is true that at Josh. 3.4, 6 and 1 Kgs 8.1ff. Dtr. had already introduced the priests as the bearers of the ark (he did not yet know of the Levites as a special class of minor clergy); however, he was not yet so dominated by the viewpoint of the strict observance of the holy that he could not take over unchanged the ancient story of the transfer of the ark (2 Sam. 6.1ff).

5. It was shown above on pp. 31ff. that the long lists of Levites, singers and the like which now appear in the traditional form of the Chronicler's work were secondary additions. There thus does not remain too much material on which to base arguments in favour of Chr.'s special Levitical interests, and what does remain can be explained quite naturally as an expression of the general conception in Chr.'s own time.

6. *Ant.* 7.2 (Niese §302).

7. Recently Abel (1935) has treated this passage from Josephus in detail. Although on this basis he seeks to rescue as historical as much as he possibly can, he nevertheless has to concede a long list of anachronisms. It was perhaps not necessary for him to include the character of Sanballat amongst these anachronisms, however, because he could refer to an historical person distinct from Nehemiah's contemporary (cf. Alt 1935: 107).

8. Cf. already Hag. 2.10-14, and later on Neh. 2.19ff. etc.

9. Alt (1935: 107ff.) has adduced the arguments which support this conclusion.

10. Cf. Bickerman 1938: 164ff.

11. So correctly Alt 1935: 109.

12. It must be assumed, therefore, that the tradition (if it can be so called)

which lies behind Josephus' story dates the start of the Gerizim cult somewhat prematurely when it links it with Alexander himself, but this sort of thing often happens in such cases. The fact that it referes to preparations for the founding of the cult starting even before Alexander appeared can hardly be accepted, with Alt (1935: 107), as historical evidence for the building of the sanctuary on Mt Gerizim as early as the late Persian period.

13. This territory was only designated as a separate province (and then only as a temporary measure at first) under Nehemiah; its extent may be gathered from Neh. 3.1-32.

14. This applies above all to the southern part of this hill-country (cf. Alt 1935: 100ff.); anyway, the *city* of Samaria with its associated territory was in a special position since it had been turned into a Macedonian military colony by Perdiccas. The town of Shechem, Gerizim's neighbour, provided the focus for the Samaritan cult community.

15. Cf. Alt 1939: 67ff., 73ff.

### Notes to Chapter 19
### The Attitude Towards the Inherited Traditions

1. On this, cf. Kropat 1909.

2. Cases of this have been collected above at p. 157, n. 18.

3. In any case, so far as scholarship goes Chr. is at a distinct disadvantage vis-à-vis Dtr. because we still have direct access to a good portion of his sources and are therefore in a position to examine him with complete precision. This is not the case with Dtr., since we can only reconstruct his sources from his work itself.

4. See below, p. 105.

5. A detail of this sort is the retention of *'ôd* at 1 Chron. 14.3 in dependence upon 2 Sam. 5.13, even though it refers back to 2 Sam. 3.2-5, which Chr. had omitted.

6. Equally at 2 Chron. 7.10 he passed over the sentence 'and they (the people) blessed the king' (1 Kgs 8.66); with his idiosyncratic inconsistency, however, he adopted without hesitation the remark of 2 Sam. 6.18b about David blessing the people (1 Chron. 16.2b).

7. Although Noth twice refers to 'David' in this sentence, the context indicates that this was a slip on his part for 'Solomon'.—Tr.

8. The omission at 1 Chron. 19.16f. of the statement in 2 Sam. 10.16f. about Helam, the site of a massacre, is probably due only to the fact that he did not realize that Helam was a place name and therefore did not understand it. In the account of Solomon's reign he omitted the section 1 Kgs 3.16–5.14 for the simple reason that it was of no importance to him.

9. By contrast he again inconsistently allowed Solomon's and the people's acts of sacrifice at the dedication of the temple (1 Kgs 8.62f.) to stand (2 Chron. 7.4f.), as he did David's sacrifice according to 2 Sam. 24.25 (= 1 Chron. 21.26).

10. Admittedly, at 1 Chron. 11.3 he took over unchanged the wording of his source (2 Sam. 5.3), according to which 'the elders anointed David king'.

11. We should scarcely include here the omission of the bulk of the Succession Narrative in David's reign; this was left out rather because it was not of importance for Chr.'s theme (so correctly Torrey 1910: 214, n. 5). There is material unfavourable to David in the account of the census which Chr. nevertheless took over because of its relevance to his theme.

12. See above, pp. 57ff.

13. He could refer for this to 2 Sam. 7.2 (= 1 Chron. 17.1). Like Dtr. (2 Sam. 7.13a=1 Chron. 17.12a), he thereby ignored the absolute nature of the rejection of temple-building in 2 Sam. 7.4-7 (= 1 Chron. 17.3-6). As is well known, Chr. explained the anomaly that David did not carry out the building himself by the excuse that this was not God's will since David had shed too much blood in his wars. In Chr.'s opinion this clearly impaired his cultic purity (1 Chron. 22.8; 28.3). Dtr. explained the situation in a similar manner, but with some differences (1 Kgs 5.17).

14. On this, see below p. 173, n. 18.

15. The similarity of Chr.'s procedure in the cases of David and Ezra may carry a certain weight as a further argument in favour of the view that Chr. was himself responsible for the Ezra narrative in Ezra 9-10 and Nehemiah 8-10, these being sections of the work whose authorship is disputed.

16. Chr. went even further than his *Vorlage* by commenting at 2 Chron. 3.1 that the site of the temple was 'Mount Moriah', a site taken from the traditional text of Gen. 22.2. This will have been a common inference in Chr.'s time.

17. It is possible that Chr. did not find Ezra 2.2 already present in his *Vorlage*, in which case he was free to give the list of those who returned whatever historical setting he chose.

18. Similar combinations are to be found in matters of detail. For instance, in 1 Chron 18.8b Chr. has Solomon use the bronze exacted as tribute from Hadadezer for the manufacture of various items of temple furnishing. Again at 2 Chron. 8.11b he gives a reason for the note about the movement of the daughter of Pharaoh to a house of her own (1 Kgs 9.24a), namely that a woman should not live in David's palace because of the proximity of the ark.

*Notes to Chapter 20*
*The Central Theological Ideas*

1. Von Rad 1930.

2. So von Rad 1930: 133.

3. He seems, however, to have regarded various other things appearing in the world as having a timeless validity; in particular he seems to have conceived of the 'Law of Moses' in this way (see pp. 83f. above).

4. At the same time Dtr. did, of course, also apply the doctrine to individuals, or at least to the kings, whose success was, for him, a yard-stick for their behaviour. Nonetheless, it must be conceded that the kings were representative of the whole and at the same time determined in a decisive way the (cultic) activities of the people.

5. Chr. thus represents an interpretation of the doctrine as it was formulated for the first time in Ezekiel 18.

6. Even von Rad (1930: 80ff., and especially p. 119) still holds this view.

7. See above p. 33 etc.

8. Cf. also pp. 79f. and 83f.

9. Monarchy and temple obviously belonged closely together for Chr. and their legitimacy was a matter of mutual dependence. Because of Deuteronomy, the temple was already of special significance to Dtr. as a legitimate sanctuary in contrast with the numerous country high places. It served Dtr. primarily, however, as the point at which the transgression of the law by most of the Judaean and Israelite kings became apparent, whereas for Chr. temple and the temple cult were of far more positive significance.

10. This opposition would become especially intelligible if, as was argued above on pp. 85ff., the Samaritan schism had only just become absolute with the founding of their own cult in Chr.'s own day. But even if we do not assume this chronological coincidence, Chr.'s opposition to the Samaritans would still stand because there had been tension between Jerusalem and Samaria throughout the whole of the post-exilic period. There is nothing to be said in favour of the suggestion that Chr.'s unnamed opposition was some cult of Yahweh which was established outside the borders of Palestine and which was regarded by Jerusalem as illegitimate, such as Elephantine. In that case Chr. could not have passed in silence over the conquest tradition with its associated concept of the promised land.

11. This was already quite rightly perceived by Torrey (1910: 208ff.).

12. Cf. von Rad 1930: 133.

13. Chr. painstakingly avoided making mention of the events of Moses' time. Whereas he admittedly referred at 2 Chron. 6.11 to God's covenant with the Israelites in dependence upon 1 Kgs 8.21, he characteristically passed over the reference there to the Exodus from Egypt. Moreover, 'the Law of Moses' was a fixed concept for him so that there was no longer any

need to give thought to the historical circumstances of its promulgation. Neh. 9.7ff. forms an exception.

14. The details are well treated by von Rad (1930: 122ff.).

15. A single detail shows the extent to which the kingdom, not the people, was at the forefront of his thought: there is a comment at 2 Kgs 8.19 that God would not destroy Judah; at 2 Chron. 21.7, however, he alters this to say that God would spare 'the dynasty of David'.

16. In an addition which derives from Chr. Solomon is designated at 2 Chron. 9.8 as 'Yahweh's king'.

17. In principle, Chr. had the Davidic dynasty rule over 'Israel', and he even regarded the state of Judah only as the surviving remnant of 'Israel' after the 'apostasy' of the other tribes; consequently, but not at all consistently, he frequently substituted the name 'Israel' where 'Judah' stood in his source without regard for the political significance of the names Judah and Israel.

18. That is why it was of such importance to him that the repatriated Judaeans should continue to be separate from the inhabitants who had remained in the land. That is also why when Ezra arrived in Jerusalem Chr. made him start with the regulating of the mixed marriages affair as a task of the utmost urgency.

19. As Chr. concluded from various statements in the sources which he took over, Gibeon was the legitimate site of Yahweh's cult before Jerusalem. Gibeon, however, also lay within the territory of the Judaeans who returned from exile (cf. Neh. 3.7) and had previously belonged to the territory of the Judaean kingdom. In Chr.'s view, therefore, the Samaritan cult could not be a continuation of some Gibeonite tradition either.

20. The passage can also be understood to mean that these pious people from the state of Israel simply came on regular pilgrimages to Jerusalem for sacrifice.

21. Cf. Alt 1935: 99f.

22. It is not easy to explain this association of Simeon with Ephraim and Manasseh. As it recurs again exactly at 2 Chron. 34.6, it is clearly not an accident or textual error. Did some kind of reflection on Genesis 34 lead Chr. to locate Simeon in the hill-country of Samaria (1 Chron. 4.28ff. being certainly a later addition)?

23. The strange story about the recruiting of mercenaries 'from Israel' (or from Ephraim, to be more exact) by the Judaean king Amaziah (2 Chron. 25.6-10, 13) could be included in this context. However, the origin of the substance of this story remains somewhat obscure.

24. In 2 Chron. 25.13 Chr. even speaks of 'the cities of Judah from Samaria as far as Beth-horon'. Evidently, therefore, he here attributes the whole of the southern part of the hill-country of Samaria to the state of Judah. Presumably Chr. did not have a precise and unified notion of the extent to which he assumed the Judaean territory stretched towards the

north.

25.  Cf. 1 Macc. 11.30ff. and Alt's comments on it (1935: 96ff.).

26.  Of course, in the context the period of Ezra/Nehemiah is being treated, but it went without saying that the judgment on it could apply, and was intended to apply, to the time of Chr. as well.

## NOTES TO THE APPENDIX

### Notes to Chapter 21
### The 'Hexateuch' in the Light of the Deuteronomistic Work

1.  The continuation of the sources of the 'Hexateuch' beyond the book of Joshua is certainly incompatible with our analysis of the work of Dtr. In any case, however, neither in detail nor as a whole can such a hypothesis be cogently substantiated and probability tells strongly against it. Our literary-critical treatment of Dtr. has already included an implicit refutation of it, so that there is no need to deal with it again separately.

2.  See Noth 1981: 34-35.

3.  It is not necessary to deal with the ups and downs of 'Hexateuchal' criticism since the definitive and comprehensive work of Holzinger 1893. Of the numerous attempts which have been undertaken in the last half-century to challenge the almost canonical form of 'Hexateuchal' criticism, those which refuse to see the literary-critical problem are naturally of no value. Taken as a whole, moreover, those which only challenge the presence of one particular 'source' throughout the whole of the 'Hexateuch' do not seem to me to hold out the prospect of much progress either, however much they frequently include important and pertinent observations at individual points; this is because for Genesis, at least, the usual source divisions seem to me to be so self-evidently correct that they can scarcely be shaken. The issue therefore boils down to how much further one can really track down the sources of Genesis. The literary situation lying behind the Sinai pericope, strongly determined as it is by P, is so obviously different from that in Genesis that one is virtually compelled to offer a special explanation for this state of affairs. For this part of the 'Hexateuch', therefore, it is necessary in the first instance to proceed without regard for the results achieved on the basis of Genesis.

4.  For details, see Noth 1938: xiii and 107f.

5.  I may be permitted to observe in this connection that I reached this conclusion on the basis of a modest literary examination of the book of Joshua even before the existence of the work of Dtr. had come within my purview (see my commentary on Joshua, cited in the previous note). From many different quarters (cf. especially de Vaux 1938) the fact has been particularly emphasized and welcomed that my commentary on Joshua

isolated the book of Joshua from the 'Hexateuch'. At the time this was at most a by-product of the attempt to deal with the problems raised by the tradition-history of the book of Joshua.

6.   Not without some justification Beer (1941) found fault with my commentary on Joshua in that it involved a measure of uncertainty and lack of clarity in the purely negative establishment of a lack of connection between the ancient conquest tradition and the sources of the 'Hexateuch'. Nevertheless, in the exegesis of an individual book it is often not possible to get beyond the necessary task of primary analysis; the presentation of more comprehensive literary connections has then to be left to a separate investigation. To that extent the present work provides the necessary expansion of my exposition of Joshua.

7.   In the present context it will not be possible to deal with the problem of the 'Hexateuch' in its full extent; nor is this necessary. It will be sufficient to suggest various new ways of looking at the question.

## Notes to Chapter 22
### The Priestly Writing in the Book of Joshua

1.   Smend 1912: 289, 290 and 304f.

2.   Eissfeldt 1922: 69f. and 73f. Rudolph (1938: 177, 179f. and 202f.) has also recognized that the theory of Smend and Eissfeldt is correct.

3.   Because of the appearance in v. 16 of the expression $^{\alpha}r\hat{o}n\ h\bar{a}\,'\bar{e}d\hat{u}th$, which elsewhere is characteristic of P, one should also include this section here. Even von Rad (1934b: 145ff.) has overlooked it, despite the fact that he has again argued strongly for the presence of P in Joshua 1–12.

4.   So von Rad 1934b: 145.

5.   For other aspects of the analysis of Joshua 3–4 I must refer the reader to my commentary on Joshua, pp. 11ff.

6.   The word $q\bar{a}l\hat{u}y$ occurs elsewhere only in Lev. 2.14, and there it is in a quite different cultic context. The word $^{\alpha}b\bar{u}r$ = 'produce (of the land)' occurs in the whole Old Testament only in this passage (vv. 11 and 12).

7.   Two of these chronological notices were not even present in the *Vorlage* of the Septuagint. The repetitious note in v. 12b is presumably an addition; the most that can be said of it is that it is formulated in P's 'style'.

8.   The alternative explanation of this passage by Rudolph (1938: 179f.) seems less probable to me, since it starts out from the erroneous statement that the passage is in the 'style of P'. Nevertheless, it also leads to the conclusion that the passage cannot have been an element of an original P-narrative.

9.   For more precise detail, see my commentary on Joshua, pp. 29ff.

10.   This includes primarily the expression 'leaders of the congregation' in vv. 15b and 18. In this way P's characteristic word $'\bar{e}d\hat{a}$ (cf. Rost 1938: 38ff.) came into the context. The expression 'to all the congregation' at the start of

v. 19 will be an addition made under the influence of v. 18.

11. This latter position was the common assumption of the 'classical' form of 'Hexateuchal' criticism (cf. the charts in Holzinger 1893). It has been taken up afresh by von Rad (1934b: 148ff.) and modified by his hypothesis of two layers in P.

12. Von Rad too (1934b: 151) adduces 'linguistic usage' as the only argument in favour of an attribution to P.

13. I believe that I have been able to demonstrate this quite clearly in Noth 1935. The reconstruction of an example of this 'line of border points' may be found in Noth 1938: 58.

14. At a pinch, one might, therefore, give credence to Rudolph's theory (1938: 219ff.) that a portrayal of the tribal territories drawn up with the help of the boundary descriptions has been secondarily expanded by the addition of the lists of towns; but the matters discussed below also tell against this.

15. The redactor attempted to create the necessary space for which allowance was not made in the system of boundary descriptions by pushing back Benjamin's western border from the coast to the edge of the hill-country. In doing so, however, he was not able completely to avoid making Dan's territory, which was determined for him on the basis of a specific part of the list of towns which he inherited, intersect in an unsatisfactory manner with the northern border of Judah, which was determined by the system of boundary descriptions. This was an inevitable consequence of constructing the whole on the basis of two quite separate sources; the lists of towns originally had absolutely nothing to do with the tribal geography.

16. Cf. the stories of Samson and Judges 17–18.

17. For the details, which are often quite complicated, I may be permitted to refer to my discussions in *ZDPV* 58 (1935), pp. 185-255 and *Das Buch Josua* (1938), pp. 47-95; I am not aware of the need to make any substantial correction to what I have written there.

18. According to Alt's illuminating demonstration (Alt 1925), the town lists derive from the time of King Josiah. Consequently this can have happened at the end of the seventh century BC at the earliest.

19. There are two reasons for this unevenness. First, the town lists were only available for part of the tribal territories. More significantly, however, the provision of a consecutive text for the lists of fixed boundary points becomes steadily more sketchy, the greater the geographical separation becomes from the standpoint of the apparently Judaean redactor and the slighter his geographical knowledge evidently becomes in consequence.

20. Joshua 20 belongs within the framework of the Deuteronomistic work as an appendix to the section about the geography of the tribes; we shall deal more particularly with this chapter and with Josh. 21.1-42 below.

21. Von Rad (1934b: 148ff.) correctly observed the literary-critical significance of the framework. He overlooked, however, one of the layers of this framework—the one treated by us in what follows as the middle

layer.

22. There is no justification for emending the qal of *nḥl* in 19.49a into the pi'el (so Eissfeldt 1922: 283* and von Rad 1934b: 150, following Dillmann); the traditional wording can be translated as it stands.

23. The fact that the description of the southern border of Joseph in Josh. 16.1-3 comes in a far more summary form than that of the identical northern border of Benjamin in Josh. 18.12-14a gives a positive indication that the original order was Benjamin–Joseph.

24. Von Rad (1934b: 150) maintains that the composition of this framework is priestly. There is no evidence for this, however, other than the presupposition of his conviction that Joshua 13–19 belongs to P.

25. There is a theoretical possibility that at this stage the section about the tribal geography should be attributed to one of the older sources of the 'Hexateuch'; however, there is absolutely no positive indication of this. We ought, therefore, to draw the conclusion that, as was the case for the corpus of ancient narratives relating to the conquest, so this section too existed as an independent unit until it was taken up by Dtr. The town lists, at any rate, cannot have stood in one of the older sources of the 'Hexateuch'; they are too recent for that.

26. For the basic form of this passage, which has been expanded with subsequent additions, cf. Noth 1938: 79f. Apparently some additions were made to parts of this second-stage framework in dependence upon the oldest layer of the framework. They have 'Israelites' as their subject and use the qal of *ḥlq* for the verb (cf. 18.2); this is the case at 14.5 and also in 19.51b, where the qal of *ḥlq* probably stood originally. The remark about Joshua's inheritance in 19.49b-50 was initially added to the older note in v. 49a under the influence of Judg. 2.8-9 (see Noth: 1981 p. 102 n. 14). The whole was then rounded off by the addition of a new conclusion in v. 51b.

27. This is probably connected with the inclusion of various items of narrative (cf. Noth 1938: x).

28. In this connection it is of no importance that this inclusion was only made subsequently into the already completed work of Dtr., a fact that can be deduced from the secondary anticipation of Josh. 23.1b in 13.1a (cf. Noth 1981: 40f.).

29. Von Rad's suggested textual emendation (1934b: 148), which would turn the relative clause into an independent sentence, is completely without foundation. The fact that this verse is without doubt badly worded is due not to subsequent textual corruption but to the character of the second half of the verse as an addition. We should therefore think of the development of Josh. 14.1-5 happening as follows: the primary component was v. 1a (first stage); to this vv. 2bβ, 3a (5) were added at the second stage and v. 1b at the third. The remainder developed in a series of later successive additions; of these, the first was the reference to the number of the tribes (vv. 3b, 4a, linking on to v. 1b; alternatively this might still belong to the third stage),

and then the comment about the lot (v. 2abα) and the addition of v. 4b with its reference to Josh. 21.1-42. (This is a somewhat different reconstruction from Noth 1938: 55f.)

30. 14.1b and 19.51a may well be dependent on Num. 34.16ff. (see below p. 125).

31. For the details cf. Noth 1938: 95ff.

32. The cities of refuge were only subsequently worked into this designation from Joshua 20; the town of Hebron was common to both of the designated groups.

33. For the post-exilic origin of the designation of the towns itself and for the development of the form of Josh. 21.1-42 which has come down to us, cf. Noth 1938: 97ff.

34. Cf. Steuernagel 1912: 283; Smend 1912: 313; Eissfeldt 1922: 75. Only von Rad (1934b: 245f.) has returned to ascribing the passage to P; indeed, he regards it as belonging to his hypothetical more recent layer of P ($P^B$), but without giving any reasons for this.

35. Josh. 22.7f. has been inserted later as a connection between Josh. 22.1-6 and 22.9ff.

36. Not even von Rad (1934b: 159f.) ascribes this passage to P. He postulates, however, a priestly report as its basis, even though this can no longer be traced in detail. But there is absolutely no reason for this.

### Notes to Chapter 23
### *The Priestly Writing in Num. 10-36 and Deut. 31-34*

1. The agreement between the two passages is so extensive that we cannot for one moment entertain von Rad's idea (1934b: 127f.) of two parallel but independent P-passages. The conclusion that a particular paragraph has been secondarily repeated elsewhere cannot be circumvented, as von Rad seeks to do, by the argument that this cannot be established elsewhere as the redactor's habit. In the first place, 'the redactor' was confronted by a peculiar and unique circumstance in the closing portion of the Pentateuch, and in addition to this 'the redactor' is hardly to be regarded as a single figure.

2. It is mostly a question of relatively insignificant expansions in wording. The specification of the place involved has been expanded in v. 49 as in Deut. 34.1, and v. 52 has been added by way of a free composition with Deut. 3.23ff. etc. in mind.

3. The unevennesses in this passage are scarcely sufficient to prove the presence of two parallel but independent narratives (so von Rad 1934b: 128ff.); it is more natural to explain vv. 19, 21a and the last two words of v. 23 as parts of a later 'clerical' reworking in connection with v. 22b.

4. Deut. 1.38 and 3.21f. are additions to the work of Dtr., as is Deut.

31.3b.

5. For the literary-critical analysis of Deuteronomy 31, cf. Noth 1981: 34f.

6. We can ignore Num. 33.1-49 from the outset. This is one of the latest parts of the Pentateuch (cf. Noth 1940/41: 171f.). It has admittedly been inserted at a suitable point following the account of the division of the land in Transjordan, but it interrrupts the original connection between Numbers 32 and Num. 33.50ff.

7. The casuistic-type instructions for the application of the laws of asylum in Num. 35.16-34 are generally correctly reckoned to be a secondary accretion to Num. 35.9-15.

8. For the details, cf. Noth 1935: 186-89.

9. Dan's settlement in the extreme north-east (cf. the Samson stories and Judges 17-18) was not yet a consideration in the time of Joshua.

10. Elliger (1936: 34ff.) has devoted a special study to the question of the border described in Num. 34.7b-11 in which he tries to show that it relates to the 'northern border of the kingdom of David' which ran along the latitude of the northern ends of the Lebanon and Antilebanon. He chooses as his starting point the incontrovertible identification of the place-name Zedad in Num. 34.8 and the present day ṣadad at the north-eastern end of the Antilebanon. This identification, however, which is the only really firm point in his demonstration, is insufficient by itself to carry the full weight of the thesis which is laid upon it. Nor is it any match for the fact that, from a literary point of view, the border of Num. 34.7b-11 can *only* be attributed to the system of the Israelite *tribal* boundaries. This conclusion follows in particular, and without any doubt, from the description of the corresponding southern boundary in Num. 34.3b-5. Moreover, even an 'ideal' tribal boundary would hardly have extended so far towards the north. Numbers 34, however, has nothing to do with the borders of David's kingdom either according to the tradition which has reached us or according to the actual facts of the case. The fact that in Ezek. 48.1 part of the boundary described in Num. 34.7b-11 is explicitly used as a boundary of the tribe of Dan may have some validity as an argument in favour of the assumption spoken of above, even though otherwise the blueprint for the new division of the land to the west of the Jordan (especially as regards the southern part of the country) takes curiously little account of the historical dwelling-places of the tribes. On the position of Lebo-Hamath, which crops up as a fixed border point in this context, I have nothing further to add to my remarks in 1935: 242ff. and 1937: 50f.

11. The same verb also intrudes into the framework (and hence once again not the basic material) of this section via the corrupt first word of v. 10. It was therefore used once more in the first heading following vv. 7b-8a.

12. There is actually no reference to fixed border points in this passage. Only 'the great sea' is mentioned, in connection with which there was

probably originally a reference only to 'the mountains' (so already Noth 1935: 247, n. 1). This is therefore certainly an addition to the boundary description. Its intention was to extend the boundary of the tribe of Dan, which did not reach the sea, so as to achieve a fully consistent overall boundary.

13. For the details, see Noth 1935: 189ff.

14. Cf. Noth 1935: 190-92.

15. In Ezek. 47.15ff. and 48.1 we do in fact have an example of a use of the system of fixed boundary points which is independent of Joshua 13ff. Here, the connecting text is phrased quite differently, besides being very meagre, and furthermore the system of fixed boundary points has been subsequently expanded in a completely different manner (cf. Noth 1935: 239ff.).

16. In Numbers 34 a new framework has been supplied with regard to the present new context. This has overlaid, if not completely obliterated, the original framework so that the latter can no longer be reconstructed. Presumably there was once a connection with Josh. 14.1a, 2bβ and 3a along the lines of 'This was the land which still remained for the Israelites to divide up (after the transjordanian tribes had already taken their share)'.

17. Verses 52, 53, 55 and 56 are generally explained as secondary; the usual reason for this is that with their Deuteronomic style they cannot have stood originally in a P-passage. This argument, of course, is invalid if the whole of Num. 33.50-56 is but a prologue to the border description which derives from Dtr.; despite this, these verses give the impression of being additions in the present context. With v. 54 compare in addition Num. 26.54, and with v. 55 compare Josh. 23.13.

18. The use here of the hithpa'el of *nḥl* (twice in v. 54) falls midway between the use of the qal in the old formulation of Josh. 14.1a; 19.49a and the pi'el of the late additions in Josh. 14.1b and 19.51a.

19. The hithpa'el of *nḥl* reappears here.

20. In the postscript (v. 29b) the pi'el of *nḥl* is used, and this is characteristic of the passages in Joshua just mentioned. Accordingly, in vv. 17 and 18 we should vocalize as pi'el rather than as the qal of the traditional text.

21. By comparison with the passages in Joshua this is possibly a more primitive characteristic; the tribes are arranged in geographical order in Num. 34.19-28, and for the Galilean tribes it is clear that the order of Joshua 19 provided the pattern.

22. On Num. 35.16-34 see above p. 179, n. 7.

23. See above, pp. 118.

24. The first formulation of the purpose of the cities of refuge in Num. 35.11b (*wᵉnās šāmmâ rōṣēaḥ*) admittedly follows the form of expression which is characteristic of Deuteronomy 19 (cf. vv. 3 and 4). The basis for all OT information about the cities of refuge is thus certainly Deuteronomic; nowhere do we find a fully independent 'priestly' treatment of this

institution. All we have are some expansions on this theme which were written in the style of the post-exilic period and which were added to Joshua 20 and to the passage which has Joshua 20 in view, namely Num. 35.9-15 (and subsequently also Num. 35.16-34).

25. There is no good reason to explain this paragraph as an addition (so de Vaux 1941: 16). The fact that Numbers 32 speaks first of Gad and Reuben does not preclude the possibility of its speaking subsequently of Manasseh as well.

26. Admittedly the clan of Nobah in v. 42 is not explicitly associated with Manasseh; v. 42 looks as though it has been added here as an appendix because of its similarity of theme. By 'Gilead' in v. 39 is certainly meant the land to the north of the Jabbok (cf. Noth 1941: 72ff.), an area in which on other grounds we should in any case locate Machir. On the neighbouring territory of Jair, cf. Noth 1941: 78ff.; and for a suggestion about the location of the clan of Nobah, cf. *ibid.*, pp. 80f.

27. Here too 'Gilead' refers to the land north of the Jabbok.

28. There is no obvious reason for regarding v. 40 as an isolated addition rather than as a component of another literary layer.

29. On the use of the name 'Amorite' as an indication of source, cf. Noth 1940/41: 182ff.

30. In the present context not much of significance hangs on these particular designations; they could only be verified by means of a comprehensive investigation into the older sources.

31. Several additions have subsequently been slotted in between these verses, as the otherwise unnecessary repetition of the verb at the start of v. 5 demonstrates. First came v. 4, which is phrased in the 'style' of P, and which still retains the singular form of address and depends on v. 1, then the introduction of Eleazar the priest and the *neśî'îm* in v. 2bβ, and finally the enumeration of various place names, which was borrowed somewhat arbitrarily from vv. 34-38 and was included here without any introduction.

32. This is the order in which these two tribes are presented here.

33. As far as this narrative layer is concerned it seems that no reason was given to explain why Gad and Reuben wanted and were allowed to remain in Transjordan.

34. This narrative layer is thus represented here by only a few brief sentences; but it will hardly have included much more. The only point that we miss is a comment to the effect that Moses did actually 'give' the Gadites and Reubenites the land which they wanted; it must have fallen victim to the secondary expansions of the chapter. The expression 'this land' must refer to something that has been related earlier; it may be related to the setting of the Balaam story or of the scene in Num. 25.1-5.

35. This is the order here, in contrast to vv. 2ff.

36. The explanation of these two names in the present context is difficult to determine and requires special investigation.

37.   In this narrative layer, too, the only item that is missing is a note about the execution of the decision of v. 16a. As the word 'to him' was most probably included only at the time when the sources were amalgamated, it is possible that Moses was not referred to in this layer at all but that Reuben and Gad simply explained their decision to the assembled tribes.

38.   For *ḥᵃmušîm* (as we should read here), compare Josh 1.14 and 4.12 (Dtr.); for marching out 'in front of the Israelites', compare Deut. 3.18 and Josh. 1.14 (Dtr.). As well as the language, the content of v. 17 also bespeaks dependence on Dtr.; an important aspect of Dtr.'s schematic presentation of the conquest was precisely the continuing involvement of the Transjordanians in the common enterprise. It is thus no wonder that Dtr.'s simple and clear presentation of the conquest should have given rise to a subsequent expansion of the older material in Numbers 32 on precisely this matter. Since v. 17 specifies that the concern of the Transjordanians was the accommodation of the little children rather than their herds of cattle, v. 16b could be attributed to the same expansion as v. 17.

39.   This verse cannot be later than vv. 20-23 (so Rudolph 1938: 133f.) because it neither presupposes nor joins on to it. Rather, it has been subsequently deprived of its introduction by this passage and detached from its original context. It belongs with vv. 16b and 17 (the focus of attention is on the children rather than the cattle).

40.   The enumeration of the tribes in v. 33 is obviously an addition in line with the familiar schema of Dtr. The original reference was to Gad and Reuben alone; then, of course, the mention here of Og signifies an inaccuracy brought about by the usual Deuteronomistic coupling of Sihon and Og. The reference to Sihon as 'King of the Amorites' shows that v. 33 is dependent on Dtr. but that it is at the same time secondary by comparison with Dtr. (on this cf. Noth 1940/41: 184 and 188, n. 1).

41.   The question of the relationship between Num. 32.34-38 and Josh. 13.15ff. is extremely difficult to answer in detail even though there can be no doubt that a close literary relationship does exist and that Numbers 32 is secondary by comparison with Joshua 13. It is precisely the fact that Moses seems to be out of place in Joshua 13 as the one responsible for apportioning the cultivated land in Transjordan because he had died long since that prevents us from following von Rad (1934b: 134ff. and 240f.) in his assumption that its original setting was in connection with Numbers 32. —Who would have transposed Josh. 13.15ff. secondarily to its present inappropriate setting? On the other hand, it would have been an obvious move secondarily to anticipate the theme of Josh. 13.15ff. by including it earlier at what seemed to be an appropriate place. The traditional setting of Joshua 13 can be explained simply enough: the section about the geography of the tribes was a unity from the very first and could not thereafter be torn apart when it was incorporated into the work of Dtr. It was thus so arranged that the allocation of the territory in Transjordan stood at the start, by way

of a resumption. The listing of the cities in Num. 32.34-38 cannot be separated from Josh. 13.17b + 19a (v. 18 was added subsequently in accordance with 21.36f.), for it is certainly no coincidence that the first name and the last three names coincide in both cases (the name of Nebo in Num. 32.38 is lacking in the original Septuagint). The whole list of names must originally have stood in Josh. 13.17-19 and only subsequently was its middle section lost by textual corruption. On the other hand several names in Numbers 32 seem to have come in secondarily: the lack of the accusative particle in front of Jogbehah (v. 35) indicates that this name is an addition, whilst the two following names (v. 36a) were included secondarily in accordance with Josh. 13.27. The way in which Numbers 32 deviates so curiously from Joshua 13 in the matter of the division of the cities between the two tribes seems to me to have been carried out subsequently in an arbitrary manner: of the *original* listing exactly the first half was attributed to Gad (who always appears in the first position in Num. 32.2ff.) and the second half to Reuben. Such an arbitrary procedure should not cause any surprise in the case of the kind of editor who was responsible for Num. 32.33-38.

42.   The use of the hithpa'el of *nḥl* establishes a link with that part of Num. *33.50-34.29 (33.54; 34.13) which does *not* belong to P.

43.   Holzinger (1903: 153) tried to avoid this difficulty by suggesting that, in complete contrast with the usual procedure in the redaction of the Pentateuch, some important elements of the P-narrative had been left out of Numbers 32. This proposal is devoid of probability and simply serves as an escape from the recognition of the dependence of vv. 18 and 19 on v. 17.

44.   There are linguistic links with the third layer of the framework of Joshua 13ff.; compare the first words of v. 22 with Josh. 18.1b.

45.   Verse 17 is echoed by the use of the niph'al of *ḥlṣ* in v. 20 (these are the only two places in the OT where this niph'al is used, since presumably Num. 31.3 is the result of a mistake in the vocalization); the secondary nature of the link is apparent from the following words, 'before Yahweh' (instead of 'before the Israelites', v. 17).

46.   In v. 28 we find the commission of Josh. 14.1b, 19.51a and 21.1; with v. 29aβ compare again Josh. 18.1b.

47.   Smend 1912: 236; our earlier remarks mean that we must dissociate ourselves from his argument that P spoke of the apportionment of land in Transjordan.

48.   Eissfeldt 1922: 65.

49.   Rudolph too (1938: 131f.) accepts this view without hesitation.

50.   The source P was a narrative work at the centre of which stood the constitution of the national and cultic community at Sinai. The laws were only loosely embedded in the historical narrative by the use of introductory formulae. It is scarcely possible now to decide with any certainty to what extent these laws were included in P or to what extent they were added at the stage of the compilation of the Pentateuch.

51. As a corrective to Num. 27.1-11, Numbers 36 would still have to be explained as secondary even if Num. 27.1-11 were ascribed to P (on which cf. p. 131 below).

52. Wellhausen 1899: 113; Holzinger 1903: 148ff.; Steuernagel 1912: 170; Smend 1912: 248; likewise Rudolph 1938: 130, n. 3.

53. Von Rad (1934b: 133) rightly rejects as being without foundation the view that v. 2b should be deleted (so, for instance, Holzinger 1903: 150). I do not quite understand, however, how he can then use this conclusion to argue that it *favours* the view that Num. 31.1-12 belonged to the basic text of P.

54. Noth 1940/41: 161ff.

55. Wellhausen 1899: 111f. In his reconstruction of this introduction which he presumed had been lost, Wellhausen made use of Num. 31.8,16 and Josh. 13.22. None of this, however, belonged to the original P-narrative.

56. Holzinger 1903: 127.

57. Cf. Holzinger 1903.

58. Rudolph (1938: 131) correctly rejects this elimination. He ascribes the whole passage to P, but fails to mention the linguistic arguments which tell against this conclusion.

59. It is quite obvious that the Levitical genealogy in vv. 57-63 is a later addition (besides which it lacks unity even within itself). The same is true of the remark in vv. 64-65 about the relationship of the census in Numbers 26 to that in Numbers 1.

60. Cf. Noth 1930: 122ff.

61. Von Rad (1934b: 121ff.) has correctly recognized that vv. 52-56 are not a unity from a literary point of view, but his analysis of them hardly hits the nail on the head: he implausibly postulates a secondary removal of the original conclusion of Num. 1.20-47 to Numbers 26. It is much more likely that vv. 52-54 belong together as the basic element in the text (v. 54 cannot possibly be separated from the last two words of v. 53). They give a clear explanation of the purpose of the census, namely that the future tribal territories are to be apportioned according to the numerical size of each of the tribes. Verses 55-56 then follow as an addition, introduced by the corrective or limiting particle *'ak* (von Rad translates this word incorrectly by 'and indeed'). They differ from the foregoing by insisting that the tribal territories should be decided by lot, a thought which appears first in a Deuteronomistic context at Josh. 18.6 (8, 10). This approach cannot be harmonized with the idea of apportioning the tribal territories by numerical size, despite the comment of Num. 26.56 which by hook or by crook combines both *modi procedendi* into one.

62. Holzinger 1903: 133; Steuernagel 1912: 169.

63. This conclusion also follows from the fact that Num. 34.54 is clearly dependent on Num. 26.52-56 in its combined state. This can be seen from the close fusion of the wording of Num. 26.54 on the one hand with a reference to the casting of lots on the other.

64. The passage about the arrangement of the camp in vv. 13-28 is correctly recognized as an addition.

65. There is general agreement regarding the separation of P in these two chapters apart from a few matters of detail which are of no consequence here.

66. Thus even P had to say in its introduction (13.2) that it was the land whose future possession had been promised that was to be reconnoitred.

67. This point derives from the fact that this was originally a Calebite tradition. It was emphasized appropriately by Dtr. at Josh. 14.6aβb-14. Without this point Caleb's role in the story lacks motivation. P simply took it over from the older tradition but at the same time he altered the original sense of the story by placing Joshua alongside Caleb. In so doing he had Joshua's role in Num. 27.15-23 and Deut. 34.9 in mind. These latter passages serve to demonstrate, however, that in mentioning Joshua he did not necessarily include any thought of the future conquest.

68. This stood in the older sources at 14.23, a verse which should be expanded with the Septuagint (cf. Smend 1912: 197), and it was then given expression especially by Dtr. in his version of the spies story (Deut. 1.39aβb).

69. This passage too has some secondary elements, for instance v. 28, and certainly also v. 34 with its address to the spies (on this, cf. von Rad 1934b: 107f.); but these are details of no great importance here.

70. Being a collection of all sorts of legal regulations, Numbers 15 does not belong to the P-narrative. This conclusion includes vv. 32-36, since it is a narrative told by way of illustration only.

71. So, correctly, von Rad (1934b: 116f.), Rudolph (1938: 277), *et al.*

72. Once again Numbers 19 with its legal content has nothing to do with the P-narrative.

73. Neither the complex of secondary items in Num. 25.6–27.11 nor that in Numbers 32-35 (36) is attached from a literary perspective to the P-narrative as such. Rather in each case they are joined to an item from the older sources which has been worked into the combined narrative.

74. This applies to the stage *before* the work of Dtr. was brought into play. The successive phases in the building up of the complex in Num. 25.6–27.11 are to be attributed to this stage, as well, presumably, as the introduction of Numbers 31.

75. To this stage belongs the complex in Numbers 32-36 which developed in various successive steps and which is joined on to a few verses of the older text in Numbers 32. Num. 14.30-33 and 21.33-35 may also have come in at this stage.

76. For clarification, cf. the diagrammatic summary on p. 148 below.

1. On Num. 27.15-23 and Deut. 34.9 see above pp. 121f., and on Num. 13-14 see above p. 132.

2. Elsewhere, too, P had traditions at his disposal which are otherwise unknown to us. Since this is the only place where Mount Hor is mentioned in an original context (the secondary occurrences in Num. 21.4, 33.37ff., and Deut. 32.50 being dependent upon it), there is no way in which the question of its location can be answered.

3. That is why it does not seem to me to be at all promising when, for instance, Löhr (1924) sets out to answer the question of the existence of P solely on the basis of Genesis.

4. On the significance of J for the development of this tradition cf. von Rad 1938: esp. pp. 46ff. (= 1966: 50ff.).

5. Von Rad 1934b: 175.

6. Wellhausen 1899: 1.

7. The covenant concept no longer played any very decisive role for P (cf. Noth 1940: 76f. =1966: 91f.); the covenant with Abraham was a datum of tradition (Genesis 15) and he introduced the story of the covenant with Noah into his presentation by way of a free composition based on some such tradition as Gen. 8.21f. Precisely at Sinai, however, where the history of God's covenant was originally rooted, P no longer knows of any covenant ratification.

8. From the very first this history belonged inseparably with that of the stay in Egypt and the Exodus from Egypt (cf. von Rad 1938: 3ff. =1966: 3ff.).

9. As a conclusion to the Sinai narrative alone the stories of the death of Aaron and Moses would, of course, have been very suitable. But P pushed the start of his narrative much further back than that.

10. We can see how little he was concerned for an historical understanding of the statutes and ordinances from the fact that he associated the law about ritual slaughter with Noah and the instructions for circumcision with Abraham even though he obviously intended both laws to be binding on the Israelite community.

11. The reason why he included the stories of the spies and of Korah first is simply that he was working in dependence upon inherited tradition. He could have quite easily done without the spies story. The story about Korah, however, enabled him at least to air in historical guise a number of questions of importance for his own time.

12. This latter point, of course, applies only to the original text. Later on Deut. 34.10-12 was attached to the end as an addition. Its aim was to correct Deut. 18.15 in the light of Exod. 33.11.

13. This conclusion is not contradicted by the possibility, which will be

discussed on p. 140 below, that a few scattered remnants of them could have been preserved as haphazard blocks of material in Joshua 1–Judges 1. In no case is there any question of these being elements of a continuous narrative thread which have been preserved.

14. I may be permitted to point out once again that I arrived at this insight solely on the basis of an exegesis of the book of Joshua (cf. Noth 1938: xiii). At that time I had no idea of the more comprehensive literary-critical theories which I have developed here.

15. Cf. von Rad 1938: esp. pp. 3ff. (= 1966: 3ff.).

16. This verse is now textually corrupt; for its probable original shape, see n. 68 to Chapter 23 above.

### Notes to Chapter 25
*The Pentateuch and the Deuteronomistic History*

1. In the case of the Pentateuchal narrative about the death of Moses, it is natural to suppose that it represents a compilation of the various sources. However in the text of Deuteronomy 34 as we have it there is no certain trace of the older sources (see the next note). Either these are victims of the losses which the Pentateuchal narrative suffered when it was combined with Dtr., or the Pentateuchal redactor's preference for P once again resulted here in the total suppression of the older sources.

2. In the analysis of Deuteronomy 34 I can only express complete agreement with Steuernagel (1923). Only under pressure from the presupposition that the older sources *must* be represented in Deuteronomy 34 could one doubt the purely Deuteronomistic origin of vv. 4–6 (on v. 4a, cf. Deut. 6.10; also 9.5; 29.12; 30.20; on v. 4b, cf. Deut. 3.27; for Moses as 'the servant of the Lord' [v. 5], cf. also Josh. 1.1; the place-names in v. 6 come otherwise only at Deut. 3.29 and 4.46 [on Num. 21.20, cf. Noth 1940/41: 178]). Verse 1 from the reference to 'the top of Pisgah' (otherwise only at Deut. 3.27 as the site of Moses' death) onwards is equally Deuteronomistic. Since the detailed description of the promised land in vv. 1bβ–3 is certainly an explanatory addition, we may conclude that vv. 1aβbα + 4–6 constitute a consecutive passage from Dtr.

3. Namely the *'arbôth Mō'āb* (cf. Num. 22.1). The phrasing at the start of this verse may as well be compared with Deut. 3.27 as with Num. 27.12. 'Mount Nebo' comes nowhere else apart from here and Deut. 32.49, and in both cases it is poorly integrated into its context. It must therefore be a later addition, based on a particular opinion regarding the site of Moses' grave. In that case, the explanatory relative clause 'which is opposite Jericho', which also occurs word for word at Deut. 22.49, must be a gloss.

4. Dtr.'s own layout, of course, does not correspond with this subsequent division. The book of Samuel, in particular, is a very curious entity. In terms

of Dtr.'s historical periods, it belongs partly to the 'Judges' period and partly to the period of the kings. No doubt the high esteem in which the figure of Samuel was held played an important part in its being separated out. This division into 'books' cannot have taken place so very long after the amalgamation of Dtr. with the Pentateuch because it is already presupposed by the addition of the concluding appendixes to the books of Joshua, Judges and Samuel.

5. It was an obvious move to put Deuteronomy 33 immediately in front of Deuteronomy 34 because of the reference to the death of Moses in its heading. However, it is such a unique passage that it is hardly possible any longer to determine within which larger literary context it was first taken up or at what stage in the process of literary development this happened.

6. Deut. 31.16-22 is a completely secondary paragraph. It introduces a subsequent interruption into material which properly belongs together.

7. Because of the intervention of vv. 16-22 the impression is given that Moses is the subject of the first two verbs in v. 23. The continuation of the verse, however, as well as the link with v. 14aβ, shows that Yahweh is intended as the subject.

8. This theme once stood in the various separate sources, and it was therefore bound to crop up repeatedly in the combined narrative if there was to be no deletion. Consequently, there was no alternative but to understand each occurrence as presenting a different nuance or separate act within the course of a single event.

9. Apart from various stylistic elaborations, these expansions include primarily the introduction of 'Mount Nebo which is in the land of Moab, that is over against Jericho' in v. 49 (this is also repeated in Deut. 34.1 and is presumably the work of a supplementary editor) and the addition of v. 52, something quite natural in view of Deut. 34.4b etc. (v. 52bβ, moreover, is an even later addition to v. 52abα.

# BIBLIOGRAPHY

Abel, F.-M.
    1935    'Alexandre le Grand en Syrie et en Palestine', *RB* 44, pp. 42-61
Alt, A.
    1925    'Judas Gaue unter Josia', *PJB* 21, pp. 100-17=*Kleine Schriften zur Geschichte des Volkes Israels* 2 (1953), pp. 276-88
    1935    'Zur Geschichte der Grenze zwischen Judäa und Samaria', *PJB* 31, pp. 94-111=*Kleine Schriften* 2, pp. 346-62
    1939    'Galiläische Probleme. 5. Die Umgestaltung Galiläas durch die Hasmonäer', *PJB* 35, pp. 64-82=*Kleine Schriften* 2, pp. 407-23
Baumgartner, W.
    1927    'Das Aramäische im Buche Daniel', *ZAW* 45, pp. 81-133 = *Zum Alten Testament und seiner Umwelt* (1959), pp. 68-123
Beer, G.
    1941    Review of Noth 1938, *TLZ* 66, pp. 78-79
Benzinger, I.
    1901    *Die Bücher der Chronik* (Kurzer Hand-Commentar zum Alten Testament)
Beyer, G.
    1931    'Beiträge zur Territorialgeschichte von Südwestpalästina im Altertum. 1. Das Festungssystem Rehabeams', *ZDPV* 54, pp. 113-34
Bickerman, E.J.
    1938    *Institutions des Séleucides* (Bibl. archéol. et hist. 26)
Driver, S.R.
    1913    *Introduction to the Literature of the Old Testament*, 9th edition (Noth himself cited J.W. Rothstein's 1896 German translation of the 5th edn [1894] of this work)
Eissfeldt, O.
    1922    *Hexateuch-Synopse*
    1934    *Einleitung in das Alte Testament, unter Einschluss der Apokryphen und Pseudepigraphen: Entstehungsgeschichte des Alten Testaments* (ET of the 3rd edn, and hence taking account of Noth's work, *The Old Testament: an Introduction* [1966])
Elliger, K.
    1935    'Die dreissig Helden Davids', *PJB* 31, pp. 29-75=*Kleine Schriften zum Alten Testament* (edited by H. Gese and O. Kaiser, 1966), pp. 72-118
    1936    'Die Nordgrenze des Reiches Davids', *PJB* 32, pp. 34-73
Gadd, C.J.
    1923    *The Fall of Nineveh: the newly discovered Babylonian Chronicle, no. 21,901, in the British Museum*
Galling, K.
    1937    'Der Tempelschatz nach Berichten und Urkunden im Buche Esra', *ZDPV* 60, pp. 177-83 (for a revised version of this study, cf. 'Das Protokoll über die Rückgabe der Tempelgeräte', in *Studien zur*

*Geschichte Israels im persischen Zeitalter* [1964], pp. 78-88)

Goettsberger, J.
1939    *Die Bücher der Chronik oder Paralipomenon* (Die heilige Schrift des Alten Testaments)

Gray, G.B.
1896    *Studies in Hebrew Proper Names*

Hjelt, A.
1925    'Die Chronik Nabopolassars und der syrische Feldzug Nechos', in K. Budde (ed.), *Vom Alten Testament. Karl Marti zum siebzigsten Geburtstag gewidmet* (BZAW, 41), pp. 142-47

Hölscher, G.
1923    'Die Bücher Esra und Nehemia', in E. Kautzsch, *Die heilige Schrift des Alten Testaments* II, 4th edn (edited by A. Bertholet), pp. 491-562

Holzinger, H.
1893    *Einleitung in den Hexateuch*
1903    *Numeri erklärt* (Kurzer Hand-Commentar zum Alten Testament)

Junge, E.
1937    *Der Wiederaufbau des Heerwesens des Reiches Juda unter Josia* (BWANT, 4/23)

Kittel, R.
1902    *Die Bücher der Chronik* (Handkommentar zum Alten Testament)
1918    *Zur Frage der Entstehung des Judentums* (Leipziger Reformationsprogramm)
1929    *Geschichte des Volkes Israel* III, 2

Klein, S.
1934    'Palästinisches im Jubiläenbuch', *ZDPV* 57, pp. 7-27

Klostermann, A.
1896    *Geschichte des Volkes Israel bis zur Restauration unter Esra und Nehemia*

Kropat, A.
1909    *Die Syntax des Autors der Chronik verglichen mit der seiner Quellen* (BZAW, 16)

Löhr, M.R.H.
1924    *Untersuchungen zum Hexateuchproblem. I. Der Priesterkodex in der Genesis* (BZAW, 38)

Noth, M.
1928    *Die israelitischen Personennamen im Rahmen der gemeinsemitischen Namengebung* (BWANT, 3/10)
1930    *Das System der zwölf Stämme Israels* (BWANT, 4/1)
1935    'Studien zu den historisch-geographischen Dokumenten des Josuabuches', *ZDPV* 58, pp. 185-255=*Aufsätze zur biblischen Landes- und Altertumskunde* I (edited by H.W. Wolff, 1971), pp. 229-80
1937    'Das Reich von Hamath als Grenznachbar des Reiches Israel', *PJB* 33, pp. 36-51=*Aufsätze zur biblischen Landes- und Altertumskunde* II (edited by H.W. Wolff, 1971), pp. 148-60
1938    *Das Buch Josua* (Handbuch zum Alten Testament. 2nd edition: 1953)
1940    *Die Gesetze im Pentateuch* (Schriften der Königsberger Gelehrten-Gesellschaft, Geisteswissenschaftliche Kl. XVII, 2) (ET 'The Laws in the Pentateuch: Their Assumptions and Meaning', in *The Laws in the*

*Pentateuch and other Studies* [1966])
1940/41  'Num. 21 als Glied der "Hexateuch"-Erzählung', *ZAW* 58, pp. 161-89=*Aufsätze* I, pp. 75-101
1941  'Beiträge zur Geschichte des Ostjordanlandes. 1. Das Land Gilead als Siedlungsgebiet israelitischer Sippen', *PJB* 37, pp. 50-101 = *Aufsätze* I, pp. 347-90
1981  *The Deuteronomistic History* (JSOT Supp, 15, ET of *Überlieferungsgeschichtliche Studien* [1943], pp. 1-110)

Oestreicher, Th.
1923  *Das Deuteronomische Grundgesetz*

Rad, G. von
1930  *Das Geschichtsbild des chronistischen Werkes* (BWANT, 4/3)
1934a  'Die levitische Predigt in den Büchern der Chronik', *Festschrift Otto Procksch*, pp. 113-24=*Gesammelte Studien zum Alten Testament* (1958), pp. 248-61 (ET 'The Levitical Sermon in *I* and *II Chronicles*', in *The Problem of the Hexateuch and Other Essays* [1966], pp. 267-80)
1934b  *Die Priesterschrift im Hexateuch* (BWANT, 4/13)
1938  *Das formgeschichtliche Problem des Hexateuchs* (BWANT, 4/26) (ET 'The Form Critical Problem of the Hexateuch', in *The Problem of the Hexateuch and Other Essays* [1966], pp. 1-78)

Rost, L.
1938  *Die Vorstufen von Kirche und Synagoge im Alten Testament; eine wortgeschichtliche Untersuchung* (BWANT, 4/24)

Rothstein, J.W.
1923  'Die Bücher der Chronik', in E. Kautzsch, *Die heilige Schrift des Alten Testaments* II, 4th edition (edited by A. Bertholet), pp. 562-677

Rothstein, J.W. and Hänel, J.
1927  *Das erste Buch der Chronik* (Kommentar zum Alten Testament)

Rudolph, W.
1938  *Der 'Elohist' von Exodus bis Josua* (BZAW, 68)

Schaeder, H.H.
1930a  *Esra der Schreiber* (Beiträge zur historischen Theologie, 5)
1930b  *Iranische Beiträge 1*

Smend, R.
1912  *Die Erzählung des Hexateuch, auf ihre Quellen untersucht*

Steuernagel, C.
1912  *Lehrbuch der Einleitung in das Alte Testament*
1923  *Das Deuteronomium übersetzt und erklärt*, 2nd edn (Göttinger Handkommentar zum Alten Testament)

Sukenik, E.L.
1931  'Funerary Tablet of Uzziah, King of Judah', *Palestine Exploration Fund Quarterly Statement for 1931*, pp. 217-21

Torrey, C.C.
1896  *The Composition and Historical Value of Ezra-Nehemiah* (BZAW, 2)
1910  *Ezra Studies*

Vaux, R. de
1938  Review of Noth 1938, *RB* 47, pp. 462-64
1941  'Notes d'histoire et de topographie transjordaniennes', *Vivre et Penser* 1 (= *RB* 50), pp. 16-47

Wellhausen, J.
1899  *Die Composition des Hexateuchs*, 3rd edn

# INDEX

## Index of Principal References

# Index of Authors

# JOURNAL FOR THE STUDY OF THE OLD TESTAMENT

## Supplement Series

* Out of print